DON GEORGE has been a pioneering travel writer and editor for more than two decades. Currently the Global Travel Editor for Lonely Planet Publications, he writes the award-winning Traveler at Large column for lonelyplanet.com and frequently appears as a travel expert in print, on radio and on TV. He has visited more than seventy countries, published more than six hundred articles in newspapers and magazines around the globe, and has won numerous awards for his writing and editing. In twenty-five years of wandering, he has lived in Paris, Athens and Tokyo, and now happily occupies his own House Somewhere in a small town outside San Francisco.

For ANTHONY SATTIN, travelling is not simply part of life but also the core of his work as a travel writer, critic and broadcaster. A contributor to several publications in the United Kingdom and abroad, he is the author of many books, including the novel *Shooting the Breeze* and the highly acclaimed *The Pharaoh's Shadow*. He is based in London and travels the world, but his heart flits between the Middle East and Africa.

A House Somewhere

TALES OF LIFE ABROAD

EDITED BY

DON GEORGE

AND

ANTHONY SATTIN

LONELY PLANET PUBLICATIONS
Melbourne • Oakland • London • Paris

A House Somewhere: Tales of Life Abroad

Published by Lonely Planet Publications
    Head Office: 90 Maribyrnong Street, Footscray, Vic 3011, Australia
                   Locked Bag 1, Footscray, Vic 3011, Australia
    Branches: 150 Linden Street, Oakland CA 94607, USA
                   10a Spring Place, London NW5 3BH,UK
                   1 rue Dahomey, 75011, Paris, France

Published 2002
Printed by The Bookmaker International Ltd
Printed in Australia

Copy-edited by Meaghan Amor
Designed by Daniel New

National Library of Australia Cataloguing-in-Publication entry

A house somewhere: tales of life abroad.

ISBN 1 74059 419 3.

1. Voyages and travels. I. George, Donald W. II. Sattin,
Anthony. (Series: Lonely Planet journeys).

910.4

Introduction, selection, arrangement and biographical notes
© Lonely Planet and Anthony Sattin 2002.
'A Home in Paradise' © ISABEL ALLENDE, 2002.
Additional copyright information precedes each story.

LONELY PLANET and the Lonely Planet logo are trade marks of Lonely Planet Publications
Pty. Ltd.

CONTENTS

INTRODUCTION

I T'S A POTENT SCENARIO: you're on a trip somewhere – rural Italy, say, or the South Pacific – and suddenly you see a place that exerts a kind of mysterious attraction on you. You stop the car and jump out, or hire a boat to take you back. It's not logical, but you're irresistibly drawn there, and after you return to wherever you came from, you spend all your time thinking about how to get back to that enchanted place. This chance encounter will change your life forever.

Some part of us has always been drawn to the idea of a House Somewhere, of a place to which we can escape, where life will be different and we can enjoy a new start, or create a new ending. The urge has been around probably as long as mankind, but in the past hundred years it has gone through a fundamental change. When the Roman Emperor Augustus built himself a magical hideaway high up on the island of Capri, a blue place where he could escape the demands of life in the ancient Roman court, he didn't write about it. When the real-life eighteenth-century sailor Alexander Selkirk was shipwrecked and marooned, alone, on a faraway island, he didn't write about it – that was left to Daniel Defoe, who used Selkirk's story as the model for his fictitious castaway Robinson Crusoe.

Then along came the twentieth century and all that changed. When Gerald Brennan decided he needed to hide away after the First World War to discover whether he had what it takes to be a poet, he went and buried himself in a small village in the Alpujarras Mountains of Andalucia, southern Spain – and then proceeded to write *South from Granada*. When Lawrence Durrell wanted to recapture the essence of the carefree years he spent at his hideaway on Corfu before the Second World War and the equally blithe spirit of the people he had shared it with, he wrote *Prospero's Cell*. By the time the upheavals of that war had subsided, there was a recognisable body of writing by and about people who had committed themselves to a place, another place, any place that wasn't their own but that had become home. This kind of narrative is usually grouped under the rubric of travel writing, but it stretches that genre in a wholly new direction, for this is not the literature of movement but rather the literature of staying put – of setting down roots in foreign soil.

It is this kind of writing that fills our anthology, but you won't find any of the writers mentioned so far in the pages that follow. When thinking about who to include in this volume and who to leave out, we recognised that a line had been drawn about halfway between Gerald Brennan in the 1920s and our own time. This was a line drawn by experience, but not the experience of the cultural revolutions of the 1960s, the Beatles, the spread of television, and student riots; rather it was drawn by the popular-isation of travel and the consequent growing popular knowledge of the world.

In the 1960s, if you had bothered to look, you could still have found Durrell's Corfu. Not so in the 1970s, for by then the island had been transformed by tourism, which has since taken the trend to its logical conclusion in our own time by putting Durrell's Corfu villa on the rental market. When Durrell moved to Greece he was considered a bohemian, a poet. When the beautiful people moved to caves on the Spanish island of Ibiza in the 1960s, they were disparagingly called hippies. Poets or hippies, they were all freaks, well outside the mainstream. But when Peter Mayle quit his job in advertising and moved to a house in southern France, he was called a visionary, and not just because of the fortune he made from the subsequent best-selling book, *A Year in Provence*. By that time a significant number of people understood the attrac-tions of trading in a high-flying job in a big city for a simpler, slower daily routine: the lure of the good life.

The popularity of *A Year in Provence* held a mirror up to many people, who realised that they too would like to opt out, or opt in. Many have done just that, and bought themselves a slice of the dream. And many who haven't actually made the move have obviously enjoyed making it vicariously because a long line of best-selling 'home abroad' authors now stretches from Peter Mayle to Frances Mayes, Chris Stewart and beyond.

In choosing the stories for *A House Somewhere*, we looked for three things in particular. We expected the writer to have made a commitment to the place, whether it was Isabel Allende falling for Marin County (and the man who first showed it to her) or James Hamilton-Paterson settling into his hut on a remote Philippine island. We wanted it to be an experience that moved them, as it did Carla Grissmann when she went to live in a remote village in Turkish Anatolya, or Paul Theroux, desperate to get on and write in Singapore, or Errol Trzebinski, facing frustration and then fathomless tragedy in Kenya. We also wanted the writing to be excellent. In this regard, we have assembled a distinguished gathering of novelists, poets, essayists and journalists – and a couple of musicians and a curator, too.

Our anthology consists of eighteen extracts and eight original essays commissioned expressly for this book. We have assembled these pieces with the goal of presenting a variety of voices and a diversity of geographical areas. But despite the differences in setting and voice, a thematic progression links all these tales, and we have ordered the book according to this progression.

It starts (doesn't it always?) with falling in love, with seeing a place and thinking, 'That's where I want to be.' Love being blind, the place is often a wreck, usually miles from the nearest electricity, and way out of the price range. Never mind, love must be obeyed. And it's just as well that it *is* love because next comes the often tricky business of buying or renting, an activity peppered with pitfalls, many of them dug by silver-tongued lawyers or notaries. After the purchase comes the even trickier business of turning that dream into reality with the help of what are called the local builders. They are local, but they rarely build, failing to turn up when they promise, insisting that what is wanted can't be done or else that a problem has been fixed when it clearly hasn't.

Now comes the concomitant challenge of language. This progresses from the first few failed attempts at communication to the gradually dawning realisation that the world around you is mostly incomprehensible and that the only way to peer into the heart of your new home is to breach the language barrier.

Miscommunications inevitably ensue; but word by word, phrase by phrase, your confidence and your knowledge grow.

At this stage, some begin to wish they had never started, but there are rewards ahead, the satisfaction that comes when the work is done, the new paint a little faded, the garden in bloom. It is the thrill of recognising that you have realised your dream, that here is your home, your future. Now, if they haven't done before, the locals tend to kick in and you get to bond with perhaps the most important and unpredictable of all the elements, your neighbours, the one part of the jigsaw that is almost never considered until it is too late. Like your family, they are something you discover you cannot change.

That should be the end of the story, but people – and life – being what they are, it rarely is. There are the doubts, dilemmas and tragedies as the world turns and what was once a very quiet House Somewhere is now in a war zone or has a highway run past it, a dam built below it, or a nightclub opened across the way.

And so the renovation of the house, the evolution of the village – in short, the story – is never finished: the plumbing always needs to be upgraded; the place always needs a new coat of paint; new neighbours move in; and new laws are passed. The only constant is change – and, well, connection.

For that original love remains, and ripens, until a last salutary lesson is revealed: home is not finally a thing of rocks and roof tiles, nails and wood; home, as the old saying has it, is where the heart resides. Or in other words: our House Somewhere is anywhere our own true love abides.

DON GEORGE AND ANTHONY SATTIN

HOME THOUGHTS

FROM ABROAD

JAN MORRIS

JAN MORRIS has written some forty books and says she will write no more. They include a major work of British imperial history; the *Pax Britannica* trilogy; studies of Wales, Spain, Venice, Oxford, Manhattan, Sydney and Trieste; two autobiographical works; two capricious biographies; five volumes of collected travel essays; a novel; and a short book about her own house in Wales. However, she defines them all as really being the 'ego-biographies' of a wandering Welsh European.

There go the swallows for Venice, the stout sea-farers –

Seeing those birds fly makes one wish for wings!

S o WROTE old Browning, sitting in his English garden one spring morning, and Oh! I know too well that delicious pull of distant parts, foreign places and different ways of living. I have watched the birds fly off too, as the drizzle falls out of a grey Welsh sky, the sheep in the field next door stand there hangdog and reproachful and whenever the telephone rings it seems to be somebody getting the wrong number – oh yes, I've wished for the wings of a 747 often enough, when the opposite of homesickness sets in!

And I know well, too, the delectable thrill of moving into a new house somewhere altogether else, in somebody else's country, where the climate is different, the food is different, the light is different, where the mundane preoccupations of life at home don't seem to apply and it is even fun to go shopping. Travel itself, after all, is largely a matter of enjoying differences – why else would those swallows migrate? Transferring one's whole being – family, possessions, bank accounts, blankets, mixers and all – gives us the same pleasure in less restless form.

It is seldom a permanent pleasure. Most people I know who move to a foreign part do not stay there forever, just as people who succumb to the allure of isolated islands generally seem to creep back sheepishly, sooner or later, to the conveniences of suburbia. All my own excursions into the expatriate condition have been temporary, but that has not made them any the less exciting. When we find our dream retreat far away, most of us know well enough that its first foreign delights are presently going to wear off, until they hardly seem foreign at all; we put that out of our minds, though, and glory in our exotic new garden, poke happily around our smoke-stained antique kitchen, peer dreamily from our lead-paned casement window, as though it is all going to be fresh and strange forever.

3

I have had many such moments of delightful self-delusion. I remember as if it were yesterday the moment I first stepped aboard the superannuated river steamer *Saphir*, moored on the banks of the Nile in Cairo, where my family and I were to spend some of the happiest years of our lives. The Egyptian sun was blazing that day, but canvas awnings cast an exotic shade over the poop, which was littered with divans and cushions like a sultan's seraglio, and in our living quarters the light streamed brazenly through the shutters in almost tangible rays. My workplace was the wheelhouse on the upper deck, all glass and blistered white paint, and here and there around the ship servants in spotless *djellabas* and turbans smilingly awaited our every pleasure.

The *Saphir* sank in the end, but we were long gone by then, and had moved into some other fascinatingly alien home. Was it the top-floor flat in the Venetian palace that came next, with the majestic view over the Grand Canal, and the soft swish of oars outside our windows that orchestrated the night hours? Or was it the apartment in the antebellum mansion in Vicksburg, Mississippi, with its high white balcony that Jefferson Davies had spoken from, and its heady scents of tobacco plant and jasmine drifting past the kitchen window? Or the house above the water in Hong Kong, the sampans clustered below the bluff, the great container ships offshore, the clink of wind chimes and the clank of cooking pots?

I forget now which came when – what about the apartment in Sydney, looking below the Harbour Bridge to the flying white wings of the Opera House beyond, or the sweet little clapboard house in Cranbury, New Jersey, or that apartment on Forty-ninth Street in Manhattan, where the fire engines triumphantly rode by, or – yes, when did we live in that adorable chalet in Haute Savoie, where we skied in our own backyard in the winter, and in the spring welcomed the itinerant distillery to the apple orchards? They were foreign places every one – alien, exotic places – and they have blurred in my memory into a glorious mosaic of new experiences and new delights.

Why is it then that I have never felt entirely comfortable, entirely natural, in those delectable foreign homes? Other people seem to be. Americans in particular, who come from restless stock by the nature of things, seem to find themselves altogether at ease putting down roots, however transient, in foreign parts. It is part of their heritage, I suppose. They are settlers by inheritance, and they are still particularly accomplished at making themselves homes away from home.

It is different for me. I am a traveller by profession but not by instinct. My people have not lived outside the British Isles since kingdom come – my English maternal forebears for at least a thousand years, my Welsh paternal ancestors probably never. In my white wheelhouse on the *Saphir*, among the magnolias of Vicksburg, watching the ships sail by in Hong Kong, wine-bibbing on my Venetian balcony, sociable in Manhattan or tobogganing in our Alpine garden of France – in none of our adopted homes, though I was always deliriously happy, was I ever entirely settled.

This is because I was always, at the back of my heart, home-sick. On another day, in another place, in another mood, Browning wrote another poem, *Home Thoughts from Abroad*, remembering the chaffinch on its English orchard bough, the blossomed pear tree in the hedge, the careless rapture of the thrush's call and all the scents and suggestions and evocations of his homeland. I am with him there, too: the swallows on their way south may call me to follow them, but that damned thrush, singing the same exuberant song over and over again, always summons me home.

Homesickness is the most delicious form of nostalgia, if only because generally speaking it really can be gratified. We cannot return to the past, but we can go home again. In my own case, homesickness is related to something the Welsh language calls *hiraeth*. This over-worked word (for the Welsh are big on emotions) means literally longing, nostalgia or sometimes plain grief. It has come to signify, however, something even less exact: longing, yes, but for nothing definite; nostalgia, but for an indeterminate past; grief without cause or explanation. *Hiraeth!* An insidious summation of all that is most poetical, most musical, most regretful, most opaque, most evasive, most inextinguishable in the character of Wales.

Hiraeth it is, then, that makes me feel, even as I unpack the bags in our new and lovely Mediterranean villa, our quaint wooden house upon the fjord, our Barbados penthouse or our attic in the Dordogne, that I shan't be there for long. I am not a settler, only a wanderer perhaps. Outsider I may be by instinct as by preference, but I am not made to be an exile, and in this I am honouring the instincts of my paternal forebears down the ages. The Welsh have never been easy migrants. They have left their homes for more prosperous, more tolerant or more easy-going countries because they have had to, but we read in their old diaries how forlornly, until the last dim line of the Welsh shoreline disappeared from view, they lingered together over the rails of their emigrant ships. Many of them presently became assimilated citizens of their new countries, but many more hoped all their lives to return to Wales, and sometimes they did. Joseph Jenkins from Tregaron, for example, who had become an archetypal Australian swagman during his long years down under, returned at last in his seventy-eighth year specifically to die in the hills of Cardiganshire.

This powerful homing instinct is inexplicable. The old Welsh emigrants had left Wales because their lives there were poor and miserable, yet nothing could suppress the *hiraeth* within them, and nothing can suppress it in me, either. Nobody, I swear, has had more pleasure from travelling than I have, and nobody has pushed more eagerly through the door of a rented house somewhere far away. Yet the old sensation nags at me always, part sweet, part sad, part consolation, part reproach. Most expatriates, if you press them, will admit to something they miss, during their idyllic residences abroad: decent eggs and bacon for the English, a proper beer cellar for the Germans, the *New York Times*, perhaps, or cornflakes for Americans. For me it is nothing so specific. A perceptive American once observed that a Welshman's truth was in the nature of a circle, and similarly what I crave when I am living abroad is rather in the form of a blur.

It is the sense of belonging that I miss, together with infusions of historical awareness and sensuality. I miss the stones of home. I miss the smell of the wood smoke and the sound of the river below the woods. I miss the murmur of the Welsh language. I miss my cat Ibsen. I miss my books. I miss the old beams of my house and the tumble of possessions, memories and reminders that tells me it is mine, all mine. I miss, of course, wherever I am, the ones I love the best, and I miss – well, not to put too fine a point upon it, I miss dear old Wales.

So I stand with Browning, either way. When the swallows fly south I want to go with them, but when I hear that chaffinch calling, I need to go the other way: up our dusty, potholed lane, through the shabby old oak gates, into the familiar, the irreplaceable embrace of home, where there is no need for *hiraeth*, where love awaits me and the kettle's always on the boil.

A HOME IN
'PARADISE'

ISABEL ALLENDE

ISABEL ALLENDE is the author of numerous works of fiction, including *The House of the Spirits*, *The Infinite Plan*, *Of Love and Shadows*, *Eva Luna*, *Daughter of Fortune* and *Portrait in Sepia*. She has also written *Aphrodite: A Memoir of the Senses*, and the autobiographical family memoir, *Paula*.

IN OCTOBER 1987, on a crisp autumn day, I saw Marin County for the first time. I had been here a year before for a fleeting moment in the midst of a hectic tour. An escort had picked me up at the airport at dusk and had driven me to the place where I was expected to speak, probably the College of Marin, although I can't be sure. By the time we got there it was dark, I was exhausted and this was just another stop in a sort of whirlwind. It was my first lecture tour, and I barely survived twelve cities in sixteen days. When I was finally back home in Caracas, where I lived at the time, I could not remember any of the places I had been. But in 1987 the circumstances were different. My first husband and I had recently divorced, after twenty-five eternal years, and we needed to have some space between us, so I accepted a book tour of Europe and the United States that kept me travelling for two months.

The last city on my journey was San Francisco. This time the travel arrangements provided for three days, so there was a chance to do some sightseeing. I had planned the usual Chinatown–Muir Woods–Napa Valley excursions, and maybe dinner at some restaurant that served California nouvelle cuisine, the rage at that moment. I soon found out how disappointing that mixture of pseudo-French and so-called ethnic flavours in small portions at exorbitant prices was. These plans were changed at the last minute because something happened that would influence the rest of my life. You have guessed: I met a man.

William Gordon was an attorney who had read one of my books and liked it, so he showed up at my reading. He was introduced to me as the last heterosexual bachelor in San Francisco. I liked him, so I accepted a bit too promptly his kind offer to show me the natural beauty of Marin County. The next day he picked me up in a car filthy with petrified fries, dog hair and broken toys, and took me to Mount Tamalpais. We drove in silence, listening to a Chopin piano concert on the radio. The day was clear, the air cool and the trees waved at us in the breeze. From the top of the mountain the view was breathtaking: the bay was laid at our feet, like an old Dutch painting. Willie pointed out each town in the county, like beads of a long rosary, and told me that it was the best place in the world to live. I looked at him and decided then and there that he was proposing to me. I took it as an invitation to stay: *Marin County was just an excuse, what he really meant was* . . . However, that was not his intention at all, he was just sharing his awe of the place where he had chosen to live for the last thirty years, after having travelled all over the world. It was one of those fortunate misunderstandings between people from different cultures. I say fortunate because it gave me determination: I was forty-five years old, I was free, Caracas was eight hours away by jet, and there was no time to waste, so I went for the jugular.

Most Chilean women are small and look rather unthreatening. Don't be fooled by appearances. They can be ferocious, especially when they fall in love. To make a long story short, let's say that Willie tried to escape, but he was no match for me. I tackled him (not immediately, a few hours later), threw him face down on the floor and forced him to love me in return. We married against his will and that is the reason why I ended up living in Marin County. I didn't know then what an extraordinary place it was, nor did I suspect that I would grow roots in it.

I have been a traveller, a political refugee and an immigrant. My family and I had to leave Chile after the military coup of 1973. We went to Venezuela, where we lived in exile for fifteen years, waiting for the dictatorship to end in Chile, so that we could return. However, when that finally happened in 1989, I was married to Willie and living in California. I did not return.

At the beginning I felt as if I were a total alien. Marin County was too safe, too clean, too pretty, too affluent, too white for me. It looked like the Côte d'Azur without tourists.

The hedonistic lifestyle was a bit of a shock. People here have time to bike, walk their dogs, surf or join a cult. Restaurants and bookstores are always full. There are plenty of mature women in yoga outfits with babies in strollers, often twins or triplets, the result of fertility drugs. Teenagers are almost nonexistent, as they prefer to hang out in San Francisco, which by comparison is much more exciting. Everywhere older folks in sweatpants are jogging their brains out, while perfectly fit men sit all day nursing cappuccinos in coffee shops. 'Don't they work?' I asked Willie. 'They are all therapists,' he informed me.

Marinites look good and dress casually; nobody wears a tie and if someone has make-up on, it's probably a female impersonator. They are healthy and educated: there are more gyms and art galleries per square mile than in any other region I know of. They treat each other kindly and everybody is politically correct; even perfume is banned in some places in consideration of the 'scent challenged'. They all seem very liberal, so it's hard to know where all the conservative votes come from. They are so open-minded that it takes a second look to see the streak of intolerance that runs under the surface and manifests itself mainly against immigrants. Most of them expect the Hispanics to do the menial work that nobody else will do and then at dusk to disappear silently into thin air . . . until the next day.

In the late eighties, when I moved to Marin County, I didn't see any homeless, and the traffic was not a subject of conversation. People talked about the stock market, food and relationships. I noticed that there were a lot of singles. The personal ads in local newspapers were quite revealing: everybody wanted to have a good time, a few females were looking for romance, and no male was willing to make a commitment.

For a while I wondered if anything ever happened in this sort of Walt Disney movie set, but soon enough I realised that Marin County is quite a Peyton Place, full of divorcées, gay/lesbian couples and Zen monks; hundreds of ecologists, vegetarians, earth mothers and masseuses; thousands of people in recovery. We even have had one or two serial killers. Half the population is into crystals, gurus, Tantric sex or saving whales. Those who are not in search of enlightenment are in search of the perfect croissant.

It is true that Marin County is the breast cancer capital of the world, but it is also one of the most beautiful inhabited places on Earth, where people still live graciously.

I am a person of rough edges. It took me a while to feel comfortable in Paradise. It was a surprise for me to learn that the American Constitution guarantees the right to search for happiness, something that Marinites take very seriously. They also want to be permanently entertained. The rest of the world accepts that life is mostly boring, and they consider themselves fortunate if they have a few moments of joy here and there. No-one expects to live happily ever after! In my Chilean family, happiness was irrelevant. Life was supposed to be tough, take it or leave it. No whining allowed. But, I am proud to say, I have adapted so well that now I expect to be happy and entertained like my fellow Marinites. If it doesn't happen, there is always counselling and Prozac.

I remember my confusion at the beginning. My English was so poor (on my lecture tours I had been reading from prepared speeches) that I could barely order food in a restaurant, and Willie had to translate the movies for me. So my first decision was to learn the language. The second was to get a driver's licence. And the third was to accept the customs. Coming from a society where things are always oblique and ambiguous, I found the direct approach of Americans offensive. Their sense of time is so different! Time is gold: fast money, fast sex, fast food. To this day I have not been able to find a translation for the words 'quickie' and 'snack'. The concepts do not exist anywhere else.

I thought I would never adapt in Marin County. I look Chilean. I cook, dream, write and make love in Spanish. My books have an unmistakable Latin American flavour. But I am greedy, I want it all. I decided to incorporate what I like about this place without renouncing any of the things I cherish about my own culture. To be totally bicultural was my goal. Why settle for less? The twentieth century was the century of refugees and immigrants; never before had the world witnessed such large numbers of displaced people. My family was part of that diaspora. It is not as bad as it sounds. I thought I could live in Marin County without losing my identity, my background, my language or my beliefs. I could simply keep adding to them.

I love this country in general and California in particular. Diversity fascinates me. All the races of the planet come here with their traditions and their dreams. Everything new or important starts here or comes here. I like the awareness, the sense of future, the generosity of the people. The young and optimistic energy of Californians is so attractive! Also their sense of freedom: this is as far West as you can get.

It didn't take me long to make friends in Marin County. One day I went to buy a pair of gloves at a small shop in Sausalito. 'They come with this hat,' the saleswoman told me. I couldn't afford the hat and bought only the gloves. Three days later the hat arrived in the mail with a note from the woman saying that she had read my first novel and the gift was a token of her affection. Thus she became my first friend. A couple of days later I went to Book Passage in Corte Madera, the liveliest bookstore in the Bay Area, where the owner treated me to mango tea and didn't charge me for the book I intended to buy. She became my second friend. My third friend is a famous jeweller, who I met at a beauty salon in San Rafael, where we both were having our hair tinted purple. She was reading one of my books and I was wearing her earrings. The rest was relatively easy. Now I know everybody: artists and writers, teachers and doctors, obsessive bikers, dog trainers, grouchy mailmen, Latino waiters, Asian acupuncturists, spiritual crones who take workshops on how to become goddesses. I am acquainted on a first-name basis with every dog on a leash on the trails and almost all of their owners. I even have a prayer group and a book club, for Pete's sake! Definitely, I am not an alien any more. Maybe it's just my imagination, but I think that in the last fifteen years the people in Marin County have not only accepted me, they have sort of adopted me.

I know every town and almost every corner in the county. I know where to find vintage clothes, the most decadent chocolate and fresh-baked bread. My vegetables and herbs come from the farmers' market on Sundays. I can tell you where you can have real Italian latte, buy Oriental furniture, get your next tattoo or have your palms read.

When an astrologer told me I should live in the north, and when Willie and I realised that, in spite of our best intentions, our lustful affair was turning into mature love, we decided to get the house of our dreams. He wanted it spacious, comfortable, full of gadgets, with a view of the bay and a garden. I simply hoped to feel at home. We found the perfect lot on top of a hill and built it, and when it was finished we hired a team to 'distress' it. They stained the walls, threw acid on the iron railings, and hammered the doors. The neighbours gathered in the street to observe this methodical destruction in amazement, asking what on Earth we were doing. If we wanted a beaten-up house, why did we build a new one? The result is a historical impossibility: a century-old Chilean house sitting on a hill in Marin County. It's a fake, but I love it.

My daughter's ashes are scattered in the woods of West Marin. My granddaughters were born here. The deepest grief and the greatest joys of my life have been in this place. My husband, my son, my grandchildren, my friends and my books are here. This is my home now.

THE ALIEN HOME

FROM

THE GLOBAL SOUL

PICO IYER

PICO IYER is the author of several books about the romance of foreign places, from *Video Night in Kathmandu* and *The Lady and the Monk* to *The Global Soul*. His most recent book, about Islam and California, is a novel called *Abandon*. He lives in suburban Japan.

AND SO OUR DREAMS of distant places change as fast as images on MTV, and the immigrant arrives at the land that means freedom to him, only to find that it's already been recast by other hands. Some of the places around us look as anonymous as airport lounges, some as strange as our living room suddenly flooded with foreign objects. The only home that any Global Soul can find these days is, it seems, in the midst of the alien and the indecipherable.

And so, a wanderer from birth, like more and more around me, I choose to live a long way from the place where I was born, the country in which I work, and the land to which my face and blood assign me – on a distant island where I can't read any of the signs and will never be accepted as even a partial native. Specifically, I live in a two-room apartment in the middle of rural Japan, in a modern mock-Californian suburb, none of whose buildings are older than I am, with a long-time love whose English is as limited as my Japanese, and her two children, who have even fewer words in common with me. Once every few months, I see a foreign face in the neighbourhood, and occasionally my second-hand laptop greets me with, 'Good morning, Dick . . . The time is 6:03 p.m. [in Houston],' but otherwise, long weeks go by without my speaking my native tongue.

You could say that much in the area is familiar – my apartment building is called the Memphis (as in the city of the hero of a thousand karaoke bars), and my girlfriend worked for years at a boutique called Gere (as in Hollywood's most famous Tibetan Buddhist). The Gere store is to be found inside the Paradis department store, which houses the Kumar Indian restaurant on its fourth floor and sits just across from a Kentucky Fried Chicken parlour, a Mister Donut shop, and a McDonald's eatery. But the very seeming familiarity of these all-American props serves only to underline my growing sense of a world that's singing the same song in a hundred accents all at once. The Kentucky Fried Chicken parlour is generally rich in young girls with black silk scarves around their throats, waiting, in thick black furs and fedoras, for the lucrative (elderly) dates they've just arranged to meet on their miniature cell phones. Mothers with silent kids beside them sip demurely at blueberry flans and pear sorbets, rice taco salads and tomato gratin, while a country-and-western singer on the sound system croons about the sorrow of lost truckers. Colonel Sanders is dressed, often, in a flowing blue *yukata*, though the recipients of his old-fashioned Southern hospitality are largely carrot-haired boys and girls in black leather microskirts slumped, in untraditional fashion, across the spotless tables.

On rainy days, the unfailingly perky cash-register girls (with TEAM MEMBER and ALL-STAR written across their chests) race out to place umbrella stands in front of the entrance, and hand out 'Gourmet Cards'. The scented autoflush toilet plays a tape of running water as soon as you go in (just past the elegant sink for washing your chicken-stained hands). And every time a cashier presents me with my change, she cups my palm tenderly to receive the coins.

I go for walks, twice a day, in and around the neighbourhood – the 'Southern Slope of Deer', as its name translates – and pass through silent, tidy streets that look like stage sets in some unrecorded 'Star Trek' episode. I pass Autozam Revues and Toyota Starlets, Debonairs and Charmants, Mazda Familias and Honda Todays (with Cat's Short Story tissues in the back). Mickey Rourke grins down at me from a bank of vending machines. The local dry-cleaner hangs out a sign that promises REFRESHING LIFE ASSISTANCE. At the intersection of School-dori and Park-dori (as these science-fictive locales are called), dogs wait patiently for the lights to change, and everything in the whole firm-bordered area is so clear-cut that every single house is identified on maps at the number twelve bus stop.

Outside my window, toddlers cry 'Mummy' and men in white shirts and black ties scale ladders to polish the sign outside the bank.

Most mornings, a truck rumbles past, playing the unbearably mournful song of a traditional sweet potato salesman.

There are two small strips of stores in my 'Western Convenience Neighbourhood' (as the Japanese might call it), and both are laid out as efficiently, as artfully, as batteries inside some mini disc player. I can get fresh bread at the Deer's Kitchen bakery and éclairs (and Mozart) at Père de Noel. The Wellness building stands just across from a twenty-second-century health club, which offers qigong classes twice a week, its grey walls thick with autumn leaves, and the man at the Elle hair salon tells me (every time I visit) about his one trip abroad, to Hawaii. Right next to the Memphis Apartments, competing with the Elle, the Louvre Maison de Coiffure, and the Musée Hair and Make, is the Jollier Cut and Parm, and I had been in the neighbourhood for three years before I realised that the name probably referred to Julia (as in Roberts). A ten-minute bus ride takes me to the Bienvenuto Californian trattoria down the street; the Hot Boy Club (with surfing shop next door); and a coffee shop, above an artificial lake, that used to be called Casablanca and contained the very piano that Dooley Wilson played for Humphrey Bogart.

At one level, of course, all these imported props could not be more synthetic or one-dimensional, and participate, as much as anything in Los Angeles or Hong Kong, in all the chill deracination of the age. The Japanese are probably less apologetic about embracing artifice and plastic replicas than anyone I know, and have few qualms about modelling their lives on the Spielberg sets they've seen on-screen. Those who worry that history is being turned into nostalgia, and community into theme park, could draw their illustrations from this suburb.

Yet the children in the neighbourhood call every older woman 'Auntie', and the Aunties feed whoever's child happens to be around. At dawn, old women take showers in freezing-cold water and shout ancestral prayers to the gods. The very cool clarity with which the neighbourhood shuts me out, calling me a *gaijin*, or outsider person, is partially what enables it to dispense courtesy and hospitality with such dependability, and to import so much from everywhere without becoming any the less Japanese. Surface is surface here, and depth is depth.

The old ceremonies are scrupulously observed in Japan, even in a place where there are no temples and no shrines. Every year when the smell of daphne begins to fade from the little lanes, and the first edge of coldness chills the air, the baseball chat shows on TV transfer their interviews to sets melancholy with falling leaves, and Harvest Newsletters appear beside the Drink Bar at my KFC. And as soon as the five-pointed maples begin to blaze in the local park, it lights up with matrons, sitting at easels, transcribing the turning of the seasons on their canvases.

And sometimes, on these sharpened sunny days, when the cloudless autumn brightness makes me homesick for the High Himalayas, I fall through a crack somehow, and find myself in a Japan of some distant century. Not long ago, as I was looking out on a light so elegiac that it made me think of the magical transformations of the Oxford of my youth (where Alice found her rabbit hole and a wardrobe led to Narnia, and where the Hobbit sprang out of some dusty Old Norse texts), I went out for my daily morning walk along the shiny, flawless streets, held as ever in a tranquil northern stillness of tethered dogs and mapled parks and grandfathers leading toddlers (in Lovely Moment hats) by the hand.

Men were washing their white Oohiro Space Project vans in the street, and girls, or sometimes robots, were crying out 'Welcome' from the computer shop with the two kittens for sale (at five hundred dollars a pop) in the window. Fred Flintstone in a White Sox cap invited me to a local softball league, and a Mormon, by a park, promised some form of enlightenment. A simple prelude of Bach's floated down from the upstairs window of the stationery shop. And, just behind the power plant, which I'd passed almost every day for five years, I chanced, for the first time ever, upon a flight of stairs, leading down into a valley.

I followed the steps down, and ended up in a thick, dark grove of trees. I passed out of it and found myself inside another country: green, green rice paddies shining in the blue-sky morning, and narrow, sloping streets leading up into the hills. Two-storey wooden houses, and a small community ringed by hills. Grandmothers were working in traditional white scarves outside their two-storey homes, and as I passed one, she favoured me with a gold-toothed smile. 'It's warm,' she said, and so was she. 'Look at me! I'm working in my socks!'

I walked on farther through the silent village streets, past flowering persimmon trees and a central oval pond. Then I turned back, and greeted the old woman – my friend now – as I passed. I climbed the fifty-four steps, and the hidden world fell behind me as a dream.

Four-year-old boys were playing catch in Harvard T-shirts; women walked with parasols to shield their faces from the sun.

TIWARIK AND KANSULAY

FROM

PLAYING WITH WATER

JAMES HAMILTON-PATERSON

JAMES HAMILTON-PATERSON is a London-born poet and novelist who has travelled widely and lived, among other places, in the Philippines. Much of his writing has taken the Philippines or water as its theme. He writes a regular column on marine and scientific topics for a Swiss-based magazine.

FOR FIVE YEARS, on and off, I had been living up in the hills behind Kansulay, another tiny village some thirty miles along the coast from Sabay and Tiwarik Island. It is yet another oddity in my relationship with the island that I should have been living so near it for so long without suspecting its existence. But thirty miles is very far in a province which has yet to build a tarmac road around its coast.

As is the way in the Philippine provinces, where everyone seems to know everybody else, I already had an introduction to the *barangay* captain at Sabay. It turned out he had long known of me because until a year ago one of his daughters had taught at the elementary school in whose catchment area Kansulay lay. The presence of a strange *'kano* living on his own in the woods was much gossiped about and in consequence Sabay knew of me before I knew of it. One day I walked down to the village and caught the first of a series of battered jeepneys which took me along the rutted coastal road for hours past anonymous villages among the palms, *barrios* and *barangays* whose names I never learnt, to ever-smaller provincial townships where I changed jeeps: Bulangan, Malubog, Sirao. After Sirao the road vanished into a track ridged with grey-black lava, on the left the slopes of the massif rising above the groves and bearing its rainforests into cloud, on the right the mobile blue of water. And there suddenly Tiwarik, placed just so on the other side of its strait the better to be seen entire.

I was received in Sabay with caution and some astonishment. The smaller children ran away and hid behind their mothers' legs or under the huts. Everyone smiled with unease. This changed to warmth and interest as soon as I had named names, spoken the magic syllables and identified myself as one encompassed – no matter how peripherally – by the huge and complex circle of family, friends and acquaintances spreading outwards from Sabay. So this was the *'kano* from Kansulay? And he wanted to live on Tiwarik? Well, why not? But on the other hand, why? There was nothing there, no hotels or discos, no white beach, not even fresh water. Captain Sanso was baffled, not unreasonably, since I could give no explanation he would find plausible, especially not when I told him of the miserable and involuntary two days I had already spent there. I just thought I'd go back for a bit, I said, and did he have any objection to my putting up a temporary hut in which to live?

Captain Sanso did not own Tiwarik but he thought this a fine idea. Already, I knew, he was working out the spin-offs of my presence for his impoverished village. I in turn had decided how much in default of rent I should contribute to the local economy. For the equivalent of twenty pounds he would provide me with materials and labour with which to build my house. Until its completion I was, of course, to stay with him. I was deeply grateful and observed that the village pump needed renewing, something which I was sure would happen in the near future if things worked out well. So a deal was struck inside his own sitting room on whose naked cement-block wall was nailed a Lions International plaque reminding the reader of the captain's subscription to the principle of mutual help. He sent his bodyguard/factotum off to the village shop for a bottle of ESQ rum with which to toast ourselves. Within an hour of arriving in Sabay I was in the middle of a drinking session.

Filipino drinking habits have a strange, intense air to them. In Europe, even when the drinking is done by the round as in an English pub, people do it mostly at their own rate and from their own glass. In the Philippines a single glass circulates, refilled as each drinker downs it at a gulp. When a spirit like rum is drunk a glass of water is on hand to act as a 'chaser'. To see a table of people knocking back slugs of spirit with a shudder and at once follow it with a slaking gulp of water makes one think of an ordeal rather than a convivial custom. The drinking takes on an insistent, almost brutal rhythm. It is as if people were drinking to become drunk, as they usually end by becoming. What makes the custom more bearable is the code which insists on a plate of *pulutan* on the table: any kind of food which people can pick at with a communal fork or spoon. This may be no more than salted peanuts or it may be a stew of chicken or dog, vegetables done in coconut milk, fried fish. There is also a formula with which a timid or queasy drinker may skip a round by nominating a *sakop* or proxy. I have frequent recourse to this system; remarkably few nominees ever decline the extra burden.

Captain Sanso introduces me to his youngest brother Arman, to Totoy and Danding and Silo and Jhoby and Bokbok. The names, at once familiar and unmemorable, slide through my rum-fumed brain. I smile until my face aches answering question after question. How old am I? Where is my companion? Why am I not married? Why do I want to live on Tiwarik? Is there treasure there? Where did I learn Tagalog? I answer some of the questions, duck others. The affability is tangible but under it curiosity runs with a hard and knowing edge: nobody does anything or is anything without good reason. From long experience I am conscious that these strangers are likely to become daily colleagues and friends. I try to make a dignified impression but merely look stupid because I keep forgetting who is who. Occasionally when I glance up from the arena of the table, now covered in puddles of rum, water and stew at which flies are sipping, I notice faces pressing in at the doorway, children's curious faces, an old man with a stick. A group of girls bursts into giggles behind me so I turn and to their embarrassment ask them what they are *really* laughing at. Eventually one of them covers her mouth with a hand, a girl of saintly beauty who asks nearly inaudibly if I am related to the actor George Hamilton. I tell her that I expect I am if one were to go back several centuries. For some reason this excites the girls still further.

In the late afternoon I strike a drunken deal with Arman to hire a small *bangka* from him, something in which I can paddle back and forth between Tiwarik and Sabay and the next morning, clear-headed and seen off from the beach by children, I head towards the island with the early sun rushing down on all sides. I bound over the wavelets; my arms seem tireless with excitement and wellbeing. I am filled with the overwhelming desire to do something, there is no telling what.

That was the day I never did do anything but climb up to the grass field and daydream. It was not until the following day I made a serious effort to acquire Tiwarik's geography. Until I knew what the island contained and how it lay I could not begin to build my house. Site is everything, of course; I had freedom of choice since I had no claim on the land and the hut I was going to put up would probably not outlive the first serious typhoon.

A position at the foot of the cliffs near where my companion and I had taken shelter had always been a possibility but I now found that the coral strand had changed its shape and position. Before, there had been a steep bank of shingle with a declivity which filled with water at high tide and became a hot lagoon before draining away at low tide. This bank had now vanished and with it the recurrent lagoon. Instead there was a spit of shingle jutting from an altogether narrower beach like a miniature port with its jetty. I soon realised that the whole coral bank shifted constantly, changing its shape with nearly every tide and during severe storms practically disappearing for a while as violent currents swirled it away. Yet it always returned. Consequently landing on Tiwarik was seldom the same twice running. I took pleasure in this feature. No sooner had the blackened corals, clumped together as supports for fishermen's cooking pots, become familiar in their disposition than the sea scoured the beach clean of all sites taking with it the carefully-collected piles of fish spines (otherwise a menace to bare feet), cigarette packets, frayed ends of nylon twine and crisp curls of abrasive skin torn off a species of triggerfish known locally and mystifyingly as *bagets* or 'teenager'. All in all, then, this strand was clearly no place for a house.

The ideal site, of course, was somewhere on the uplands where with the sea eagles I could command the bright gulfs to every horizon. However, my scrambles up the cliffs had made it clear that convenience would have to take priority over enchantment: the thought of carrying water daily up to the top of the island was too forbidding. It was going to be enough to fetch it from the mainland in the first place. Eventually I compromised and chose a spot above one end of the strand where a prehistoric fall of Tiwarik's black igneous rock had left a ledge, roughly level and some twenty feet deep, covered in shingle and a scatter of topsoil on which grew a succulent mat of vines. From here I could gaze across the strait to Sabay, watch the comings and goings on its beach or let my eyes travel up the great slopes of the cordillera behind it, past the tilted prairies of *cogon* to the gorges of scree and observe the veilings and vanishings of cloud about the peaks. Even the most unsatisfied eye might not grow restless at such an outlook.

I gave Captain Sanso money, he gave orders. Soon *bangkas* laden with helpers landed on Tiwarik's strand and the cliffs echoed to the sound of bamboos being split. Several sorties to the top of the island were organised and various stout timbers borne back from the forest, dripping with sap which dangled snot-like from their cut ends. Apart from nails, tools and nylon line little had to be brought from the mainland. The one exception was palm fronds for weaving the panels of *sulirap* with which to cover the bare bones of roof and walls. The lack of a single palm tree on Tiwarik was fairly conclusive proof that the island had never been inhabited. There was not even a wild papaya tree, which surprised me for I had already noticed the steady traffic of birds across the strait and would have imagined they had long since brought in their gut the seeds of this ubiquitous tree. The papaya, like the dragonfly, is unchanged from its fossil predecessors: a survivor which seems to suggest it is perfect in some way not immediately apparent (certainly not in the boringly-flavoured, cheesy-textured fruit it bears like skin tags around its bole).

At the end of three days I have a simple house and several new friends. Arman, perhaps by virtue of being the Captain's brother, has about him an ease and openness which makes him accessible. He is immediately recognisable as a fisherman for instead of the uniform Asian black, his hair is a strange layered thatch of brown with auburn tints and streaks of authentic dark blond. Only the fisher-boys' hair goes this colour, and only if their fishing is full-time and involves diving. Ordinary fishermen – generally the older ones – who sit in boats for hours with a hook and line remain largely unaffected. Arman also has a diver's physique: deep chest and shoulders, slender waist, powerful thighs. At twenty-seven he must be past his physical peak but is still probably the fittest of all Sabay's fishermen because – as I discover later – he alone does not smoke.

Arman has brought with him his young cousin Intoy, a boy in his earliest teens whose hair is also tawny. Intoy is unabashed by my foreignness, is openly curious about the whim which has brought me here, wants to know if I have any *komiks* with me. He laughs a good deal and leaps about like a sprite. Once he discovers I am a spear-fisherman we have an earnest discussion about techniques and trigger design which brings Arman and the others over. This of all subjects seems to be the great ice-breaker. We might have had one of those knowing, raunchy conversations about sex which occasionally serve but I would not have been treated as seriously as I now am when I describe my own method of waterproofing a cheap Chinese flashlight for night diving. Intoy asks about the commonest species of fish 'where you come from'. He means Kansulay and makes it sound as remote and vague as England (which everyone in the provinces here thinks is one of the states of the Union).

When finally my house is complete Intoy walks all round it appraisingly and announces he will live here. Arman promotes this idea.

'You can't live without a companion,' he says.

I tell him I am quite used to it. Everyone is aghast so it is clear they had none of them believed me at the drinking session that first afternoon.

'At least you must have a *bantay*,' somebody suggests.

I don't think I will need a guard, there being no-one else on Tiwarik.

'Ruffians come here,' says Arman darkly. 'All sorts of criminals from the Visayas. They may land one night, creep up and cut your throat.'

I say I think I am more likely to die several fathoms down than have my throat cut.

'Well then, you must have a servant. Intoy here will keep you in firewood and bring your water across each day. He's a good boy, quite strong.'

'About as strong as boiled seaweed,' agrees another boy whose job has been to cook rice for the construction team. Amidst laughter he and Intoy tussle and roll down the shingle spit into the shallows where they thrash like porpoises. I know why Arman is insisting. It is partly that my payment of his cousin for houseboy duties would bring some money into the child's family but also it is a matter of propriety. That a visitor – especially a *'kano* – should live nearby unaided is not correct. I recognise this; it has taken me several years to establish my independence at Kansulay in a way which merely makes people rueful and indulgent rather than giving offence.

I explain I am a writer who needs time and space to himself. Intoy comes up and dumps himself down, dripping and panting, and says I can send him away whenever I wish. And in fact at that moment I want them all to go away and leave me alone with my new house.

After a bit they do and I lie on my stomach on the floor and watch from the open doorway their little flotilla nearing Sabay. The bamboo strips beneath me smell sweetly of sap, their curved surfaces still green. It will be some weeks before they turn to blond and the nail heads to black.

Later that same evening after eating fish and rice by firelight I go back down to the shore to clean the dishes in the lapsing wavelets, scrubbing them with handfuls of gravel. They remain coated with a film of cooking oil which will stay constant day after day. The moon is dazzling, awesome, full this very night. A drift of silver molecules washes away from the dishes; it will be broken down by marine organisms within the hour.

First nights in strange places can determine how one sees them for ever after. This is my second first night on Tiwarik and it is determined not to efface itself into just another tropic nocturnal. The puddled mercury which is the sea, the wheeling galaxies above and the island at my back full of the metallic sheen of leaves give off the strangest light. It is as if everything generated its own luminescence which the moon then gathers into its brilliant lens. Tonight the moon stimulates the secretion of light from things much as the regular use of a well encourages the flow of its own waters. The whole of Tiwarik, that irregular bulk of rock and soil jutting from the ocean, must be veined with capillaries along which this light leaks and gathers and overflows from cliff face and grass blade and forest canopy. The serenity and clearness seem a good omen and I go back up to my hut with the dishes, content to be here.

But the omens are not yet finished. I blow out the lamp and lie on the floor listening to the slow breathing of the sea below, the crickets in the grass around the house. From nearby a gnarled rattling prefaces a tree lizard's loud repeated call as it names itself in Tagalog: tu-ko, tu-ko, tu-ko . . . American troops in Vietnam knew it as the *fuck-you* lizard but the sound of these syllables is less close, maybe saying more about the namer than about the named. As I lie pleasurably adrift I become aware of change. The noises are fewer, the chirpings and chitterings are stilled, the harsher cries from up in the island's cap of jungle die away. Even the sea sounds muffled. I open my eyes. Instead of brilliant chinks of moonlight in walls and roof there is nothing but dark. I get up, open the door and fumble down the bamboo steps into a weird landscape.

The moon is still there but it has nearly gone out. Its flawless disc is still flawless but now dulled to a deep amber as if seen through a piece of broken beer bottle. A primaeval shiver runs over me, a sense of having been transported a million years forwards to the Earth's end. It would be more bearable if the insect noises were still confidently asserting independence of such cosmic trivia. But nothing moves. It is as if all living creatures together with the sea and the wind were silenced by the desolation of total eclipse.

As the minutes go by and the Earth is held motionless I recover sufficiently to reflect on my amazing good fortune. At school there had occasionally been announcements that everyone could skip the class immediately following break in order to watch a partial eclipse of the sun, and we had dutifully gathered outside with pieces of smoked glass. But it had always been cloudy, that grey overcast which conspires to shield Britain from the universe. After half an hour we all trooped in again, not even particularly disappointed and with our faces smeared with lampblack. Yet here, my second first night on Tiwarik, there is a total eclipse of a full moon in a cloudless sky which lasts for nearly two hours. It is astounding.

Certainly it is easy to understand people's terror of eclipses, even of the moon. When on my ninth birthday I was given an army signal lamp I was enraptured by it and its accessories but became wary of one particular piece of equipment. This was a pair of rubber goggles with deep red lenses for use when a red glass cap was fitted over the lamp, enabling the signaller to send without the beam giving away his position. The first time I went out into the garden on a sunny day wearing them I was seized with a complete terror of the apocalypse. The world had turned to blood. The tennis lawn and the cherry trees were an alien landscape, as if it were Mars at war. Above it flamed a terrifying sky, raging with billows of incandescent gases. I was suddenly the last person alive anywhere, my parents and sister and dog a million years dead on another world and I condemned to witness the destruction by fire of the universe before myself being consumed. I tore the goggles from my face and surfaced into warm June sunlight. Beneath its reassuring lambency the lawn was now a luscious green while in the sky overhead the boiling smoke had changed to mild heaps of drifting cumulus. Thereafter whenever I wished to frighten myself I would walk about wearing the goggles, sweat pooling in the rubber eyecups, partially emboldened by the spicules of white light leaking in at the side of the lenses through ventilation holes.

Now on Tiwarik I note the reddish tinge of the eclipsed moon and understand the biblical references to its turning to blood. At the same time, of course, I am captivated by the oddness of the phenomenon. It is so rare and completely unexpected I do not know quite what to do with it, so after walking about experimentally for some time I come back and sit on the top step and watch the first splinter of silver as the untrammelled disc begins at last to slide clear of the shadow. No doubt about it, this heavenly body has nothing whatever to do with the bleak satellite on which men landed nearly twenty years ago. That was merely the Earth's moon. But the brilliant mandala whose last segment of tarnish is wiped clear as I watch, this is The Moon. The Moon is an act of the imagination and will remain forever unmarked by the cleated boot prints of interlopers. And from all around crickets burst back into song, the *tuko* calls, the sea breathes again. Now I can go to sleep.

FEBRUARY

FROM

A YEAR IN PROVENCE

PETER MAYLE

PETER MAYLE is credited with re-creating the 'house book' with *A Year in Provence*, his account of how he left his job and home in London and relocated to southern France. He has since written several other books, including the sequels *Encore Provence* and *Toujours Provence*.

THE FRONT PAGE of our newspaper, *Le Provençal*, is usually devoted to the fortunes of local football teams, the windy pronouncements of minor politicians, breathless reports of supermarket hold-ups in Cavaillon – '*le Chicago de Provence*' – and the occasional ghoulish account of sudden death on the roads caused by drivers of small Renaults trying to emulate Alain Prost.

This traditional mixture was put aside, one morning in early February, for a lead story which had nothing to do with sport, crime or politics: PROVENCE UNDER BLANKET OF SNOW! shouted the headline with an undercurrent of glee at the promise of the follow-up stories which would undoubtedly result from nature's unseasonable behaviour. There would be mothers and babies miraculously alive after a night in a snowbound car, old men escaping hypothermia by inches thanks to the intervention of public-spirited and alert neighbours, climbers plucked from the side of Mont Ventoux by helicopter, postmen battling against all odds to deliver electricity bills, village elders harking back to previous catastrophes – there were days of material ahead, and the writer of that first story could almost be seen rubbing his hands in anticipation as he paused between sentences to look for some more exclamation marks.

Two photographs accompanied the festive text. One was of a line of white, feathery umbrellas – the snow-draped palm trees along the Promenade des Anglais in Nice. The other showed a muffled figure in Marseille dragging a mobile radiator on its wheels through the snow at the end of a rope, like a man taking an angular and obstinate dog for a walk. There were no pictures of the countryside under snow because the countryside was cut off; the nearest snowplough was north of Lyon, three hundred kilometres away, and to a Provençal motorist – even an intrepid journalist – brought up on the sure grip of baking tarmac, the horror of waltzing on ice was best avoided by staying home or holing up in the nearest bar. After all, it wouldn't be for long. This was an aberration, a short-lived climatic hiccup, an excuse for a second café crème and perhaps something a little stronger to get the heart started before venturing outside.

Our valley had been quiet during the cold days of January, but now the snow had added an extra layer of silence, as though the entire area had been soundproofed. We had the Lubéron to ourselves, eerie and beautiful, mile after mile of white icing marked only by occasional squirrel and rabbit tracks crossing the footpaths in straight and purposeful lines. There were no human footprints except ours. The hunters, so evident in warmer weather with their weaponry and their arsenals of salami, baguettes, beer, Gauloises and all the other necessities for a day out braving nature in the raw, had stayed in their burrows. The sounds we mistook for gun shots were branches snapping under the weight of great swags of snow. Otherwise it was so still that, as Massot observed later, you could have heard a mouse fart.

Closer to home, the drive had turned into a miniature mountainscape where wind had drifted the snow into a range of knee-deep mounds, and the only way out was on foot. Buying a loaf of bread became an expedition lasting nearly two hours – into Ménerbes and back without seeing a single moving vehicle, the white humps of parked cars standing as patiently as sheep by the side of the hill leading up to the village. The Christmas-card weather had infected the inhabitants, who were greatly amused by their own efforts to negotiate the steep and treacherous streets, either teetering precariously forward from the waist or leaning even more precariously backward, placing their feet with the awkward deliberation of intoxicated roller skaters. The municipal cleaning squad, two men with brooms, had cleared the access routes to essential services – butcher, baker, épicerie and café – and small knots of villagers stood in the sunshine congratulating each other on their fortitude in the face of calamity. A man on skis appeared from the direction of the Mairie and, with marvellous inevitability, collided with the only other owner of assisted transport, a man on an ancient sled. It was a pity the journalist from *Le Provençal* wasn't there to see it: SNOW CLAIMS VICTIMS IN HEAD-ON COLLISION, he could have written, and he could have watched it all from the steamy comfort of the café.

The dogs adapted to the snow like young bears, plunging into the drifts to emerge with white whiskers and bucking their way across the fields in huge, frothy leaps. And they learned to skate. The pool, that just days before I had been planning to clean and make ready for some early spring swimming, was a block of blue-green ice, and it seemed to fascinate them. On to the ice would go the two front paws, then a tentative third paw, and finally the remaining leg would join the rest of the dog. There would be a moment or two of contemplation at the curiosity of a life in which you can drink something one day and stand on it the next before the tail would start whirring with excitement and a form of progress could be made. I had always thought that dogs were engineered on the principle of four-wheel drive vehicles, with equal propulsion coming from each leg, but the power appears to be concentrated in the back. Thus the front half of the skating dog may have the intention of proceeding in a straight line, but the rear half is wildly out of control, fishtailing from side to side and sometimes threatening to overtake.

The novelty of being marooned in the middle of a picturesque sea was, during the day, a great pleasure. We walked for miles, we chopped wood, we ate enormous lunches and we stayed warm. But at night, even with fires and sweaters and yet more food, the chill came up from the stone floors and out of the stone walls, making the toes numb and the muscles tight with cold. We were often in bed by nine o'clock and often, in the early morning, our breath was visible in small clouds over the breakfast table. If the Menicucci theory was correct and we were living in a flatter world, all future winters were going to be like this. It was time to stop pretending we were in a sub-tropical climate and give in to the temptations of central heating.

I called Monsieur Menicucci, and he asked anxiously about my pipes. I told him they were holding up well. 'That pleases me,' he said, 'because it is minus five degrees, the roads are perilous and I am fifty-eight years old. I am staying at home.' He paused, then added, 'I shall play the clarinet.' This he did every day to keep his fingers nimble and to take his mind off the hurly-burly of plumbing, and it was with some difficulty that I managed to steer the conversation away from his thoughts on the baroque composers and towards the mundane subject of our cold house. Eventually, we agreed that I should pay him a visit as soon as the roads had cleared. He had all kinds of installations at his house, he said – gas, oil, electricity and, his latest acquisition, a revolving solar heating panel. He would show them all to me and I could also meet Madame his wife, who was an accomplished soprano. I was obviously going to have a musical time among the radiators and stopcocks.

The prospect of being warm made us think of summer, and we started to make plans for turning the enclosed courtyard at the back of the house into an open-air living room. There was already a barbecue and a bar at one end, but what it lacked was a large, solid, permanent table. As we stood in six inches of snow, we tried to picture lunchtime in mid-August, and traced on the flagstones a five-foot square, large enough to seat eight bronzed and barefooted people and with plenty of room in the middle for giant bowls of salad, pâtés and cheese, cold roasted peppers, olive bread and chilled bottles of wine. The Mistral gusted through the courtyard and obliterated the shape in the snow, but by then we had decided: the table would be square and the top a single slab of stone.

Like most people who come to the Lubéron, we had been impressed by the variety and versatility of the local stone. It can be *pierre froide* from the quarry at Tavel, a smooth, close-grained pale beige; it can be *pierre chaude* from Lacoste, a rougher, softer off-white, or it can be any one of twenty shades and textures in between. There is a stone for fireplaces, for swimming pools, for staircases, for walls and floors, for garden benches and kitchen sinks. It can be rough or polished, hard-edged or rolled, cut square or in voluptuous curves. It is used where, in Britain or America, a builder might use wood or iron or plastic. Its only disadvantage, as we were finding out, is that it is cold in winter.

What came as a real surprise was the price. Metre for metre, stone was cheaper than linoleum, and we were so delighted by this rather misleading discovery – having conveniently over-looked the cost of laying stone – that we decided to risk the elements and go to the quarry without waiting for spring. Friends had suggested a man called Pierrot at Lacoste, whose work was good and whose prices were correct. He was described to us as *un original*, a character, and a rendezvous was made with him for eight-thirty in the morning, while the quarry would still be quiet.

We followed a signpost off the side road out of Lacoste and along a track through the scrub oak towards the open countryside. It didn't look like a light industrial zone, and we were just about to turn back when we nearly fell into it – a huge hole bitten out of the ground, littered with blocks of stone. Some were raw, some worked into tombstones, memorials, giant garden urns, winged angels with intimidating blind stares, small triumphal arches or stocky round columns. Tucked away in a corner was a hut, its windows opaque with years of quarry dust.

We knocked and went in, and there was Pierrot. He was shaggy, with a wild black beard and formidable eyebrows. A piratical man. He made us welcome, beating the top layer of dust from two chairs with a battered trilby hat which he then placed carefully over the telephone on the table.

'English, eh?'

We nodded, and he leant towards us with a confidential air.

'I have an English car, a vintage Aston Martin. *Magnifique.*'

He kissed the tips of his fingers, speckling his beard with white, and poked among the papers on his table, raising puffs from every pile. Somewhere there was a photograph.

The phone started to make gravelly noises. Pierrot rescued it from under his hat and listened with an increasingly serious face before putting the phone down.

'Another tombstone,' he said. 'It's this weather. The old ones can't take the cold.' He looked around for his hat, retrieved it from his head, and covered the phone again, hiding the bad news.

He returned to the business at hand. 'They tell me you want a table.'

I had made a detailed drawing of our table, marking all the measurements carefully in metres and centimetres. For someone with the artistic flair of a five-year-old, it was a masterpiece. Pierrot looked at it briefly, squinting at the figures, and shook his head.

'*Non*. For a piece of stone this size, it needs to be twice as thick. Also, your base would collapse – *pouf!* – in five minutes, because the top will weigh . . .' he scribbled some calculations on my drawing '. . . between three and four hundred kilos.' He turned the paper over, and sketched on the back. 'There. That's what you want.' He pushed the sketch across to us. It was much better than mine, and showed a graceful monolith; simple, square, well-proportioned. 'A thousand francs, including delivery.'

We shook hands on it, and I promised to come back later in the week with a cheque. When I did it was at the end of a working day, and I found that Pierrot had changed colour. From the top of his trilby down to his boots he was stark white, dusted all over as though he had been rolling in confectioner's sugar, the only man I have ever seen who aged twenty-five years in the course of a working day. According to our friends, whose information I didn't entirely trust, his wife ran the vacuum cleaner over him every night when he came home, and all the furniture in his house, from armchairs to bidets, was made from stone.

At the time, it was easy enough to believe. Deep winter in Provence has a curiously unreal atmosphere, the combination of silence and emptiness creating the feeling that you are separated from the rest of the world, detached from normal life. We could imagine meeting trolls in the forest or seeing two-headed goats by the light of a full moon, and for us it was a strangely enjoyable contrast to the Provence we remembered from summer holidays. For others, winter meant boredom or depression, or worse; the suicide rate in the Vaucluse, so we were told, was the highest in France, and it became more than a statistic when we heard that a man who lived two miles from us had hanged himself one night.

A local death brings sad little announcements, which are posted in the windows of shops and houses. The church bell tolls, and a procession dressed with unfamiliar formality makes its slow way up to the cemetery, which is often one of the most commanding sites in the village. An old man explained why this was so. 'The dead get the best view,' he said, 'because they are there for such a long time.' He cackled so hard at his own joke that he had a coughing fit, and I was worried that his turn had come to join them. When I told him about the cemetery in California where you pay more for a tomb with a view than for more modest accommodation he was not at all surprised. 'There are always fools,' he said, 'dead or alive.'

Days passed with no sign of a thaw, but the roads were now showing strips of black where farmers and their tractors had cleared away the worst of the snow, making a single-lane passage through the drifts either side. This brought out a side of the French motorist that I had never expected to see; he displayed patience, or at least a kind of mulish obstinacy that was far removed from his customary Grand Prix behaviour behind the wheel. I saw it on the roads round the village. One car would be driving cautiously along the clear middle lane and would meet another coming from the opposite direction. They would stop, snout to snout. Neither would give way by reversing. Neither would pull over to the side and risk getting stuck in a drift. Glaring through the windscreens at each other, the drivers would wait in the hope that another car would come up behind them, which would constitute a clear case of *force majeur* and oblige the single car to back down so that superior numbers could proceed.

And so it was with a light foot on the accelerator that I went off to see Monsieur Menicucci and his treasure house of heating appliances. He met me at the entrance to his storeroom, woollen bonnet pulled down to cover his ears, scarf wound up to his chin, gloved, booted, the picture of a man who took the challenge of keeping warm as a scientific exercise in personal insulation. We exchanged politenesses about my pipes and his clarinet and he ushered me inside to view a meticulously arranged selection of tubes and valves and squat, mysterious machines crouched in corners. Menicucci was a talking catalogue, reeling off heating coefficients and therms which were so far beyond me that all I could do was to nod dumbly at each new revelation.

At last the litany came to an end. '*Et puis voilà*,' said Menicucci, and looked at me expectantly, as though I now had the world of central heating at my fingertips, and could make an intelligent and informed choice. I could think of nothing to say except to ask him how he heated his own house.

'Ah,' he said, tapping his forehead in mock admiration, 'that is not a stupid thing to ask. What kind of meat does the butcher eat?' And, with that mystical question hanging unanswered in the air, we went next door to his house. It was undeniably warm, almost stuffy, and Monsieur Menicucci made a great performance of removing two or three outer layers of clothing, mopping his brow theatrically and adjusting his bonnet to expose his ears to the air.

He walked over to the radiator and patted it on the head. 'Feel that,' he said, 'cast iron, not like the *merde* they use for radiators nowadays. And the boiler – you must see the boiler. But *attention*,' he stopped abruptly and prodded me with his lecturer's finger, 'it is not French. Only the Germans and the Belgians know how to make boilers.' We went into the boiler room, and I dutifully admired the elderly, dial-encrusted machine which was puffing and snorting against the wall. 'This gives twenty-one degrees throughout the house, even when the temperature outside is minus six,' and he threw open the outside door to let in some minus six air on cue. He had the good instructor's gift for illustrating his remarks wherever possible with practical demonstration, as though he was talking to a particularly dense child. (In my case, certainly as far as plumbing and heating were concerned, this was quite justified.)

Having met the boiler, we went back to the house and met Madame, a diminutive woman with a resonant voice. Did I want a *tisane*, some almond biscuits, a glass of Marsala? What I really wanted was to see Monsieur Menicucci in his bonnet playing his clarinet, but that would have to wait until another day. Meanwhile, I had been given much to think about. As I left to go to the car, I looked up at the revolving solar heating apparatus on the roof and saw that it was frozen solid, and I had a sudden longing for a house full of cast-iron radiators.

I arrived home to discover that a scale model of Stonehenge had been planted behind the garage. The table had arrived – five feet square, five inches thick, with a massive base in the form of a cross. The distance between where it had been delivered and where we wanted it to be was no more than fifteen yards, but it might as well have been fifty miles. The entrance to the courtyard was too narrow for any mechanical transport, and the high wall and tiled half-roof that made a sheltered area ruled out the use of a crane. Pierrot had told us that the table would weigh between six and eight hundred pounds. It looked heavier.

He called that evening.

'Are you pleased with the table?'

Yes, the table is wonderful, but there is a problem.

'Have you put it up yet?'

No, that's the problem. Did he have any helpful suggestions?

'A few pairs of arms,' he said. 'Think of the Pyramids.'

Of course. All we needed were fifteen thousand Egyptian slaves and it would be done in no time.

'Well, if you get desperate, I know the rugby team in Carcassonne.'

And with that he laughed and hung up.

We went to have another look at the monster, and tried to work out how many people would be needed to manhandle it into the courtyard. Six? Eight? It would have to be balanced on its side to pass through the doorway. We had visions of crushed toes and multiple hernias, and belatedly understood why the previous owner of the house had put a light, folding table in the place we had chosen for our monument. We took the only reasonable course of action open to us, and sought inspiration in front of the fire with a glass of wine. It was unlikely that anyone would steal the table overnight.

As it turned out, a possible source of help was not long in coming. Weeks before, we had decided to rebuild the kitchen, and had spent many enlightening hours with our architect as we were introduced to French building terminology, to *coffres* and *rehausses* and *faux-plafonds* and *vide-ordures*, to *plâtrage* and *dallage* and *poutrelles* and *coins perdus*. Our initial excitement had turned into anti-climax as the plans became more and more dog-eared and, for one reason or another, the kitchen remained untouched. Delays had been caused by the weather, by the plasterer going skiing, by the chief *maçon* breaking his arm playing football on a motorbike, by the winter torpor of local suppliers. Our architect, an expatriate Parisian, had warned us that building in Provence was very similar to trench warfare, with long periods of boredom interrupted by bursts of violent and noisy activity, and we had so far experienced the first phase for long enough to look forward to the second.

The assault troops finally arrived, with a deafening clatter, while the morning was still hesitating between dawn and daylight. We went outside with bleary eyes to see what had fallen down, and could just make out the shape of a truck, spiked with scaffolding. A cheerful bellow came from the driver's seat.

'Monsieur Mayle?'

I told him he'd found the right house.

'*Ah bon. On va attaquer la cuisine. Allez!*'

The door opened, and a cocker spaniel jumped out, followed by three men. There was an unexpected whiff of aftershave as the chief *maçon* mangled my hand and introduced himself and his team: Didier, the lieutenant Eric and the junior, a massive young man called Claude. The dog, Pénélope, declared the site open by relieving herself copiously in front of the house, and battle commenced.

We had never seen builders work like this. Everything was done on the double: scaffolding was erected and a ramp of planks was built before the sun was fully up, the kitchen window and sink disappeared minutes later, and by ten o'clock we were standing in a fine layer of preliminary rubble as Didier outlined his plans for destruction. He was brisk and tough, with the cropped hair and straight back of a military man; I could see him as a drill instructor in the Foreign Legion, putting young layabouts through their paces until they whimpered for mercy. His speech was percussive, full of the onomatopoeic words like *tok* and *crak* and *boum* that the French like to use when describing any form of collision or breakage – and there was to be plenty of both. The ceiling was coming down, the floor was coming up and all the existing fittings coming out. It was a gutting job, the entire kitchen to be evacuated – *chut!* – through the hole that used to be a window. A wall of polythene sheeting was nailed up to screen the area from the rest of the house, and domestic catering operations were transferred to the barbecue in the courtyard.

It was startling to see and hear the joyful ferocity with which the three masons pulverised everything within sledgehammer range. They thumped and whistled and sang and swore amidst the falling masonry and sagging beams, stopping (with some reluctance, it seemed to me) at noon for lunch. This was demolished with the same vigour as a partition wall – not modest packets of sandwiches, but large plastic hampers filled with chickens and sausage and *choucroute* and salads and loaves of bread, with proper crockery and cutlery. None of them drank alcohol, to our relief. A tipsy mason nominally in charge of a forty-pound hammer was a frightening thought. They were dangerous enough sober.

Pandemonium resumed after lunch, and continued until nearly seven o'clock without any break. I asked Didier if he regularly worked a ten- or eleven-hour day. Only in the winter, he said. In the summer it was twelve or thirteen hours, six days a week. He was amused to hear about the English timetable of a late start and an early finish, with multiple tea breaks. *'Une petite journée'* was how he described it, and asked if I knew any English masons who would like to work with him, just for the experience. I couldn't imagine a rush of volunteers.

When the masons had gone for the day, we dressed for a picnic in the Arctic and started to prepare our first dinner in the temporary kitchen. There was a barbecue fireplace and a fridge. A sink and two gas rings were built into the back of the bar. It had all the basic requirements except walls, and with the temperature still below zero walls would have been a comfort. But the fire of vine clippings was burning brightly, the smell of lamb chops and rosemary was in the air, the red wine was doing noble work as a substitute for central heating, and we felt hardy and adventurous. This delusion lasted through dinner until it was time to go outside and wash the dishes.

The first true intimations of spring came not from early blossom or the skittish behaviour of the rats in Massot's roof, but from England. With the gloom of January behind them, people in London were making holiday plans, and it was astonishing how many of those plans included Provence. With increasing regularity, the phone would ring as we were sitting down to dinner – the caller having a cavalier disregard for the hour's time difference between France and England – and the breezy, half-remembered voice of a distant acquaintance would ask if we were swimming yet. We were always non-committal. It seemed unkind to spoil their illusions by telling them that we were sitting in a permafrost zone with the Mistral screaming through the hole in the kitchen wall and threatening to rip open the polythene sheet which was our only protection against the elements.

The call would continue along a course that quickly became predictable. First, we would be asked if we were going to be at home during Easter or May, or whichever period suited the caller. With that established, the sentence which we soon came to dread – 'We were thinking of coming down around then . . .' – would be delivered, and would dangle, hopeful and unfinished, waiting for a faintly hospitable reaction.

It was difficult to feel flattered by this sudden enthusiasm to see us, which had lain dormant during the years we had lived in England, and it was difficult to know how to deal with it. There is nothing quite as thick-skinned as the seeker after sunshine and free lodging; normal social sidesteps don't work. You're booked up that week? Don't worry – we'll come the week after. You have a house full of builders? We don't mind; we'll be out by the pool anyway. You've stocked the pool with barracuda and put a tank trap in the drive? You've become teetotal vegetarians? You suspect the dogs of carrying rabies? It didn't matter what we said, there was a refusal to take it seriously, a bland determination to overcome any feeble obstacle we might invent.

We talked about the threatened invasions to other people who had moved to Provence, and they had all been through it. The first summer, they said, is invariably hell. After that, you learn to say no. If you don't, you will find yourselves running a small and highly unprofitable hotel from Easter until the end of September. Sound but depressing advice. We waited nervously for the next phone call.

Life had changed, and the masons had changed it. If we got up at six-thirty we could have breakfast in peace. Any later, and the sound effects from the kitchen made conversation impossible. One morning when the drills and hammers were in full song, I could see my wife's lips move, but no words were reaching me. Eventually she passed me a note: Drink your coffee before it gets dirty.

But progress was being made. Having reduced the kitchen to a shell, the masons started, just as noisily, to rebuild, bringing all their materials up the plank ramp and through a window-sized space ten feet above the ground. Their stamina was extraordinary, and Didier – half-man, half fork-lift truck – was somehow able to run up the bouncing ramp pushing a wheelbarrow of wet cement, a cigarette in one side of his mouth and breath enough to whistle out of the other. I shall never know how the three of them were able to work in a confined space, under cold and difficult conditions, and remain so resolutely good-humoured.

Gradually, the structure of the kitchen took shape and the follow-up squad came to inspect it and to co-ordinate their various contributions. There was Ramon the plasterer, with his plaster-covered radio and basketball boots, Mastorino the painter, Trufelli the tile-layer, Zanchi the carpenter, and the *chef-plombier* himself, with *jeune* two paces behind him on an invisible lead, Monsieur Menicucci. There were often six or seven of them all talking at once among the debris, arguing about dates and availabilities while Christian, the architect, acted as referee.

It occurred to us that, if this energy could be channelled for an hour or so, we had enough bodies and biceps to shift the stone table into the courtyard. When I suggested this, there was instant co-operation. Why not do it now, they said. Why not indeed? We clambered out of the kitchen window and

51

gathered round the table, which was covered with a white puckered skin of frost. Twelve hands grasped the slab and twelve arms strained to lift it. There was not the slightest movement. Teeth were sucked thoughtfully, and everyone walked round the table looking at it until Menicucci put his finger on the problem. The stone is porous, he said. It is filled with water like a sponge. The water has frozen, the stone has frozen, the ground has frozen. *Voilà!* It is immovable. You must wait until it has thawed. There was some desultory talk about blow-lamps and crowbars, but Menicucci put a stop to that, dismissing it as *patati-patata*, which I took to mean nonsense. The group dispersed.

With the house full of noise and dust six days a week, the oasis of Sunday was even more welcome than usual. We could lie in until the luxurious hour of seven-thirty before the dogs began agitating for a walk, we could talk to each other without having to go outside, and we could console ourselves with the thought that we were one week closer to the end of the chaos and disruption. What we couldn't do, because of the limited cooking facilities, was to celebrate Sunday as it should always be celebrated in France, with a long and carefully judged lunch. And so, using the temporary kitchen as an excuse, we leapt rather than fell into the habit of eating out on Sunday.

As an appetiser, we would consult the oracular books, and came to depend more and more on the Gault-Millau guide. The Michelin is invaluable, and nobody should travel through France without it, but it is confined to the bare bones of prices and grades and specialities. Gault-Millau gives you the flesh as well. It will tell you about the chef – if he's young, where he was trained; if he's established, whether he's resting on his past success or still trying hard. It will tell you about the chef's wife, whether she is welcoming or *glaciale*. It will give you some indication of the style of the restaurant, and if there's a view or a pretty terrace. It will comment on the service and the clientele, on the prices and the atmosphere. And, often in great detail, on the food and the wine list. It is not infallible, and it is certainly not entirely free from prejudice, but it is amusing and always interesting and, because it is written in colloquial French, good homework for novices in the language like us.

The 1987 guide lists 5,500 restaurants and hotels in a suitably orotund and well-stuffed volume, and picking through it we came across a local entry that sounded irresistible. It was a restaurant at Lambesc, about half an hour's drive away. The chef was a woman, described as *'l'une des plus fameuses cuisinières de Provence'*, her dining room was a converted mill, and her cooking was *'pleine de force et de soleil'*. That would have been enough of a recommendation in itself, but what intrigued us most was the age of the chef. She was eighty.

It was grey and windy when we arrived in Lambesc. We still suffered twinges of guilt if we stayed indoors on a beautiful day, but this Sunday was bleak and miserable, the streets smeared with old snow, the inhabitants hurrying home from the bakery with bread clutched to the chest and shoulders hunched against the cold. It was perfect lunch weather.

We were early, and the huge vaulted dining room was empty. It was furnished with handsome Provençal antiques, heavy and dark and highly polished. The tables were large and so well-spaced that they were almost remote from each other, a luxury usually reserved for grand and formal restaurants. The sound of voices and the clatter of saucepans came from the kitchen, and something smelt delicious, but we had obviously anticipated opening time by a few minutes. We started to tiptoe out to find a drink in a café.

'Who are you?' a voice said.

An old man had emerged from the kitchen and was peering at us, screwing up his eyes against the light coming through the door. We told him we'd made a reservation for lunch.

'Sit down, then. You can't eat standing up.' He waved airily at the empty tables. We sat down obediently, and waited while he came slowly over with two menus. He sat down with us.

'American? German?'

English.

'Good,' he said, 'I was with the English in the war.'

We felt that we had passed the first test. One more correct

answer and we might be allowed to see the menus which the old man was keeping to himself. I asked him what he would recommend.

'Everything,' he said. 'My wife cooks everything well.'

He dealt the menus out and left us to greet another couple, and we dithered enjoyably between lamb stuffed with herbs, *daube*, veal with truffles and an unexplained dish called the *fantaisie du chef*. The old man came back and sat down, listened to the order and nodded.

'It's always the same,' he said. 'It's the men who like the *fantaisie*.'

I asked for a half-bottle of white wine to go with the first course, and some red to follow.

'No,' he said, 'you're wrong.' He told us what to drink, and it was a red Côtes du Rhône from Visan. Good wine and good women came from Visan, he said. He got up and fetched a bottle from a vast dark cupboard.

'There. You'll like that.' (Later, we noticed that everybody had the same wine on their table.)

He went off to the kitchen, the oldest head waiter in the world, to pass our order to perhaps the oldest practising chef in France. We thought we heard a third voice from the kitchen, but there were no other waiters, and we wondered how two people with a combined age of over 160 managed to cope with the long hours and hard work. And yet, as the restaurant became busier, there were no delays, no neglected tables. In his unhurried and stately way, the old man made his rounds, sitting down from time to time for a chat with his clients. When an order was ready, Madame would clang a bell in the kitchen and her husband would raise his eyebrows in pretended irritation. If he continued talking, the bell would clang again, more insistently, and off he would go, muttering '*j'arrive, j'arrive*'.

The food was everything the Gault-Millau guide had promised, and the old man had been right about the wine. We did like it. And, by the time he served the tiny rounds of goats' cheese marinated in herbs and olive oil, we had finished it. I asked for another half-bottle, and he looked at me disapprovingly.

'Who's driving?'

'My wife.'

He went again to the dark cupboard. 'There are no half-bottles,' he said, 'you can drink as far as here.' He drew an imaginary line with his finger halfway down the new bottle.

The kitchen bell had stopped clanging and Madame came out, smiling and rosy-faced from the heat of the ovens, to ask us if we had eaten well. She looked like a woman of sixty. The two of them stood together, his hand on her shoulder, while she talked about the antique furniture, which had been her dowry, and he interrupted. They were happy with each other and they loved their work, and we left the restaurant feeling that old age might not be so bad after all.

Ramon the plasterer was lying on his back on a precarious platform, an arm's-length below the kitchen ceiling. I passed a beer up to him, and he leant sideways on one elbow to drink it. It looked like an uncomfortable position, either for drinking or working, but he said he was used to it.

'Anyway,' he said, 'you can't stand on the floor and throw stuff up. That one who did the ceiling of the Sistine Chapel – you know, that Italian – he must have been on his back for weeks.'

Ramon finished the beer, his fifth of the day, handed down the empty bottle, belched lightly and returned to his labours. He had a slow, rhythmical style, flicking the plaster on to the ceiling with his trowel and working it into a chunky smoothness with a roll of his wrist. He said that, when it was finished, it would look as though it had been there for a hundred years. He didn't believe in rollers or sprayers or instruments of any sort apart from his trowel and his eye for a line and a curve, which he said was infallible. One evening after he had gone I checked his surfaces with a spirit level. They were all true, and yet they were unmistakably the work of a hand rather than a machine. The man was an artist, and well worth his beer ration.

A breeze was coming through the hole in the kitchen wall, and it felt almost mild. I could hear something dripping. When I went outside I found that the seasons had changed. The stone table was oozing water, and spring had arrived.

FESTINA TARDE

(MAKE HASTE SLOWLY)

FROM

UNDER THE TUSCAN SUN

FRANCES MAYES

Like many other people, FRANCES MAYES and her husband bought a house in Tuscany. Unlike most others, Mayes, a poet, then proceeded to write two bestsellers describing the renovation of the house and the life they have enjoyed in it since then.

HOPING FOR MIRACLES, we go to Italy for Christmas. Elizabeth has offered us her house in Cortona, which is partly packed for her move. She also wants to give us a great deal of her furniture, since her new house is smaller. As we drive out of the Rome airport, rain hits the windshield like a hose turned on full blast. All the way north we face foggier and foggier weather. When we arrive in Camucia, we head straight to the bar for hot chocolate before we go to Elizabeth's. We decide to unpack, have lunch, and face Bramasole later.

The house is a wreck. Canals for the heating pipes have been cut into the inside walls of every room in the house. The workers have left rock and rubble in piles all over the unprotected floors. The plastic we'd requested was simply tossed over the furniture so every book, chair, dish, bed, towel and receipt in the house is covered in dirt. The jagged, deep, floor-to-ceiling cuts in the wall look like open wounds. They are just beginning on the new bathroom, laying cement on the floor. The plaster in the new kitchen already is cracking. The great long sink has been installed and looks wonderful. A workman has scrawled in black felt-tip pen a telephone number on the dining room fresco. Ed immediately wets a rag and tries to rub it clean but we're stuck with the plumber's number. He slings the rag onto the rubble. They've left windows open all over and puddles have collected on the floor from this morning's rain. The carelessness apparent everywhere, such as the telephone being completely buried, makes me so angry I have to walk outside and take gulps of cold air. Benito is at another job. One of his men sees that we are extremely upset and tries to say that all will be done soon, and done well. He is working on the opening between the new kitchen and the cantina. He's shy but seems concerned. A beautiful house, beautiful position. All will be well. His bleary old blue eyes look at us sadly. Benito arrives full of bluster. No time to clean up before we arrived, and anyway it's the plumber's responsibility, he has been held up himself because the plumber didn't come when he said he would. But everything is *perfetto*, *signori*. He'll take care of the cracked plaster; it didn't dry properly because of the rains. We hardly answer. As he gestures, I catch the worker looking at me. Behind Benito's back he makes a strange gesture; he nods towards Benito, then pulls down his eyelid.

The upstairs patio seems perfect. They've laid rose-coloured brick and reattached the rusty iron railings so that the patio is secure but still looks old. Something was done well.

By four, twilight begins; by five, it's night. Still, the stores are opening after siesta. A morning of work, siesta, reopening at dark for several hours: the winter rhythm unchanged from the massively hot summer days. We stop by and greet Signor Martini. We're cheered to see him, knowing he'll say, '*Boh*,' and '*Anche troppo*,' one of his all-purpose responses that means yes, it's too bloody much. In our bad Italian we explain what's going on. As we start to go, I remember the strange gesture. 'What does this mean?' I ask, pulling down my eyelid.

'*Furbo*,' cunning, watch out, he answers. 'Who's *furbo*?'

'Apparently our contractor.'

Warm house. Thank you, Elizabeth. We buy red candles, cut pine boughs and bring them in for some semblance of Christmas. Our hearts are not into cooking, although all the winter ingredients in the shops almost lure us to the kitchen. We love the furniture Elizabeth has given us. Besides twin beds, coffee table, two desks, and lamps, we'll have an antique *madia*, whose top part was used to knead bread and let it rise. Beneath the coffin-shaped bread holder are drawers and cabinet. The chestnut's warm patina makes me rub my hand over the wood. On the list she's left for us, we find her immense *armadio*, large enough to hold all the house linens, a dining room table, antique chests, a *cassone* (tall storage chest), two peasant chairs, and wonderful plates and serving pieces. Suddenly we will live in a furnished house. With all our rooms, there will be plenty of space, still, for acquiring our own treasures. Amidst all the restoration horrors, this great act of generosity warms us tremendously. Right now, the pieces seem to belong to her orderly house, but before we leave we must move everything over to the house full of debris.

As Christmas nears, work slows then stops. We had not anticipated that they would take off so many holidays. New Year's has several holidays attached to it. We'd never heard of Santo Stefano, who merits one day off. Francesco Falco, who has worked for Elizabeth for twenty years, brings his son Giorgio and his son-in-law with a truck. They take apart the *armadio*, load everything into the truck except the desk, which is too wide to exit the study. Elizabeth has written all her books at that desk and it seems that it was not meant to leave the house. I'm taking boxes of dishes to our car when I look up and see them lowering a desk by rope out the second-floor window. Everyone applauds as it gently lands on the ground.

At the house, we cram all the furniture into two rooms we've shovelled out and swept. We cover everything with plastic and shut the doors.

There is absolutely nothing we can do. Benito does not answer our calls. I have a sore throat. We've bought no presents. Ed has grown silent. My daughter, sick with flu in New York, is spending her first Christmas alone because the construction debacle threw off her plans to come to Italy. I stare for a long time at an ad for the Bahamas in a magazine, the totally expected photo of a crescent of sugar-sand beach along clear, azure water. Someone, somewhere, drifts on a yellow striped float, trailing her fingers in a warm current and dreaming under the sun.

On Christmas Eve we have pasta with wild mushrooms, veal, an excellent Chianti. Only one other person is in the restaurant, for *Natale* is above all a family time. He wears a brown suit and sits very straight. I see him slowly drink wine along with his food, pouring out half glasses for himself, sniffing the wine as though it were a great vintage instead of the house carafe. He proceeds through his courses with care. We're through; it's only nine-thirty. We'll go back to Elizabeth's, build a fire, and share the *moscato* dessert wine and cake I bought this afternoon. While Ed waits for coffee, our dinner partner is served a plate of cheese and a bowl of walnuts. The restaurant is silent. He cracks a shell. He cuts a bit of cheese, savours it, eats a walnut, then cracks another. I want to put my head down on the white cloth and weep.

According to Ian, the work finished satisfactorily at the end of February. We paid for the amount contracted but not for the exorbitant extra amount Benito tacked on. He listed such charges as a thousand dollars for hanging a door. We will have to be there to determine exactly what extra work he did. How we'll settle the final amount is a mystery.

In late April, Ed returns to Italy. He has the spring quarter off. His plan is to clear the land and treat, stain and wax all the beams in the house before I arrive on June first. Then we will clean, paint all rooms and windows, and restore the floors to the condition they were in before Benito's restoration. The new kitchen has in it only the sink, dishwasher, stove and fridge. Instead of cabinets, we plan to make plastered brick columns with wide plank shelves and have marble cut for countertops. We have a major incentive: At the end of June, my friend Susan has planned to be married in Cortona. When I asked why she wanted her wedding in Italy, she replied cryptically, 'I want to get married in a language I don't understand.' The guests will stay with us and the wedding will take place at the twelfth-century town hall.

Ed tells me he's confined to the room on the second floor that opens onto the patio, his little haven amidst the rubbish. He cleans one bathroom, unpacks a few pots and dishes, and sets up rudimentary housekeeping. Benito hauled several loads out of the house but only made it as far as the driveway, now a dump. On the front terrace he left a small mountain of stone that was taken out of the wall. The patio and bedroom brick form another small mountain. Even so, Ed is elated. They're gone! The new bathroom, with its foot square tiles, belle époque pedestal sink, and built-in tub, feels large and luxurious, a stark contrast to the former bucket-flush bathroom. Spring is astonishingly green and thousands of naturalised irises and daffodils bloom in long grass all over our land. He finds a seasonal creek pouring over mossy rocks where two box turtles sun themselves. The almond and fruit trees are so outrageously beautiful that he has to tear himself away from working outside.

We try not to call; we tend to get into long conversations, then decide that we could have done x at the house for the money the call has cost. But there is a great need to recount what you've done when you're working on a house. Someone needs to hear that the beams look really great after their final waxing, that your neck is killing you from working above your head all day, that you're on the fourth room. He relates that each room takes forty hours: beams, ceiling, walls. Floors will come last. Seven to seven, seven days a week.

Finally, finally, June – I can go. With all the work Ed has described, I expect the house to glow when I arrive. But, naturally enough, Ed has concentrated on telling me his progress.

When I first arrive, it's hard to focus on how far he has come. The beams look beautiful, yes. But the grounds are full of rubbish, plaster, the old cistern. The electrician has not shown up. Six rooms haven't been touched. All the furniture is piled into three rooms. It's strictly a war zone. I try not to show how horrified I am.

I'm ready for R and R. Unfortunate, because there's nothing to do but launch into this work. We have about three weeks to get ready for our first major onslaught of guests. The wedding! It seems ludicrous that anyone could stay here.

Ed is six foot two inches. I am five foot four. He takes the ceiling: I take the floor. Biology is destiny – but which is better? He actually loves finishing the beams. Painting the brick ceiling is less fun but is rewarding. Suddenly the gunky beams and flaking ceiling are transformed into dark substantial beams, pristine white-brick ceiling. The room is defined. Painting goes quickly with the big brushes made of wild boar hair. Pure white walls –

white on plaster is whiter than any other white. As each room is finished, my job is to paint the *battascopa*, a six-inch-high grey strip along the bases of the walls, a kind of pseudo-moulding that is traditional in old houses of this area. Usually it's a brick colour but we prefer the lighter touch. The word means broom-hit. The darker paint doesn't show the marks of the mops and brooms that must constantly pass over these floors. Almost upside down, I measure six inches in several places, tape the floor and wall, then quickly paint and pull off the tape. Naturally, the tape pulls off some white paint, which then has to be retouched. Twelve rooms, four walls each, plus the stairwell, landings and entrance. We're leaving the stone cantina as is. Next, I decalcify the floor. The first step is to sweep up all the large chunks and dirt, then vacuum. With a special solution I spread, the residue from dirt, plaster and paint drippings is dissolved. After that, I rinse the floor with a wet mop three times, the middle time with a mild soap solution. I'm on my knees. Next: mop again with water and a little muriatic acid. Rinse, then paint the floor with linseed oil, letting it soak in and dry. After it dries for two days, I wax. On the floor again, char style. My knees, totally unused to this, rebel and I suppress groans when I stand up. Last step: buff with soft cloth. The floors come back, rich and dark and shiny. Each room pops into place, looking very much as they did when we bought the house, only now the beams are right and the radiators are in place. '*Brutto*,' ugly, I said to the plumber when I saw them. 'Yes,' he replied, 'but beautiful in winter.'

As Ed told me, seven to seven: seven days a week. We spread the rubble down the driveway, which is chewed up anyway from all the trucks. We dig in the larger stones and bricks, spread grass cuttings on top. Gradually, it will settle in. We hire someone to take away a truckload that Benito failed to haul. On a walk a few days later, we see a pile of awful rubble dumped along a road about a mile from our house, and to our horror, spot our plaster with the madonna blue coat of paint underneath.

From high school through graduate school, Ed worked as a house mover, busboy, cabinetmaker, refrigerator hauler. A friend calls him 'the muscular poet'. He's thriving on this work, though he, too, is sapped at night. I never have done manual labour, except spurts of refinishing furniture, pruning, painting and wall-papering. This is an order of bodily exertion to shock my system. Everything aches. What *is* water on the knee? I think I may get it. I die at night. In the mornings, we both have surges of new energy that come from somewhere. We plug right back in. We're consumed. I'm amazed: the relentlessness we've developed. I never will feel the same towards workers again; they should be paid fortunes.

When I seal the patio bricks with linseed oil, the sun feels espe-cially deadly. I'm determined to finish and keep working until I start to reel with the fumes and the heat. Now and then I stand up and breathe in great draughts of the honeysuckle we've planted in an enormous pot, stare off into the great view, then dip the brush into the pot again. Who would think to ask, when paying a lot for a new patio, whether the job included finishing the brick's sur-face? It never occurred to either of us that we would have to treat the kitchen and patio bricks to several coats of this gloppy stuff.

After we clean up late in the day, we walk around assessing what's left, how we've done. We will not have any children together but decide that this is the equivalent of having triplets. As each room is finished, we get to bring in the furniture for it. Gradually, rooms are set up, still spare but basically furnished. I've brought over white bedspreads for the twin beds. We take a morning in Arezzo and buy a few lamps from a place that still makes the traditional majolica vases of the area into lamps. A fabulous feeling – things are shaping up, they're done, it's clean, we'll be warm in winter – we've done it! This feels giddy and fuels us to keep going.

A week before the wedding, our friends Shera and Kevin arrive from California. We see them get off the train way down the track. Kevin is manoeuvring something enormous that looks like a coffin for two. His bicycle! We keep working while they go to Florence, Assisi and on the Piero della Francesca trail. At night we make great meals together and they tell us all the wonders they've seen and we tell them about the new faucet we want to install for the hip bath. They fall instantly in love with the whole area and seem to want to hear our daily saga of cleaning the new bricks on the kitchen floor. When they're not travelling, Kevin is off on long bicycle trips. Shera, an artist, is captive here. She is painting milky blue half circles over the windows in a bedroom. We've picked a star from one of Giotto's paintings and she makes a stencil of it and fills the half domes with gold leaf stars. A few stars 'fall' out of the dome and onto the white walls. We're preparing the bridal chamber. At an antique shop near Perugia, I buy two coloured prints of the constellations with mythological beasts and figures. At the Cortona market, I find pretty linen and cotton sheets in pale blue with cutwork in white. We're preparing, too, for our first houseparty. We buy twenty wineglasses, linen tablecloths, pans for baking the wedding cake, a case of wine.

There is no way everything can be finished in time for the wedding (or ever?), but we manage an extraordinary amount. The day before everyone arrives, Kevin comes downstairs and asks, 'Why does the toilet steam? Is there something peculiar about Italian toilets?' Ed brings in the ladder, climbs up to the wall-mounted tank, and dips in his hand. Hot water. We check the other bathrooms. The new one is okay but the other old one also has hot water. We hardly have used those bathrooms and had not let water run long enough for the hot water to arrive, so we had not noticed that neither bathroom had cold water at all. As soon as guests started using the baths, it became noticeable. Shera says she thought the shower was awfully hot, once it finally warmed up, but hadn't wanted to complain. The plumber cannot come for a few days, so we will go through the wedding with quick showers and smoking toilets!

The front terrace is still rough but we have potted geraniums along the wall to distract from the torn-up ground. At least we removed the rubble. Four rooms have beds. Susan's two cousins from England and Cole's brother and sister-in-law are arriving. Shera and Kevin will move to a hotel in town for a couple of days. Other friends are coming from Vermont.

By day, we are twelve in the house. Many hands to help with drinks and lunch. The cake must be improvised because the oven is small. I envisioned three tiers of sponge cake with a hazelnut butter-cream frosting, to be served with whipped cream and cherries steeped in sugared wine. We couldn't find a large pan for the bottom and finally bought a tin dog dish to bake it in. The cake is lovely, if a bit lopsided. We decorate it with flowers all around. Everyone is running off in different directions sight-seeing and shopping.

We're having the prenuptial dinner here on a clear warm night, everyone in pale linens and cottons. Many photos are taken of us arm in arm on the steps and leaning over the balcony. Susan's cousin brings out champagne he has brought from France. After drinks with *bruschette* and dry olives, we start with cool fennel soup. I've made a rustic casserole of chicken, white beans, sausage, tomatoes and onions. There are tiny green beans, baskets of bread, and a salad of arugula, radicchio and chicory. Everyone tells wedding stories. Mark was to have married a Colorado girl who ran away on the wedding day and married someone else in a week. Karen was a bridesmaid on a boat wedding and the bride's mother, in teal chiffon, tipped into the drink. When I married at twenty-two, I wanted a midnight wedding with everyone wearing robes and carrying candles. The minister said absolutely not, that midnight was a 'furtive hour'. Nine was as late as he'd go. And instead of a robe, I wore my sister's wedding dress and carried a leatherbound Keats down the aisle. My mother pulled my skirt and I leaned over for her words of wisdom. She whispered, 'It won't last six months.' But she was wrong.

We should have an accordion player, à la Fellini, and maybe a white horse for the bride to ride, but we do well with the fabulous night, and the CD player inspires a little dancing in the dining room. The white peach tart with pine nuts should end this dinner but Ed's description of the *crema* and the hazelnut *gelati* in town sends everyone to the cars. They're amazed that such a small town is still hopping at eleven, everyone outdoors with coffee, ice cream, or perhaps an *amaro*, an after-dinner bitter. Babies in strollers still as wide-eyed as their parents, teenagers sitting on the town hall steps. The only thing sleeping is a cat on top of the police car.

The morning of the wedding Susan, Shera and I pick a bouquet of lavender, pink and yellow wildflowers for Susan to carry.

When we're all dressed in silks and suits, we walk into town over the Roman road. Ed carries our good shoes in a shopping bag. Susan has brought Chinese painted paper parasols for everyone because of the midday sun. We walk through town and up the steps of the twelfth-century town hall. It's a dark, high-ceilinged room with tapestries and frescoes and high judicial-looking chairs, an impressive room to sign a treaty in. The city of Cortona has sent red roses and Ed has arranged for Bar Sport to come over right after the ceremony with cold *prosecco*. Susan's cousin Brian runs all around with his video camera, getting shots from every angle. After the brief ceremony, we cross the piazza to La Logetta for a Tuscan feast beginning with a selection of typical *antipasti*: *crostini*, little rounds of bread topped with olives, peppers, mushroom or chicken liver; *prosciutto e melone*, fried olives stuffed with *pancetta* and spicy bread crumbs; and the local *finocchiona*, a salami studded with fennel seeds. Next they bring out a selection of *primi*, first courses to try, including ravioli with butter and sage, and *gnocchi di patate*, little 'knuckles' of potato served here with pesto. Course after course arrives, culminating in platters of roast lamb and veal and the famous grilled Val di Chiana steak. Karen notices the grand piano in the corner under a massive vase of flowers and prevails upon Cole, who is a pianist, to play. Ed is at the other end of the table but he catches my eye as Cole begins Scarlatti. Three weeks ago this was a dream, a long shot, a frightening prospect. 'Cheers!' the English cousins call out.

Back at home, we're all stunned by the food and heat and decide to postpone the wedding cake until late afternoon. I hear someone snoring. In fact, I hear two people snoring.

Though the cake lacks that professional touch, it may be the best cake I ever tasted. I'll credit our tree for the nuts. Shera and Kevin are dancing in the dining room again. Others stroll out to the point where our land ends for the view of the lake and valley. We can't decide whether to eat again or forget it. Finally we run down to Camucia for pizza. Our favourite places are closed, so we end up in a definitely downscale, unatmospheric place. The pizza is excellent, however, and no-one seems to notice the dust grey curtains or the cat who has leapt on the adjoining table and is polishing off the remains of someone's dinner. At the end of the table our bride and groom, holding hands, are in a charmed circle of two.

Susan and Cole have headed to Lucca then back to France; their family guests are gone.

Shera and Kevin are here for a few more days. Ed and I visit the *marmista* and choose thick white marble for the countertops. The next day he cuts and bevels them and Ed and Kevin load them into the back of the car. Suddenly the kitchen looks the way I thought it would: brick floor, white appliances, long sink, plank shelves, marble counters. I sew a blue plaid curtain to go under the sink and hang a braid of garlic and some dried herbs from the wall shelves. In town we find an old peasant dish and cup rack. The dark chestnut looks great against the white walls. At last, a place for all the cups and bowls we're buying in the local ceramic patterns.

Everyone has gone. We eat the last of the wedding cake. Ed begins one of his many lists – we should paper a room with them – of projects he hopes to accomplish now. The kitchen is looking irresistible and we're moving into high season for vegetables and fruit. July fourth: Much of summer is left. My daughter is coming. Travelling friends will stop in for lunch or for a night. We're ready.

FROM

CITY OF DJINNS

WILLIAM DALRYMPLE

WILLIAM DALRYMPLE is the author of several highly acclaimed and best-selling books, including *In Xanadu* (a journey to China), *City of Djinns* (life in Delhi), *From the Holy Mountain* (surviving Christians in the Holy Land) and, most recently, *White Mughals*. He lives in London and is a Fellow of the Royal Society of Literature and the Royal Asiatic Society.

Extract from *City of Djinns* reprinted by permission of
HarperCollins Publishers Ltd.
© William Dalrymple 1993.

THE FLAT perched at the top of the house, little more than a lean-to riveted to Mrs Puri's ceiling. The stairwell exuded sticky, airless September heat; the roof was as thin as corrugated iron.

Inside we were greeted by a scene from *Great Expectations*: a thick pall of dust on every surface, a family of sparrows nesting in the blinds and a fleece of old cobwebs – great arbours of spider silk – arching the corner walls. Mrs Puri stood at the doorway, a small, bent figure in a *salwar kameez*.

'The last tenant did not go out much,' she said, prodding the cobwebs with her walking stick. She added: 'He was not a tidy gentleman.' Olivia blew on a cupboard; the dust was so thick you could sign your name in it.

Our landlady, though a grandmother, soon proved herself to be a formidable woman. A Sikh from Lahore, Mrs Puri was expelled from her old home during Partition and in the upheavals of 1947 lost everything. She arrived in Delhi on a bullock cart. Forty-two years later she had made the transition from refugee pauper to Punjabi princess. She was now very rich indeed. She owned houses all over Delhi and had swapped her bullock for a fleet of new Maruti cars, the much coveted replacement for the old Hindustan Ambassador. Mrs Puri also controlled a variety of business interests. These included the Gloriana Finishing School, India's first etiquette college, a unique institution which taught village girls how to use knives and forks, apply lipstick and make polite conversation about the weather.

Mrs Puri had achieved all this through a combination of hard work and good old-fashioned thrift. In the heat of summer she rarely put on the air-conditioning. In winter she allowed herself the electric fire for only an hour a day. She recycled the newspapers we threw out; and returning from parties late at night we could see her still sitting up, silhouetted against the window, knitting sweaters for export. 'Sleep is silver,' she would say in explanation, 'but money is gold.'

This was all very admirable, but the hitch, we soon learned, was that she expected her tenants to emulate the disciplines she imposed upon herself. One morning, after only a week in the flat, I turned on the tap to discover that our water had been cut off, so went downstairs to sort out the problem. Mrs Puri had already been up and about for several hours; she had been to the *gurd-wara*, said her prayers and was now busy drinking her morning glass of rice water.

'There is no water in our flat this morning, Mrs Puri.'

'No, Mr William, and I am telling you why.'

'Why, Mrs Puri?'

'You are having guests, Mr William. And always they are going to the lavatory.'

'But why should that affect the water supply?'

'Last night I counted seven flushes,' said Mrs Puri, rapping her stick on the floor. 'So I have cut off the water as protest.'

She paused to let the enormity of our crime sink in.

'Is there any wonder that there is water shortage in our India when you people are making seven flushes in one night?'

Old Mr Puri, her husband, was a magnificent-looking Sikh gentleman with a long white beard and a tin zimmer frame with wheels on the bottom. He always seemed friendly enough – as we passed he would nod politely from his armchair. But when we first took the flat Mrs Puri drew us aside and warned us that her husband had never been, well, quite the same since the riots that followed Mrs Gandhi's death in 1984.

It was a rather heroic story. When some hooligans began to break down the front door, Mr Puri got Ladoo (the name means Sweety), his bearer, to place him directly behind the splintering wood. Uttering a blood-curdling cry, he whipped out his old ser-vice revolver and fired the entire magazine through the door. The marauders ran off to attack the taxi rank around the corner and the Puris were saved.

From that day on, however, the old man had become a fervent Sikh nationalist. 'Everyone should have their own home,' he would snort. 'The Muslims have Pakistan. The Hindus have Hindustan. The Punjab is our home. If I was a young man I would join Bhindranwale and fight these Hindu dogs.'

'It is talk only,' Mrs Puri would reply.

'Before I die I will see a free Khalistan.'

'You are daydreaming only. How many years are left?'

'The Punjab is my home.'

'He may have been born in the Punjab,' Mrs Puri would say, turning to me, 'but now he could not go back to village life. He likes flush toilet and Star TV. Everybody likes flush toilet and Star TV. How can you leave these things once you have tasted such luxury?'

Since the riots, Mr Puri had also become intermittently senile. One day he could be perfectly lucid; the next he might suffer from the strangest hallucinations. On these occasions conversations withhim took on a somewhat surreal quality:

MR PURI (up the stairs to my flat) Mr William! Get your bloody mules out of my room this minute!

WD But Mr Puri, I don't have any mules.

MR PURI Nonsense! How else could you get your trunks up the stairs?

During our first month in the flat, however, Mr Puri was on his best behaviour. Apart from twice proposing marriage to my wife, he behaved with perfect decorum.

It had been a bad monsoon. Normally in Delhi, September is a month of almost equatorial fertility and the land seems refreshed and newly-washed. But in the year of our arrival, after a parching summer, the rains had lasted for only three weeks. As a result dust was everywhere and the city's trees and flowers all looked as if they had been lightly sprinkled with talcum powder.

Nevertheless the air was still sticky with damp-heat, and it was in a cloud of perspiration that we began to unpack and to take in the eccentricities of our flat: the chiming doorbell that played both the Indian national anthem and 'Land of Hope and Glory'; the geyser, which if left on too long, would shoot a fountain of boiling water from an outlet on the roof and bathe the terrace in a scalding shower; the pretty round building just below the garden which we at first took to be a temple, and only later discovered to be the local sewage works.

But perhaps the strangest novelty of coming to live in India – stranger even than Mrs Puri – was getting used to life with a sudden glut of domestic help. Before coming out to Delhi we had lived impecuniously in a tiny student dive in Oxford. Now we had to make the transition to a life where we still had only two rooms, but suddenly found ourselves with more than twice that number of servants. It wasn't that we particularly wanted or needed servants; but, as Mrs Puri soon made quite clear, employing staff was a painful necessity on which the prestige of her household depended.

The night we moved in, we spent our first hours dusting and cleaning before sinking, exhausted, into bed at around 2 a.m. The following morning we were woken at seven-thirty sharp by 'Land of Hope and Glory'. Half asleep, I shuffled to the door to find Ladoo, Mr Puri's bearer, waiting outside. He was holding a tray. On the tray were two glasses of milky Indian *chai*.

'*Chota hazari*, sahib,' said Ladoo. Bed tea.

'What a nice gesture,' I said returning to Olivia. 'Mrs Puri has sent us up some tea.'

'I wish she had sent it up two hours later,' said Olivia from beneath her sheets.

I finished the tea and sank down beneath the covers. Ten seconds later the Indian national anthem chimed out. I scrambled out of bed and again opened the door. Outside was a thin man with purple, betel-stained lips. He had a muffler wrapped around his head and, despite the heat, a thick donkey-jacket was buttoned tightly over his torso. I had never seen him before.

'*Mali*,' he said. The gardener.

He bowed, walked past me and made for the kitchen. From the bedroom I could hear him fiddling around, filling a bucket with water then splashing it over the plants on the roof terrace. He knocked discreetly on the bedroom door to indicate he had finished, then disappeared down the stairs. The *mali* was followed first by Murti, the sweeper, then by Prasad, the *dhobi*, and finally by Bahadur, Mrs Puri's Nepali cook. I gave up trying to sleep and went downstairs.

'Mrs Puri,' I said. 'There has been a stream of strange people pouring in and out of my flat since seven-thirty.'

'I know, Mr William,' replied Mrs Puri. 'These people are your servants.'

'But I don't want any servants.'

'Everyone has servants,' said Mrs Puri. 'You must have servants too. This is what these people are for.'

I frowned. 'But must we have so many?'

'Well, you must have a cook and a bearer.'

'We don't need a bearer. And both of us enjoy cooking.'

'In that case you could have one cook-bearer. One man, two jobs. Very modern. Then there is the *mali*, the sweeper, and a *dhobi* for your washing. Also you must be having one driver.' Mrs Puri furrowed her brow. 'It is very important to have good chauffeur,' she said gravely. 'Some pukka fellow with a smart uniform.'

'I haven't got a car. So it's pointless having a driver.'

'But if you have no car and no driver,' said Mrs Puri, 'how will you be getting from place to place?'

🚪

Balvinder Singh, son of Punjab Singh, Prince of Taxi Drivers, may your moustache never grow grey! Nor your liver cave in with cirrhosis. Nor your precious Hindustan Ambassador ever again crumple in a collision – like the one we had with the van carrying Mango Frooty Drink.

Although during my first year in Delhi I remember thinking that the traffic had seemed both anarchic and alarming, by my second visit I had come to realise that it was in fact governed by very strict rules. Right of way belongs to the driver of the largest vehicle. Buses give way to heavy trucks, Ambassadors give way to buses, and bicyclists give way to everything except pedestrians. On the road, as in many other aspects of Indian life, Might is Right.

Yet Mr Balvinder Singh is an individualist who believes in the importance of asserting himself. While circumstances may force him to defer to buses and lorries, he has never seen the necessity of giving way to the tinny new Maruti vans which, though taller than his Ambassador, are not so heavily built. After all, Mr Singh is a *kshatriya* by caste, a warrior, and like his ancestors he is keen to show that he is afraid of nothing. He disdains such cowardly acts as looking in wing mirrors or using his indicators. His Ambassador is his chariot, his klaxon his sword. Weaving into the oncoming traffic, playing 'chicken' with the other taxis, Balvinder Singh is a Raja of the Road.

Or rather was. One month after our arrival in Delhi, Mr Singh and I had an accident. Taking a road junction with more phlegm than usual, we careered into the Maruti van, impaling it on its bows, so that it bled Mango Frooty Drink all over Mr Singh's bonnet. No-one was hurt, and Mr Singh – strangely elated by his 'kill' – took it stoically. 'Mr William,' he said. 'In my life six times have I crashed. And on not one occasion have I ever been killed.'

Although I am devoted to him, Olivia is quick to point out that Mr Singh is in many ways an unattractive character. A Punjabi Sikh, he is the Essex Man of the East. He chews *paan* and spits the betel juice out of the window, leaving a red 'go-fast' stripe along the car's right flank. He utters incoherent whoops of joy as he drives rickshaws on to the pavement or sends a herd of paper boys flying into a ditch. He leaps out of his taxi to urinate at traffic lights, and scratches his groin as he talks. Like Essex Man, he is a lecher. His eyes follow the saris up and down the Delhi avenues; plump Sikh girls riding side-saddle on motorbikes are a particular distraction. Twice a week, when Olivia is not in the car, he offers to drive me to G.B. Road, the Delhi red light district:

'Just looking,' he suggests. 'Delhi ladies very good. Having breasts like mangoes.'

Yet he has his principles. Like his English counterpart, he is a believer in hard work. He finds it hard to understand the beggars who congregate at the lights. 'Why these peoples not working?' he asks. 'They have two arms and two legs. They not handi-crafted.'

'Handicrafted?'

'Missing leg perhaps, or only one ear.'

'You mean handicapped?'

'Yes. Handicrafted. Sikh peoples not like this. Sikh peoples working hard, earning money, buying car.'

Ignoring the bus hurtling towards us, he turns around and winks an enormous wink. 'Afterwards Sikh peoples drinking whisky, looking television, eating tandoori chicken and going G.B. Road.'

The house stood looking on to a small square of hot, tropical green: a springy lawn fenced in by a windbreak of champa and ashok trees. The square was the scene for a daily routine of almost Vedic inflexibility.

Early in the morning, under a bald blue sky, the servants would walk plump dachshunds over the grass, or, duties completed, would stand about on the pavements exchanging gossip or play-ing cards. Then, at about nine o'clock, the morning peace would be broken by a procession of bicycle-powered vendors, each with his own distinctive street-cry: the used-newspaper collector ('Paper-wallah! Paper-wallah! Paper-wallah!') would be fol-lowed by the fruit seller ('Mangoes! Lychees! Bananas! Papaya!'), the bread boy and the man with the vegetable barrow. My favourite, the cotton-fluffer, whose life revolved around the puffing up of old mattresses, would twang a Jew's harp. On Sunday mornings an acrobat would come with his dancing bear; he had a pair of drums and when he beat them the whole square would miraculously fill with children. Early that afternoon would follow a blind man with an accordion. He would sing hymns and sacred qawwalis and sometimes the rich people would send down a servant with a handful of change.

In the late afternoon, a herd of cattle twenty or thirty strong could be seen wandering along the lane at the back of the house. There was never any herder in sight, but they would always rumble slowly past, throwing up clouds of dust. Occasionally they would collide with the household servants wobbling along the back lane on their bicycles, returning from buying groceries in Khan Market. Then followed the brief Indian dusk: a pale Camembert sun sinking down to the treeline; the smell of woodsmoke and dung cooking fires; the last raucous outbursts from the parakeets and the brahminy mynas; the first whirring, humming cicadas.

Later on, lying in bed, you could hear the *chowkidars* stomping around outside, banging their sticks and blowing their whistles. There were never any robberies in our part of New Delhi, and the *chowkidars* were an entirely redundant luxury.

But, as Mrs Puri said, you had to keep up appearances.

Mr Singh also had strong views about appearances.

'You are Britisher,' he said, the very first time I hailed him. 'I know you are a Britisher.'

It was late afternoon at the end of our first week in Delhi. We had just moved in and were beginning the gruelling pilgrimage through Indian government departments that all new arrivals must perform. We were late for an appointment at the Foreigners Regional Registration Office, yet Mr Singh's assertion could not go unquestioned.

'How do you know I'm a Britisher?'

'Because,' said Mr Singh, 'you are not sporting.'

'Actually I am quite sporting,' I replied. 'I go for a run every day, swim in the summer . . .'

'No Britisher is sporting,' said Mr Singh, undaunted.

'Lots of my countrymen are very keen on sport,' I retorted.

'No, no,' said Mr Singh. 'You are not catching me.'

'We are still a force to be reckoned with in the fifteen hundred metres, and sometimes our cricket team . . .'

'No, no,' said Mr Singh. 'Still you are not catching me. You Britishers are not *sporting*.' He twirled the waxed curlicues of his moustache. 'All men should be sporting a moustache, because all ladies are liking too much.'

He indicated that I should get in.

'It is the fashion of our days,' he said, roaring off and narrowly missing a pedestrian.

Mr Singh's taxi stand lay behind the India International Centre, after which it took its name: International Backside Taxis. The stand was run by Punjab Singh, Balvinder's stern and patriarchal father, and manned by Balvinder and his two plump brothers, Gurmuck and Bulwan. There was also a rota of cousins who would fill in during the weekends and at nights. Over the following months we got to know them all well, but it was Balvinder who remained our special friend.

FROM

O COME YE BACK
TO IRELAND

NIALL WILLIAMS AND
CHRISTINE BREEN

NIALL WILLIAMS and CHRISTINE BREEN gave up their jobs in publishing in New York to get back to the land of their forefathers – literally so – by buying a farm in County Clare, Ireland, that had belonged to Christine's great-grandfather. They have since co-authored several books of non-fiction and Niall has written several internationally acclaimed novels set in Ireland.

O Come Ye Back to Ireland by Niall Williams and Christine Breen, published by Soho Press 1987. Copyright © 1987 by Niall Williams and Christine Breen.

ARE YE GOING on the cuaird tonight?

When we first arrived in Kiltumper we knew nothing of the *cuaird* and when first invited had no idea of the full meaning of the word. We were new to the western landscape of field, hedgerow and silence, and found ourselves missing the variety of entertainment we had grown so used to. Looking out on the approaching night there was no movie theatre close by to escape to, no string of restaurants along a well-lit street – only the distant lights of separate houses on a hill and a sense of great stillness. So we decided to go on the *cuaird* that night with Mary and Joe. Venturing with lamp in hand, we were led along the *botharins* with a sense of great expectation. It was seven o'clock and the evening mists rolled across Hayes' Hill. Down our road men and women finished up the day's chores and got ready for the *cuaird*. Hens were locked up for the night, the range was loaded with turf, the night lamp and the warm overcoat or bicycle were made ready. As darkness narrowed the townland into a tight little community of kitchen-lit windows and turf smoke, there was a bustle of activity and the *cuaird* began to take shape.

The word *cuaird* derives from the Irish *cuairt*, the old Gaelic word for visiting. It is among the oldest living traditions of the West. The sound of it – a sound at once songlike and pleasurable – reminds me of other old-fashioned words, of courtesy, courtliness and courtship, all of which, I believe, are in some way related to the *cuaird*. But *cuaird* means more than visit, and more, too, than any one of the English words it resembles. It's a way, a habit of being in a small community that has been passed down for so long that no-one is quite certain when it started.

No word had been sent ahead, no appointment made, for none was necessary. Inside the back door of nearly every house is a chair, often a súgán, empty and waiting for the night-time visitor. No explanation is required: you simply come in the door, sit down and pull a chair to the fire – for the *cuaird* is the night's entertainment. It's a scene set for conversation, for story-telling and laughter, for tall talk of fairies or ghosts, as well as for cattle prices or the weather. As we sat to our welcome in a neighbour's house we were introduced and, even though Mary had brought a half-dozen fresh eggs to our hostess, we came to understand that the *real* gift a visitor brings is news. How are your chimneys pulling? How are ye managing? Everyone wanted to know, and all of a sudden we realised that we possessed a world of news, a whole host of ordinary subjects waiting to be shared. Here, on the *cuaird*, you can broach any subject, share any joke, any problem, and know that you will always have an attentive, and often helpful, audience.

As we sat in the parlour at Dooley's warmed by a great glowing turf fire, Nora was brought out to join us. She had welcomed people to her house for sixty years and we had heard warm tales in the village of men and women coming down across the mountain to her kitchen to hear her play the concertina and to dance the winter night away. We thought she was the embodiment of the *cuaird*. Her great bony hands shook ours and she smiled at us. Welcome, welcome. Did we like music? We did. Did we dance the sets? We didn't. Well, we must. A concertina was brought from a cupboard. She hadn't played in two years with the arthritis in her fingers, she complained, and she might not be able to get a tune. But all the company urged her, and, unsnapping the fasteners of the concertina, she began to play and that parlour in the middle of the west Clare countryside was suddenly concert hall and dance hall. The *cuaird* had come alive.

We stepped to the floor for our first lesson. Chairs were moved back, voices lilted the tune, and with a little stiff awkwardness we began to step a Clare set. Everyone smiled and laughed as we lost the air and came asunder. There was more music and more dancing and laughter. The dark was forgotten, the rain unheard, the wind that tunnelled along the black and winding roads blew unnoticed, for the *cuaird* was on, the kettle was boiling above the turf fire, and the tart was being brought from the oven.

CHRIS'S JOURNAL

A new meaning to a familiar word: *Feather dusting*. The cottage is inches deep in dust. Mary presented me with a gift of a semi-fresh, white-feathered goose wing.

'There, Crissie, there's a grand brush for ye now.'

I tried it out immediately, secretly and alone. It worked marvellously well. But who from my Westchester days of only a month ago would ever believe the sight of me, bent down over the hearth and sweeping up the finest of dust with an old greying, feathered goose wing? I guess its use for small jobs could be compared with the battery-operated Dust Buster we used to have in New York.

Thursday, April eleventh: another day of lashing rain. And still our bed had not arrived. I called Fast Sea and Air (ironic name!) and heard weak excuses: it was Easter time, customs had it, it was a bad time of the year. At long remove, over a static-laden telephone line, my anger was impotent. The bed had been in the country two weeks and was still no nearer to Kiltumper. Chris was shattered by the news of further delay, and wanted to cancel the order, get our money back, threaten action, write to Gay Byrne, Ireland's Phil Donahue. It was hopeless. We needed the bed and had no means of getting it. It was promised for the following Tuesday. After all, we would not be moved in by Chris's birthday. More gloom, disappointment and rain.

In the afternoon we drove to the Garda station, the police force in the village, to hand over our notification of Intent to Burn Bogland. But surprisingly to us, at mid-afternoon the Garda station was closed. We had planned later to drive to Kilrush, a fairly large town by Irish country standards, ten miles to the west of us. But our good intentions were forestalled again when we learnt, just as we were about to go, that Thursday was a half-day in Kilrush. The entire town was closed for the afternoon.

So much for plans for the most efficient use of time we had become predisposed to by our urban existences.

April twelfth was Chris's birthday, and the world's worst day. Sheets of rain streamed from a dark sky and wind flew fiercely at all living things. Mary, however, slow to condemn the weather, said, 'If there's enough blue in the sky to make a sailor's jacket the day will be fine.' And so, sitting late over breakfast with several cups of tea, we watched the sky like lookouts for any clearing. And still the rain rained.

Against the disappointment of being unable to move into the cottage, I had booked us into the Old Ground Hotel in Ennis for the night. An extravagance, but I judged we needed it. Chris especially, for the comforts of Kiltumper fall far short of anything vaguely American. In some of our neighbours' homes bathwater comes brown and uninviting from the taps. Many rooms are damp and dark, and after years in America the small details of hygiene and comfort are sorely missed. There are no cottony soft toilet tissue rolls here, no handy paper napkins, no supersoft fluffy towels.

Against our expectations, the van delivering the vinyl for the kitchen and the carpet for the bedroom *did* arrive in the morning as promised. Once the floor was laid the house immediately seemed friendlier and more intimate. We *were* making our mark on Kiltumper Cottage.

The sky, naturally, cleared. Doesn't it always? asked Mary. Heartened and hopeful and ready for a treat, we drove to Ennis. The Old Ground Hotel was originally a private mansion built in the early eighteenth century. It has over forty rooms, and sitting in the very heart of the lively town it looks grand and elegant. The outer grey stone walls speak of age and history, and inside the furnishings and paintings match this mood. Everything is a piece of Irish history, Irish culture. Poems by Yeats hang framed in the hall and a great turf fire in the foyer is encircled by large soft chairs.

From our new perspective of Kiltumper, the Old Ground was a palace. The moment we entered our room, Chris charged into the bathroom, turned on the taps and ran herself an immense hot bubble bath. Later, laughing, she ran to the bed. White cotton towels, cotton sheets and colour television! And direct-dial telephones! It hardly mattered that the television only had the two channels, or that the wallpaper was peeling a little in the corners, or that the brown-flowered carpet (identical to the wallpaper) was somewhat worn. For in the wilds of rural Kiltumper, Chris and I had put behind us our American perspectives. We were in heaven. I mean, there were even a kettle and teapot awaiting us in the room! Dinner was superb. The dining room was high-ceilinged and lighted with chandeliers. The menu was French and the food exquisite. And over cups of dark brewed coffee – our first *real* coffee in Ireland – the manageress presented Chris with a box of Cadbury's chocolates in honour of her birthday. There we were, foundlings in the West of Ireland, impatient, frustrated and still lonely. And at just that moment the surprise of chocolates endeared the place to us and made us welcome. We felt like peasants become lords. For all the time we were there – and we stayed until the very minute before noon checkout and bathed three times in sensual luxuriance – we were conscious of the staggering contrast between Kiltumper and the Old Ground. It seemed we had travelled a world away in just thirty minutes. Kiltumper Cottage and the Old Ground date from roughly the same period, but between the echoes of vanished aristocrats, whose portraits line the stone stairway of the hotel, and the bellowings of beasts in the field behind our bedroom, lies the entire history of Ireland. Gentry, farmers and gombeenmen. Our brief stay reminded us over and over of the complex and embittered past, of the Anglo-Irish and the Gaelic peasantry. The great gilt-framed portraits that hang on the hotel's walls contrast with the walls of country cottages we visit, covered very differently with simple pictures of Jesus, Mary and Joseph.

CHRIS'S JOURNAL

'Mary, what's that *white* bush that's in bloom now? *White*thorn?'

'No,' replied Mary, 'that's the *black*thorn tree, Crissie.'

We were finally all set to move in. The bed was in Limerick and had been promised to be delivered in the afternoon. In the spirit of things Chris cut some of our abundant rhubarb and tied the sticks in small bundles. Then, we were off to the village in the big blue Peugeot to market. We walked into one of the several small shops that has a little of everything, leaving the rhubarb outside.

'I see you don't have any rhubarb,' I said.

'No,' said the shopkeeper hesitantly, 'it's early yet for that.'

Chris smiled at me. We were going to pull it off – our first time bartering and we were nervous with the thrill of it. 'How would you like some of Kiltumper's best?'

The deal was done. The shopkeeper was delighted to be able to offer her customers early rhubarb for the Sunday dinner and Chris ran out to the car to bring in the clean red sticks. Like merchants we counted them out and tied them again. One pound forty-five pence was our price, and it seemed good as a fortune to us as it bought milk, butter and biscuits. We had picked the rhubarb only an hour earlier, and there it suddenly was on the grocer's shelf. As we drove away we were both thinking that we would come back tomorrow to see if it were sold. Wherefore goes our rhubarb? Who sits down to it today?

Back in the garden we looked at every growing thing in a new light. Everything that rises greenly above the soil is intimately a part of our life here. We were newly conscious of cycles, rhythms and patterns. There is a wonderful sense of closeness between earth and human. All old clichés perhaps, but to the person who actually grows the thing and cares for it through good and bad this is an undeniable truth. And that afternoon in the sunshine it filled Chris and me with deep satisfaction. It seemed a fitting prologue to the imminent arrival of the bed and our first night in the cottage. We had the fire in the stove burning warmly, and all eyes were on the road from the east waiting for the van. All our friends in the village were waiting, too. Mary from her kitchen window down the road was waiting for it. Pauline, next along the road, was waiting, too. In the front green garden, where we stood with ears pricked for any sound, nothing came or went. Time ran on and still nothing came, and a familiar sinking feeling crept into our hearts. Everyone had an opinion: it could be delivered as late as eight in the evening. It could be held up somewhere back up the road. It could be broken down. It could be lost. But of course it was not lost, just delayed once again. It did not come that day. Nor had we any news of it, and letting the fire burn low and returning to Mary's for the night, we were downhearted.

'You can get nothing done in this country,' Chris said angrily. 'Nothing. They've had our bed three weeks. They're only in Limerick, an hour away now. It's so bloody Irish, so incompetent! Анн!'

The curses continued. Mary, fretting and unhappy for us, drew us off to Dooley's for tea. There Chris voiced her fury and Michael Dooley sat silver-haired by the turf fire listening while she ranted. Once she had finished he looked over to her with his lovely, lively blue eyes and said, 'Crissie, have ye heard the cuckoo?'

CHRIS'S JOURNAL

And when it was good, it was very, very good. At last the bed arrived. The long delay has filled us both with hesitation and doubt, but once I had unpacked and assembled the unpainted blond ash headboard and frame, it fitted perfectly with the mood of our farmhouse cottage. Once the quilts and pillows that we had carried across the Atlantic were arranged on the mattress, the scene looked picture-perfect, just like the Conran's catalogue. All day I thought of it, proof that we were now inhabitants. We left Mary's, blessed with holy water from the local blessed well, and drove back up the road to our cottage in a high pitch of excitement. So there we finally were. We had no television, our radio was broken. There was not a sound, and earlier, writing in my journal, I had felt the unsettling sensation of the loudness of my pen as it scraped softly upon the paper.

The stove was burning over five hundred degrees. A hot-water bottle readied the chilly sheets. Hot milk preceded, and when we finally laid down our heads, the room with the three-foot thick walls was absolutely still and quiet. It felt like a cave, but with one long window to the sky of deepest blue patterned with infinitesimal stars. Gusts of wind rustled in the bedroom's old chimney, and with our heads beside it, we vaguely thought of birds or bats descending in the night. The ceiling above us, Chris said, seemed to breathe and sigh and she heard soft shuffling sounds somewhere in the rafters. The sense of disturbing ancestral ghosts snuggled us closer together. Don't go to sleep until I'm asleep, she said to me. And so, alert and listening to every sound, from the thrashing branches of the sycamore trees to the distant bellowing roar of some bull, we lay in the dark, waiting, waiting, waiting for the silent visitor of sleep on our first night in Kiltumper Cottage.

DIGGING MR BENNY'S
DEAD UNCLE

ROLF POTTS

ROLF POTTS writes a column on independent travel for *National Geographic Adventure*. His work has also appeared in *Salon*, *Condé Nast Traveler*, *National Geographic Traveler* and *Best American Travel Writing 2000*. His first book, *Vagabonding: An Uncommon Guide to the Art of Long-Term Travel* – which was written in Ranong, Thailand – will be published by Random House/Villard in January 2003. In addition to Thailand, Rolf feels somewhat at home in Egypt, South Korea and Kansas. His virtual home can be found at http://rolfpotts.com.

FROM THE OUTSET, my reasons for moving to Ranong had nothing to do with the town itself. I hadn't moved there to shop in the fish markets, explore the tidal flats or hike into the rainforest. I hadn't even moved there to meet the locals or learn about Thai culture. Rather, I'd moved to the sleepy southern Thailand border town to rent a room for a few months and write my first book. Seeking the right blend of isolation and convenience, I'd located a cheap, quiet studio at the edge of town, where I set up my laptop on a wobbly kitchen table, spread my notes out on the worn wooden floorboards and immersed myself in my work.

My plan had been to live like an obsessive and industrious hermit – and I regarded Ranong as little more than a static backdrop for my labours. Each morning I did a simple regimen of push-ups and went for a run along a jungle-fringed road outside of town; the rest of the day was given to writing. Time spent away from my laptop, I reasoned, was time wasted – and apart from simple restaurant transactions, I didn't meet, talk to or even think about anyone in the town. At night, when my work was finished, I would lie in my bed and stare at the ceiling until I fell asleep, content in my creative solitude.

Such blissful isolation might have lasted, too, had I not required a haircut ten days into my sojourn.

Although Ranong was home to several modern hair salons, I opted for a dowdy old barbershop that fitted my *jungle noir* ideals: battered iron barber's chairs in a dim, humid storefront; slippery pomade bottles clustered around dented washbasins; idle men in sweat-soured T-shirts puffing on cheroots in the corners. Lording over this scene was a thin, sexagenarian Burmese émigré who introduced himself as Mr Benny. He wore thick spectacles and sported a wispy black moustache. Faded crucifix tattoos danced on his forearms as he pinned a frock around my neck.

'Where you from?' he asked in slow, slurry English. 'Australia?'

'Nope,' I replied. 'America.'

'America. I always want to go there and see cowboys.' Mr Benny paused in concentration as he took out a pair of shears and began to snip at the side of my head. 'My great-aunt was marry to a man from Boston once. His name is Benedict, same as me. He do a business for many years on the Burma side of the river.'

'Did you know him well?'

'No, not well. He is much older than me. In 1993, I have to go find him and take him back to Thailand. Very difficult.'

'Why was it difficult?'

'Well, nobody in my family can tell me where he is.'

'Didn't he keep in contact with you?'

Mr Benny let out a slurry giggle. 'Of course not! My Uncle Benedict been dead for forty years. But my England cousin write to me that year and she ask to have his bones.'

'So you went over and dug them up?'

'Yes, but it is a big problem. My cousin become angry with me.'

'Why, what happened?'

The old Burmese barber paused and wrinkled his brow. 'It's a difficult story. Maybe you not want to hear it.'

'No, no, it sounds interesting,' I said.

With a sigh, Mr Benny started to snip at my hair again. 'I hire a boat and go across to Burma. It is not hard to find my Uncle Benedict. He's in a Christian cemetery at Victoria Point. But the cemetery mans want money to dig the bones. I not have any money, so I take a shovel and sneaked my uncle out when it get dark.'

'You dug up the bones in the middle of the night?'

'Yes. It take me all night to dig, and then I leave Burma in the morning with my uncle in this sack. The border police stop and ask me what's in this sack, and I tell them it is Burma whisky.'

'Did they believe you?'

'No! They say "Open that sack!" I open that sack a little bit and give them one bottle of whisky. Then they tell me, "Go home."'

'But I thought your sack was full of bones.'

The old Burmese barber raised an eyebrow and caught my eye in the mirror. 'Mr Benny is a clever man. He put one whisky in with his dead uncle, because he knows how police mans think. You make present for them, and they not care what's in that sack.'

'So you didn't get in trouble?'

'No problem with the police mans.'

'So your story has a happy ending,' I said. 'You were a successful grave-robber.'

Mr Benny looked at the floor and blushed. 'Happy ending,' he repeated uncertainly.

The haircut ended up costing me forty baht (slightly less than a dollar) and left me with the close-cut, whitewall coiffure of a Thai senior citizen. Bidding Mr Benny farewell, I walked back to my studio and returned to work.

Now that I'd heard Mr Benny's story, however, my work wasn't quite so focussed. Sometimes, during my morning runs or while organising note cards in my studio, I'd get the urge to go back and ask Mr Benny more about his Uncle Benedict. I wanted to know why the shadowy old Bostonian had come to Burma and how he'd died. Moreover, I realised that I'd never coaxed Mr Benny into telling me the entire story. What, I wondered, had happened to Benedict's remains once Mr Benny brought them back to Thailand? Did the cousin just show up from England, plunk the old bones into a suitcase and fly them home? Furthermore, why had Mr Benny insinuated that his family was angry with him, when it was obvious he'd gone to so much trouble to help them out?

I did my best to ignore these issues as I toiled away on my book. The isolation of my little studio had allowed me to concentrate entirely on writing, and I was determined not to compromise this by walking back into town and delving into the apocryphal family life of my Burmese barber.

After about three weeks of flawless discipline, however, I woke up one morning and decided that my hair looked a bit tousled at the edges. Seeing this as a fine excuse, I wandered into town to have Mr Benny trim my hair.

'I have a question about your story,' I said as Mr Benny pinned the frock around my neck.

'What story?'

'The story about going to Burma and digging up the bones of your Uncle Benedict.'

Mr Benny gave me a quizzical look. 'Do I tell you that story?'

'Yes, you told me the last time you cut my hair. It was very interesting. But I forgot to ask what happened when you got back to Thailand with your uncle's bones. Did your family come and get them?'

'No. They not get them.'

'Why not? What happened to your English cousin?'

'It's difficult. Maybe you not want to hear about it.' Mr Benny took out his shears and started in on his work, as if hoping I'd change the subject.

'No, of course I want to hear about it,' I insisted.

'It is a big problem,' he said. 'My family become angry with me.'

'Yes, but *why* did they get angry?'

Mr Benny sighed fatalistically. 'Because I throw my Uncle Benedict's bones into the sea.'

This bit took me by surprise. 'Why did you do that? Didn't your family want the bones?'

'Oh, my England cousin want those bones. She write me a letter and say she come to Ranong and get them from me. But when I come home from Burma with those bones I get scared. In Thailand, everyone is Buddhist – and Buddhist people burn up the body when it dies. Nobody ever see no bones except for in murders. So if the police mans come to my house and see my uncle's bones, I worry they think I kill him.'

'So you decided to throw the bones in the sea?'

Mr Benny blushed as he snipped at my hair. 'Before I throw the bones in the sea, I take them up to my cousin's cousins in Bangkok. Benedict is great-grandfather to them, so I think maybe they can take those bones and wait them for my England cousin.'

'So did they take the bones?'

'Well, I give them that sack and say, "This is your great-grandfather Benedict." But my Bangkok cousins are Buddhists, so they think I'm giving them a goats.'

'They thought you were giving them *goats*?'

'A goats.'

'Oh, you mean a *ghost*.'

'Yes, a goats. They get scared and call a monk to chase the goats out from their house. They yell and tell me to take those bones and go home. So I took the bus back to Ranong.'

'You took the bones back to Ranong on the *bus*?'

'Yes! Mr Benny not have car! I hold that sack on my legs like a baby the whole way. Ten hours on that bus. And no sleep for Mr Benny, because he not want that sack to open and his uncle's bones fall out.'

'But you made it home okay?'

'I make it home. But then I not know where to put those bones. There are many dogs in Ranong. They come and sniff that sack. They *know* about my Uncle Benedict inside.' Mr Benny swapped his shears for a hard-razor and started shaping my sideburns. 'When I fall asleep in my home that night, I dream of dogs eating those bones. So I wake up and get a rock for that sack and go find a boat.'

'And you threw the bones into the sea?'

'Yes. I threw my uncle down into the sea.'

'Wow. That's quite a story.'

'Quite a story,' Mr Benny shot me a weak smile in the mirror. 'Very difficult.'

As Mr Benny continued his work with the hard-razor, I quizzed him about his great-uncle's life – but he didn't know much beyond the fact that Benedict was from Boston and had worked as a trader. Mr Benny then proceeded to tell me about his own life in Burma: how the Irish priests at his grammar school had taught him English; how, at age fourteen, he'd been recruited to fight with Kuomintang nationalists against the Red Chinese in northern Burma; how he'd slipped out of his troubled homeland as a young man and eventually settled in Thailand.

I went home that morning with another garish, senior-citizen haircut, but I was happy I'd taken the trouble to chat to Mr Benny. Now that my lingering questions about his dead American uncle had been addressed, I figured I could return my full energies to working on my book.

The problem, of course, was that I kept thinking up new questions for Mr Benny. I found myself curious about the Irish priests who'd tutored him, and his days as a teen solider. I wanted to know what had finally made him leave his homeland for Thailand, and if he ever missed it. What's more, I realised that I still hadn't let the recalcitrant old barber tie up the loose ends of his grave-robbing story. He'd dropped the bones into the sea, yes, but I suddenly remembered he'd left out certain details about his English cousin. What, I wondered, had she done when she arrived in Thailand to find the bones missing?

This time, I didn't have the discipline or patience to wait for another haircut. The following morning I walked into town and found Mr Benny unlocking the folding iron gate in front of his barbershop. He cheerfully invited me in and served me a cup of coffee thickened with condensed milk. He asked me a bit about America, and when I told him I hailed from the prairie, he told me that his favourite English-language book was an old cowboy novel called *The Big Sky*.

Eventually I steered the conversation over to his dead American kinsman. 'I'm still curious about what happened with your Uncle Benedict,' I said to him.

Mr Benny sipped his coffee and smiled cautiously. 'I tell you: I throw his bones into the sea.'

'Yes, but what about your English cousin? Wasn't she going to come to Ranong and get the bones? What happened to her?'

Mr Benny gave me a bashful look. 'It's difficult,' he said. 'A difficult story.'

'You mean your cousin was angry to hear that you'd thrown the bones into the sea?'

'No.'

'Oh. Then what's difficult about the story?'

Mr Benny leaned in with just the trace of a smile. 'I *never tell* my England cousin about throwing those bones in the sea.'

'I don't understand. Didn't she come to Ranong?'

'Yes, she *did* come! But I feel too bad to tell her that grandfather Benedict is down under the water. So I say, "See me tomorrow and I give you the bones."'

'But you didn't have the bones.'

'Yes. I don't have no bones. So I go to my Chinese friend and ask *him* for bones.'

'Why would your Chinese friend have the bones? Was he a scuba diver?'

'He is a meat man.'

'What, like a butcher?'

'Yes, butcher. He give me some *pig bones*. He say, "Tell your cousin that this pig bones is Uncle Benedict."'

'But surely your cousin could tell the difference between pig bones and human bones.'

'Yes. So my Chinese friend and me, we smash up the pig bones and put them in a pretty jar. I give that pretty jar to my England cousin, and I say, "These are the bones that I digged for you." So she give me one thousand baht and she go home with my Uncle Benedict in that jar.'

'But it wasn't really your Uncle Benedict.'

'Yes. And I didn't know about NDA.'

'NDA?'

'I didn't know the scientist can check if those bones are her family.'

'Oh, right. DNA testing.'

'Yes. My cousin go to the NDA, and the scientist say to her, "Your grandfather is a pig."'

'Wow. And she was angry with you?'

'Very, very. She send a letter and say I am a liar. She say I try and trick her for money. And I never heared from her again.'

With a guilty giggle, Mr Benny finished off his coffee and got up to prepare his barbershop for a day of business.

After that morning, my isolationist work ethic never quite recovered. In sharing the bizarre tale of his dead uncle, Mr Benny had broken through my tunnel vision and allowed me to glimpse a piece of Ranong for the first time. In the weeks that followed, I found myself growing more gregarious and more distracted. One day in the central market, a passing conversation with a policeman led to a raucous evening at Ranong's kick boxing venue. Another time, a moto driver (whose English was as limited as my Thai) invited me to spend an afternoon with his family at a city park. I began to take my long-distance runs in the evenings, when I could join groups of Thai joggers along the road to the local hot springs. My landlady, sensing my new openness, had me over for dinners and offered to let me spend my weekends at her beach house on the Andaman Sea coast. Over time, I found myself lingering longer at restaurants and returning smiles on the street. Bit by bit, my loner pretensions dried up, and I began to feel more a part of Ranong.

Naturally, my writing output suffered as a result. What I'd hoped would be an intense four-month creative brainstorm ultimately ballooned into nine haphazard months. Rainy season stretched into dry season. Deadlines passed. Return tickets were rescheduled and rent fees were renegotiated. Dry season began to stretch its way back into rainy season.

And, amidst all of this, I made a habit of visiting Mr Benny's barbershop whenever I passed through central Ranong. There, we'd offhandedly talk about sports or politics, and I'd wheedle him into sharing more quirky tales from his life.

Sometimes, when the tales were particularly interesting, I'd even let him cut my hair.

TROPPO GENTILE

FROM

ITALIAN NEIGHBOURS

TIM PARKS

TIM PARKS has lived and taught in Italy for many years. His experiences both as a teacher and as a foreigner in Italy have provided the material for several of his highly acclaimed novels and non-fiction works, among them *Italian Neighbours*. His latest book describes time he spent following the Verona football club and its fans.

Extract from *Italian Neighbours* by Tim Parks published by Heinemann 1992. Used by permission of The Random House Group Limited and Anthony Harwood Ltd.

To BE EARTHQUAKE-PROOF, modern Italian buildings are legally required to be constructed around a reinforced concrete frame. In the event of tremors, the whole structure should thus shift as one unit, rather than crumbling into its separate parts. And, indeed, as one walks about the outskirts of Montecchio and on into the surrounding hills, builders are eagerly pouring cement into columns of roughly nailed planks, in a hurry to get things done before the November rains.

Concrete the columns and the beams, where shortly before were olive trees; concrete the roofs, too, of these new *palazzine* and *case a schiera*; and likewise concrete the floors, all wires and plumbing laid forever inaccessible in the cement. Gaunt frames take over a vineyard. Up go the walls between one beam and the next. The roof is then topped with terracotta, the living space inside tiled with ceramics: sombre colours and smaller tiles in the seventies, brighter gloss-finish colours and much larger tiles in the eighties.

It makes for some rather curious acoustics. With no wood, you are saved the creaking board, the moaning stair. If you want to sneak in to check on a sleeping baby, or, God forbid, sneak out on wife or husband, there is no danger of the floor betraying you. In stockinged feet you are soundless. On the other hand, a hard object dropped on that ceramic-on-concrete floor, even a coin, will be heard in every room in the building, volume and intensity depending on the vicinity to a load-bearing beam or column. Patent leather soles clicking across the tiles will thus click across all the floors and ceilings of the condominium. A lavatory flushing in the dead of night is an explosion, an act of terrorism. And if you should take a drill to the wall and, after penetrating the plaster, happen upon one of those steel-reinforced columns, then

TIM PARKS

all over the building, from *taverna* to *solaio*, it will seem that the eventuality for which the structure was designed is in full swing. The air vibrates. Soundwaves oppress the ear. It is as if one were caught inside a guitar with some naughty Brobdingnagian child incessantly twanging the bass string.

We did experience a couple of small quakes in Via Colombare. The *palazzina* shuddered and sang. Patuzzi's wineglasses tinkled on their shelves. Apparently, columns of trucks were passing in the night, or ships' engines starting up in the basement.

Lying down to sleep of an October evening, thankful that we can now close the windows against the TVs, accordions and ping-pong of the velvety dark outside, we hear instead an unmistakeable fierce trickling, coming, well, presumably from below us. At eleven-thirty every night. Trickle trickle trickle, dribble dribble, drop, drop, stop. We hold our breath. But there is no explosion of flushing, for unspoken condominium etiquette requires that the toilets *tacciono* – fall silent – after eleven o'clock. It's a special kind of intimacy this concrete brings.

Trying to sleep again after being woken by Vega in the early hours, I begin to hear footsteps going back and forth in our *solaio* under the roof above. This is alarming. Slow heavy footsteps, back and forth, back and forth, above our heads. Rita confirms, they definitely come from our *solaio*, supposedly an empty attic. And in the dead of night one believes in *fantasmi*. Vega has been moaning rather than barking this evening, howling and wailing at the moon.

I get up, pull on a pair of trousers, then slippers against the cold tiles, and go out of the flat and up the stairs. Where I slip and fall on the highly polished marble. This particular flight to the roof is rarely used, but Lucilla waxes it regularly just the same. Everything must always be just so, a mausoleum odour. Cursing and rueful, I reach the iron door of the *solaio*, open it, and then remember I still haven't put a light bulb in. At which point the timed landing light goes out. I grope for the switch, but don't know where it is on this floor. So I go into the *solaio* blind.

I stare, waiting for my pupils to dilate, recognising a smell of geranium cuttings and thick dust. A dark, softly shifting light, filtering from the attic's one window, finally enables me to see the shadows of untidily piled boxes, an ancient bed, a crucifix, a pair of bellows unaccountably left on the windowsill, and rows and rows of *il professore's* old climbing boots. None of them moving, thank God. I cock my head. No sound.

But back downstairs, the footsteps go on and on above us.

Talking to Orietta, the quiet repository of all condominium gossip, we discover that Lucilla suffers from insomnia. The footsteps are hers, the ventriloquist building sends the sound where it will.

Orietta is loosening up. She is losing her suspicion of my Englishness. She recognises the advantage of having other non-Montecchiesi to make friends with. Giampaolo, she tells us, has frequently complained about those footsteps. Getting up in the night, it seems, Lucilla will put on her fur coat, partly against the cold, partly because she likes her fur coat; she finds its luxury comforting, its moneyed smell reassuring. But since she is small and bought the coat long, she puts her heels on so as not to have it trail on the floor. And paces up and down.

Another night it is the squeal of heavy furniture being scraped above our heads. Bumps and banging. Thud, scrape, squeal. Yes, Lucilla tells us brightly on the stairs, she decided to rearrange the sitting room, do we want to come and see it?

Please would we come and see it?

Perhaps we would take a little drink with her? She has some *Lacryma Christi*.

Or perhaps we would like to have a piece of her *pastafrolla*?

Surely, if she isn't disturbing us, we would like to come and see her new curtains, eat her shortbread? Also, if we could explain something in the instruction book to her steam iron . . .

There is a scene in Fellini's film, *La Voce della Luna*, where a local politician, fallen upon hard times, is seen returning to his dreary flat in an old *palazzotto* in some tiny town of the Po valley. But every time he climbs the stairs and approaches his door, whether it be two in the afternoon or two in the morning, four ancient neighbours will appear at the door opposite and, like awful decaying sirens, try to lure him into their flat to share some

TIM PARKS

old-fashioned dainty: a thimbleful of some sweet forgotten liqueur, a morsel of traditional crumbliness. Their faces are pictures of decrepit flattery and seduction. Close to obscenity. The furniture, dingily glimpsed behind them, is sombre and coffin-inspired with candlesticks in abundance, photographs of dead relatives on lace doilies. 'Would a small glass of sherry be to your liking, your honour? Would a small slice of *pan di spagna*, councillor, be acceptable as our humble offering?' Their veiny hands are outstretched in supplication. Which is immediately perceived as a trap, as if a whole culture were refusing to lie down in its grave, but were rising ghoulish to eat our contemporary flesh. Horrified and furious, the man manages to escape into his room, slams and bolts the door behind him. But already the four leathery faces are down by the keyhole. 'Would your honour be so kind as to take a glass of brandy with some humble folk . . .' They haunt his dreams. He sees their faces floating outside his window at night with the moon behind, luring him back into some archaic, provincial Italy of polished woodwork and thickly smoking candle wax, flattery, favours, back-stabbing.

Such, for me, were Lucilla's insistent invitations. So that I almost looked back with regret on her ravings from the balcony, her confiscation of the dustbin. Those days when I at least knew where I stood.

Barely has she got us inside her polished door – *troppo gentile*, too kind, *Signor Tino* (she never registered the name Tim) – than she is leaning out into the stairwell calling down to Vittorina. She has a direct intercom connection with Vittorina's flat, but prefers to call down the stairwell, if only to remind all residents in the condominium of her existence. 'Rina! Rina! Come and have something to drink with *i signori inglesi*.' Is she calling up reinforcements? Or just increasing the size of her audience?

We walk in, and promptly slither on imitation animal skin rugs strewn over the usual lethally waxed floor. Lucilla is clearly nostalgic for her cleaning days. The year before we arrived, she slipped on the rug in the entrance and broke her hip. But this has not deterred her. I all but come a cropper on the synthetic white hairy thing between low glass table and imitation leather sofa.

Vittorina, who has now appeared in a nightgown, hair thinner than ever, frowns with the air of one who is wiser than the person she is used to being bossed about by. And indeed, she doesn't even try to remove her moustache as Lucilla does. A vanity beneath her.

We are shown round the flat. The walls are simple whitewash, as in almost every Italian house. The furniture is what a local Veronese would laughingly describe as *stile Bovolone*. Bovolone being an industrial settlement twenty kilometres away in the foggy *bassa* where scores of busy companies produce clunky replicas of antique furniture. A Louis XIV dresser, bright and new, features prominently in the entrance way. There is a Renaissance chest in polished pine, and Lucilla's is the first home, aside from paying visits to Waltham Abbey and Hatfield House, where I have seen a bed with a canopy curtain affair over the headboard, here upholstered in electric nylon pink. The room is about ten by twelve.

Il professore was a great man, she begins impulsively, having put little red glasses of *gingerino* in our hands. A great man. Of culture. She speaks in fierce dialect. I strain my ears to distinguish the words, my mind to understand. It is not unlike trying to make out a strange landscape through thick fog. Was that a house or a tree, a tail-light or shop neon? And we are going so fast. My head starts to ache. Still, at the end of an hour or so of non-stop haranguing, I do manage to discern the following salient landmarks, if only because Lucilla goes round and round them so insistently, not unlike Pooh Bear following his own tracks in the snow: so, *il professore*, that is, Patuzzi, had written a will and put it in his deposit box in the bank (half of Montecchio seems to have a deposit box at the bank). He then died quite suddenly, of a heart attack, breathing his last on the ambulance stretcher right outside her door, *poveretto* (obligatory epithet for describing the dear departed). And what a fright for her! *Comunque*, the will had clearly stated that the wife would have use of the property only until her death, after which it would pass to her, Lucilla. Such an exquisite man, *il professore*. As had been agreed of course. Because it was her money, her money had paid for the *palazzina*. She had worked her fingers to the bone all her life. So cultured. We would have admired him immensely. But no sooner had he passed away than Signora Marta and Maria Rosa were off to the bank, had opened the deposit box and promptly burnt the will. For which they themselves would burn in hell. Whereas we would never meet anybody more *gentile*, more *generoso*, than *il professore*.

Lucilla's bosom began to heave, it wasn't clear whether out of love or anger or some dangerous blood-dark cocktail of the two. Then Maria Rosa had herself fallen ill and become infirm. Lucilla had looked after her, as was her duty towards another 'Christian', taking her meals which she handed over at the door whose threshold she was never to pass. Because that woman put on airs, while *il professore*, who might have had good reason to be haughty, was *dolcezza* itself. And when things got worse, Maria Rosa had come and more or less lived in her own, Lucilla's flat; slept there for months, being nursed and helped to the toilet and so on. Until, finally, Lucilla could cope no more and the woman had had to go into a home. But towards the end of that period, in a fit of remorse, Maria Rosa had told Lucilla the story of the will and how it had been burnt and had agreed to write a further will herself.

Lucilla fiddles under the flap of a rather oversized new Regency writing desk, bringing out a furry-grey piece of notepaper which she then waves under our noses. '*Ecco, legga, legga, Signor Tino.*' Her fingers are stubby and impressively bejewelled. I take the *documento* with due respect. Uncertain handwriting announces the last will and testament of Maria Rosa Griminelli. The whole of Via Colombare number ten belongs and always has belonged to Lucilla Zambon who built it with her own money. There is a single indecipherable signature, no lawyer, only the beneficiary as a witness.

But Lucilla's hopes are pinned on that scrap of paper. She raises her voice. She is furious, defiant. Her bony teeth are in evidence. 'The flat is mine, mine, mine.' But we are nice people, and when she finally gets hold of the property, on Maria Rosa's death, she will allow us to stay, although she will have to ask us to buy it rather than rent. But we can discuss all this at a later date.

Would we like a *cioccolatino*, a San Pellegrino Bitter? Would we like to watch television with her of an evening? She would be grateful if we could adjust her set. There is a programme on Tele Montecarlo with a man just like her beloved husband, here he is in this photograph. *Così bello!* Why did the men always die first? But she can never get a good picture on Tele Montecarlo. Signor Giampaolo has put up that new motorised aerial on the roof and it is sucking all the goodness from hers. Do I know anything about aerials? And could Rita perhaps phone her lawyer for her to have him explain something she can't understand, and tell him to hurry up with the case.

Lucilla talks on and on. There is simply no chink in her verbal armour, no hesitation into which one might thrust the dagger of a request to leave. Vittorina watches, silent, dark, with those sudden smiles when she catches your eye, smiles which say she understands your suffering, but this is Lucilla, this is how she is, *porti pazienza*.

In desperation, we begin our long retreat. First simply getting to our feet, then edging out of the lounge and across the dining room with its dark, dying plants, its sad canary, heading towards the entrance. Along a low wall is an array of those tiny twisted-glass Venetian ornaments, reminding me of my infancy in Blackpool, when we visited a Great-Aunt Esther who had row upon row of the things on a dresser.

Do we think she should ask for the *condono edilizio*, the building pardon? You see, she had this wall knocked down, that's why it is different from our flat, didn't we notice, between the entrance and the kitchen . . . So much more space. But without asking for planning permission . . . and now with this pardon . . .

Does she have the right lawyer? What do we think? Perhaps he isn't being tough enough. Surely the rent we are paying should go to her. How much are we paying? *Il professore* only left the flat to his wife for use while she wanted to live there, but any rent should go to her, Lucilla. And, of course, in that home Maria Rosa is in, Signora Marta is putting pressure on her to sign another will leaving everything to her. But it wouldn't be right, because Rosa isn't capable of exercising free will now. She is senile. Though the doctors are all *in complicità* clearly, with what's being paid for her to be there. All *il professore's* fortune. The priest said . . .

Finally we make it to the hall. We are repeating *arrivedercis*, *buona nottes*, when I finally remember the purpose behind our visit, the subject I had originally come to broach. The nocturnal noises. We hope, I say, that we never, er, bother them, when we play our stereo, when we type late at night, when we have friends over. Noise carries so much in these buildings. One can hear everything. We wouldn't like . . . 'But no, Signor Tino, no, no, no, *troppo gentile, troppo gentile!* We like to hear noise. We like to hear footsteps, laughter, banging. The more the merrier. We're two old ladies. It keeps us company. We feel less lonely. *Ma troppo gentile, ma che signore!*'

And somehow Signor Tino just can't bring himself to say what he wants to say. The way he can never quite make up his mind to poison that dog.

AT HOME
ON THE SEINE

MORT ROSENBLUM

MORT ROSENBLUM is a special correspondent for the Associated Press, based in Paris, and former editor of the *International Herald Tribune*. Amongst the many books he has written are *The Secret Life of the Seine*, *A Goose in Toulouse: And Other Culinary Adventures in France* and *Olives: The Life and Lore of a Noble Fruit*, for which he won the James Beard Award.

EVERY OTHER MORNING, my friend Paul slouched into the office with yet another hard luck story about the boat he loved. The *something-something* had clogged and frozen his family overnight. A *bateau-mouche* had decked his poop, or pooped his deck. The river had risen, and he needed a dinghy to get home.

Paul slouched because he was six feet one inch high, and the saloon ceiling of *La Vieille* was not. Winter or summer, his clothes were ripe with mildew and diesel. One sleeting December night, his clothes smelled even worse. He had slipped on the gangway and belly-flopped into the Seine.

Paul could talk your ear off about epoxy resin fatigue and wet carpets. He and his wife, Jill, had lived aboard *La Vieille* since the time they nursed her ancient teak timbers across the English Channel in 1967 and tied her up in the middle of Paris. That they had a son to rear on a fifty-four-foot boat didn't faze them, not even when young Ozzie grew so tall he could stand erect only with the hatch open.

During the decade that Paul and I worked together, I could never fathom his devotion to *La Vieille*. But I knew why he loved the Seine. There is not a river like it in the world for beauty and passion along its banks. Its history is as old as the Jordan's, and it is no muddy stream across moonscape. If hardly a Mississippi, it still conceals treacherous sandbanks that keep boatmen anxiously marking their twain.

From the time I first gasped at the view from the Pont Marie, years ago, I was smitten by the Seine. And back then, I didn't know the half of it.

While Paul and Jill lived on *La Vieille*, I rented a country cottage four floors up in an old building in the heart of Paris, on the

Île Saint-Louis. Each time Paul lamented over his Webasto diesel heater, I thought of my cheery steam radiators and fireplaces on two floors. When winds and waves rocked the boat, I shut double doors to a terrace rose garden. I was a happy landlubber, and my clothes did not smell.

Late one night I walked home across the Pont Sully. Golden light from the Quai d'Anjou glittered on the Seine. The narrow street curved by the slate-roofed stone mansions that had sheltered the families, from the Voltaires to the Rothschilds, who had made France into France. Climbing the last steps to my door, I figured I had found the loveliest speck of real estate in the world. With any luck, I'd live there forever.

Inside, I exulted on the subject to my friend and roommate. 'We have to leave,' she said.

It was a typical low Parisian story. A local reptile who inherited some money had heard about the apartment and visited our landlord. The short version of the story is that we had a few months to clear out, with no idea where to go. I only knew that I had to be near the Seine.

Paul showed up for work, as usual, with another *La Vieille* hard luck story. 'You don't want to sell that old wreck, do you?' I asked. 'I just might,' he said. Not long after, I was the one telling the stories and reeking of old boat.

Paul and Jill had decided to move to England, and they were looking for friendly hands to take the helm. I was a reluctant candidate, a son of Arizona desert and a klutz with a wrench or varnish brush.

It took only one lunch on deck. The spring air was electric. Dutch barges lazed past, piloted by housewives in slippers and patrolled by stubby dogs trained to coil rope with their teeth. Tugs puffed by, their wakes sloshing the Burgundy in our glasses. On the neighbouring boats and along the quay, I watched characters Hugo had missed and Flaubert never imagined. Along with foul water, I saw waterfowl. It had to be Paris because the Eiffel

Tower loomed over the golden cherubs on the Pont Alexandre III. But we were also somewhere else, in a place most Parisians seldom see.

Only a few nylon ropes, a power cable and a garden hose connected us to the real world. Suddenly, I understood why my friends loved *La Vieille* and had resolved to sell her with lumps in their throats. I had discovered the secret life of the Seine.

During the fifteen years that followed, I acquired a corner of overgrown land in Provence which looked like Cambodian jungle but turned out – after much hard labour – to be a lovely olive farm. Then my persistent search for roots brought me back to Arizona, where I bought a small bit of Tucson desert.

My problem is that I am home-impaired. As a foreign correspondent, much of my life is spent on aeroplanes, in hotels, under jeeps. I've often been homesick, but I've never been able to say for where.

In the end, I discovered that my roots are planted in water, about as firmly as a hydroponic tomato's. If anyone forgets to shut a seacock, or one of those dreaded logs finally hits the mark, my home may end up to be no more than a patch of dirty river water. Until then, however, it is bobbing happily on the Seine.

Things are a bit different, I found. When you live on the river, other Parisians constantly ask two questions: *Isn't it damp?* (the answer is yes) and *Where do you get your croissants in the morning?* (the answer is: at the bakery). Occasionally, some kindred spirit has a third: *When are you going to die and leave this to me?*

It is agreeable, as the French say, to take a candlelight cruise without leaving home. You can go away for a weekend and not pack. Your morning alarm is ducks quacking. Friends visit without coaxing. My pal Barbara fled a Stockholm winter and dropped into the nearest deck chair. When a *bateau-mouche* passed, she flung out her arms and yelled, 'Envy me.'

There are drawbacks, of course. A boat is not a great place for people who tend to drop their keys. Sleepwalkers, too, ought to think twice. Life afloat is like living in a small apartment, in a zone of frequent, quiet earthquakes.

Boats are also not the best place to teach an old cat new tricks. This lesson was made manifest early on, when a Marin County feline named Princess took up residence. Among other adjustment problems, she fell into the river one night. No-one knew it until she jumped back through a porthole onto the bed, her fluffy long hair matted and stinking, and produced a plaintive meow. She was on penicillin for two weeks. And we learned that cats, when pressed, can do the backstroke and chin-ups.

In time, a cat named Miranda moved aboard. She has fallen in five times, each time hanging onto the rudder with her claws until someone figures out how to save her. The last time, a treasured friend named Dev leapt into the Seine, ignoring a swift, roiling current, and was nearly washed towards the English Channel.

Aboard *La Vieille*, I started talking funny. When I remarked to a normal person, 'I've got dry rot in my head,' he nodded in agreement, not aware that I was referring to the bathroom ceiling.

When I moved to the river, I found a cast of old characters right off the end of my gangway. There was, for instance, Jacques Donnez, who spelt his name 'Jack', even though no-one else did. He looked like a cross between Jean-Paul Sartre and Popeye, with a raspy voice and a craggy squint behind opaque glasses. At first, for me, he was a pleasant curiosity. By the third time he spared me from making chopsticks of a fine old boat, he was captain, sir and a friend.

Jacques was born afloat in 1939, an eighth-generation Seine boatman. He and his wife, Lisette, married on a floating church barge, and made a decent income ferrying coal, sand, grain and wine while their laundry flapped in the wind on the aft deck. But trucks and trains cut deeply into the market. In 1976, they sold the barge for scrap and came ashore. He took a job on the quay, where he could fix anything made by man and wait out anything delivered by nature. He started work early, finished late and did his level best to make the Burgundy vineyards prosper.

'*Ouuaais, je l'aime,*' Jacques replied once when I asked him to rhapsodise on the Seine. Trick was to watch him look at the river;

his eyes were as expressive as temperature gauges. When he furrowed his brow at the rising current, it was time to get the car off the quay. He was like most hearty old marine equipment – utterly dependable as long as you check the meters. When his nose flashed red, for instance, it was not the time to have him change your bilge pump.

As 2000 approached, Jacques and the rest of us shuddered at the writing on our old quay walls. Our boat owners' association charter ran out and port management went to a band of government bureaucrats. Captain Jacques retired to disappear somewhere upriver. And it was then that we lost the redoubtable Philippe.

For years after I moved aboard, *La Vieille* was tied up to a 126-foot barge, the standard French workhorse. Its master was Philippe, a perfect neighbour who was not wild about me writing a book. When I told him the title, *The Secret Life of the Seine,* he recoiled. 'But if you write about it,' he reasoned, 'it's not secret. Be sure to tell them about floods and leaks.' I resolved to spare his privacy, just as everyone aboard my boat was schooled not to see into his uncurtained windows. In France you can do that.

'Please understand if I do not seem to see you when we look at each other,' Philippe said when we first met. I loved him instantly. Two boats tied alongside are like Siamese twins, and I am no Rotarian. Imagine the perils of proximity. You could not get to my boat without walking across his bow. He could not leave the quay unless I went first.

Carefully, like two porcupines sharing a den, we found a happy symbiosis. I didn't sand my rails when he was sleeping in. He shrugged when I parked my car on his hose during his shower. Every so often, he came aboard to dislodge debris about to tear off my portside prop – a hazard I tended not to notice – while muttering, 'Unaware. Completely unaware.'

You never knew. One Sunday evening, he emerged blearily at five o'clock, unwound six feet of hung-over party victim, wandered below to get my guitar, and announced, in G, 'I'm a little red rooster.'

Philippe pioneered the port. For years, he kept his barge discreetly under a bridge. Then he painted it white – sort of like a yacht – and tied up at the quay. By the time Paul and Jill arrived, he was the old-timer who set the tone of the place.

Then a state agency called Voies Navigables de France took over the port, and Philippe lost his ebullience. We would have to leave the heart of our little floating village to make room for a water-bus stop that could easily have been put elsewhere. New management tore up plants that Philippe had put in and tended over the years. He was never the same.

Things changed after that. Boat life was less of a lark than a sacred duty. People had lived on the Seine for two thousand years, and those few of us left were not about to abandon that tradition to functionaries who wanted to replace us with noisy restaurant barges.

But in the place where *plus ça change* is an unchanging cliché, much also remains the same. In a new location, with different neighbours and a new batch of ducks, there is the lovely, ageless river. Mostly, I love it as much as I always did. On bad days, I can still manage a philosophic shrug.

In the heart of Paris, I had found a separate *arrondissement* of the spirit. For years, I had watched the Seine from above, treasuring the river as a lovely but inanimate path through the centre of the most thrilling settlement I knew. It took moving onto it, having it seep into my bilges and turn my underwear green, for me to realise that it was alive, a settlement in its own right. That was home enough for me.

TENMANGU

FROM

LOST JAPAN

ALEX KERR

ALEX KERR is an American specialising in East Asian art and culture, who first came to Japan in 1964. For *Lost Japan* (written in Japanese), he became the first foreign recipient of the Shincho Gakugei Literature Prize. His recent book *Dogs and Demons* takes a controversial look at contemporary Japanese culture. He is resident in Bangkok and Kyoto.

Lost Japan by Alex Kerr, published by Lonely Planet 1996.
Copyright © Alex Kerr 1996.

FINDING THIS HOUSE was a piece of great good luck. At the end of the Oomoto seminar in 1976, the foundation suggested that I come to work there after going down from Oxford, and without thinking much about it, I agreed. Over the next year, when people asked me for whom I would be working, I had pleasure in telling them, 'For the Mother Goddess of Oomoto.' But I had neglected to discuss my salary. When I arrived in 1977 to take up my position in Oomoto's International Department, I discovered that all those who worked at the foundation were considered to be 'contributors of service'; in other words, the pay was nominal. I found to my horror that my monthly salary was to be 100,000 yen (about $400 a month). Art activities were all very fine, but how was I going to pay the rent?

For the first two or three weeks I stayed in the Oomoto dormitory, but one day near the end of summer I had an inspiration. A friend from Thailand, Ping Amranand, was taking the seminar. I said to him, 'Ping, let's go look for a house!' So we set out, walking away from the Oomoto grounds. Kameoka is a flat-bottomed bowl of rice paddies, and you cannot walk for long without running up against mountains. As we walked towards them, I noticed an unusual building. Through a gate in a white wall was a large garden, rank with weeds, and by it an empty house. Drawing on my wealth of experience in breaking into abandoned houses in Iya, we were inside the house in a matter of moments. It was dark and dusty inside, and spider webs clung to our hands and faces. Walking gingerly across the floor of the dim living room, which winced and threatened to collapse at every step, we came out onto the back verandah, which was sealed shut with a row of heavy wooden doors. I gave one of the doors a shove, and the entire rotten row collapsed and fell into the garden in a heap. In that instant, warm green light from the back garden flooded the living room. Ping and I looked at each other: in a single summer day, we had found my house.

The old woman who lived next door told me that the caretaker of the house was the head priest of the nearby Kuwayama Shrine, so I paid him a visit. The priest explained the history of the house to me. It was very old, having been built around four hundred years before. It had originally been a Buddhist nunnery, but around the end of the Edo period it was dismantled and moved to its current site in the grounds of the Tenmangu Shrine. The gate, from another temple further into the mountains, was moved here at about the same time. The house then took on a second life as the shrine-keeper's home, and also doubled as the village school. But after the 1930s there was no more shrine-keeper, so the house was rented out to local residents. In recent years, nobody had wanted to live in such an old and dirty house, so it lay vacant. Though at a loss to imagine why a foreigner would want to live in such a place, the priest decided then and there that I could rent it.

Although the Tenmangu Shrine, which is tended by the villagers, is separate from the house, my friends and I have taken to calling the house 'Tenmangu' as well. Today, it looks considerably better than it did in 1977. Guests arrive and think, 'Ah, a quaint country residence', but they can have no idea of the long years of toil it took to bring the house to its present state. At first there was not even running water; there was only a well, which dried up in the winter months. Although I don't mind 'run-down', I do mind 'dirty'. So I invited a group of friends from Oomoto over for a house-cleaning party. Carrying buckets of water from the well, we wiped the ceilings, pillars and tatami mats until they gleamed. Happily, the roof did not leak, so the tatami had not rotted and I did not face the horrific roofing problems which had coloured my experience in Iya. Gradually, I brought in running water, repaired the doors and walls, and weeded the garden. The back garden which Ping and I had discovered that first day was an impenetrable mass of weeds and vines. A few months after moving in, I took sickle and machete to it, and saw for the first time the stepping stones, lanterns and azaleas that are typical of a Japanese garden.

However, on a salary of only 100,000 yen a month, the repair of the house could not be done all at once. As a result, for the first three or four years, life in Tenmangu was very much like dwelling in a haunted house. Not long after I moved in, an eighteen-year-old friend named Diane Barraclough came to live with me. Diane was a blonde British–French girl who had been raised in Kobe and spoke a colourful form of Kobe dialect. Although her Japanese lacked delicacy, she was certainly fluent. She had also inherited French from her mother and an upper-class British accent from her father, doctor to the expatriates in Kobe. Diane was the sort of long-haired beauty who inhabits the comic books which are popular among young girls in Japan. She was pure Edgar Allan Poe, and completely happy in the dark and dilapidated atmosphere of Tenmangu.

I was initially unable to replace the rotten verandah doors, so the entire eight-metre expanse of the verandah was left open facing the garden. On summer evenings, hordes of moths and mosquitoes would come flying in, so I went to one of the second-hand shops in Kyoto and bought a couple of old mosquito nets. These nets were among the most hauntingly beautiful objects in old Japanese life. They were like enormous square tents, each one the size of a whole room, and they hung from hooks high up on the ceiling. The body of the net was pale green linen, and the borders were of brilliant red silk. We laid our bedding inside the green tents and set out floor lamps. Dressed in a kimono, Diane would sit inside her tent to read, a silver *kiseru* pipe dangling from her lips. The view of her silhouette, filtered through the green netting, was pure romance, the sort of thing you might find in an Edo woodblock print. In fact, years later, when nets like these had become scarce, I lent one to the Kabuki actor Kunitaro for a performance of *Yotsuya Kaido* in Kyoto. *Yotsuya Kaido* is a ghost story, commonly performed in summer to give the audience a 'chill', and the ghostly green netting with blood red borders is considered an indispensable backdrop.

One night I brought a Japanese friend over to visit. When our taxi pulled up in front of Tenmangu, all the lights were off in the house, and there was just the sound of wind and waterfall. Diane was standing in the doorway dressed in a black kimono, her long blonde hair falling over her shoulders. In her outstretched hand she held a rusty old candle stand, over which spiders crawled. My friend took one look, shuddered, and hastily returned to the station in the same taxi we had come in.

In the evening, Diane and I would light a candle and sit out on the verandah talking, while watching the spiders spin their webs. Diane had a talent for vivid bons mots, most of them as politically incorrect as they could possibly be. Some prey on my mind even now. 'Tea ceremony,' she once said, 'is aesthetics for unaesthetic people.' What she meant was that tea tells you what to do about everything – where to put the flowers, which art objects should be displayed and how to use even the tiniest division of space. This is very comforting for people who have never thought about such things and have no idea what to do on their own.

Another time, she said, 'Zen is profundity for shallow people.' That is the sort of comment which the old Zen master Ikkyu would have loved. What sticks in my mind most of all, however, is when Diane said, 'You know, Westerners with their full-blown personalities are infinite in interest as human beings. But Western culture is so limited in depth. The Japanese, on the other hand, so restricted by their society, are limited as human beings. But their culture is infinitely deep.'

In retrospect, the late 1970s in Kyoto were the turning point of an era. Diane, David Kidd, many of my other foreign friends and I were all living in a dream of ancient Japan, because in those days it was still possible to believe in the dream. Around Tenmangu was wilderness and rice paddies, and the streets of Kameoka were still lined with wooden houses and the big *kura* of saké-makers, lending it the feel of a feudal castle town. The mountains had yet to be covered with steel pylons, and the wave of concrete and plastic had yet to overtake the town. Our actions at the time may have been a bit eccentric, but they still had some air of reality. It was possible, as we sometimes did on summer nights during the seminar at Oomoto, to walk all the way through town back to Tenmangu wearing kimono and *hakama* (trousers). To do so today would be so divorced from modern Japanese surroundings as to seem wholly ridiculous.

Time passed, and the early 1980s saw the renovation of Tenmangu advance steadily. I wired the house for electricity, swept away the cobwebs and installed glass doors along the verandah. With the exit of the spiders, Diane did not feel quite at home any more and she moved out as well. I turned my attention to the *doma*, an earthen-floored room used as the kitchen, which took up about a third of the floor space in Tenmangu.

First, the head priest of Kuwayama Shrine, my landlord, performed a Shinto purification ritual for the old earthen oven and the well – fire and water. Then my friends and I set about transforming the *doma* into a studio space by removing the oven and capping the well. I put in a long table where I could do calligraphy, and mount and back paintings. The other rooms of the house had ceilings, but the *doma*, in order to allow smoke from the oven to escape, was open all the way up to the rafters, like Chiiori. But the rafters were so crammed with lumber and old sliding doors that it was impossible to see them. We carried out the detritus, and swept down one hundred and fifty years of accumulated soot, enough to fill ten large garbage bags. In doing so, a wide expanse of rafters and crossbeams magically appeared. This airy room is now my workspace.

Though the age of mosquito nets, candles and kimonos has ended, a special world lives on at Tenmangu even now. This is a very simple thing: nature. When I return to Tenmangu after a trip to Tokyo or abroad, I always find that the cycle of the seasons has shifted a bit, and new natural phenomena await me. According to the old Chinese calendar, the year is divided into twenty-four mini-seasons, with names like 'Clear and Bright', 'White Dew', 'Great Heat', 'Little Cold' and 'Squirming Insects'. Each has its own flavour.

The god of Tenmangu was originally a tenth-century courtier named Michizane, famed for his love of plum blossoms; as a result, the thousands of Tenmangu shrines across the country invariably have a plum tree planted in the grounds. The mystique of plums is that they bloom at the end of winter, when snow is still on the ground. Soon spring comes, and the old cherry tree in the garden blooms, along with azaleas, peaches and wildflowers. But my favourite season comes later, around the end of May or the beginning of June, when the rainy season starts. The frogs in the surrounding paddies start croaking, and my friends calling from Tokyo are amazed to find that they can hear them even over the phone line. Little emerald gems, the frogs hop about and ornament the leaves and stepping stones. Then lotuses burst into bloom, and the heavy rain drums pleasantly on the roof of my bedroom. Sleeping during the rainy season is always a joy.

Then one evening, a lone firefly appears in the garden. With a friend, I climb down behind the garden to the creek bed below, and we wait in silence in the darkness. After a while, from the thickets on either side of the ravine, glowing clouds of fireflies come floating out. In the summer, the village children come to swim in the pool below the waterfall. My cousin Edan, a little blond imp, spent a whole summer playing under the waterfall. From my living room I can hear the children's voices as they dive into the pool. The trees on the mountain slope beyond sway in the breeze, and a black kite lazily spreads its long wings high above. The end of the summer brings typhoons and autumn's crimson maple leaves, yellow gingko, ruby nandina berries and, at the end, hanging onto the bare branches of winter, orange persimmon fruit. On winter days, frost descends on the garden, and each blade of grass sparkles like diamonds in the morning sun. Frog emeralds, frost diamonds, nandina rubies – these are Tenmangu's jewel box.

But these seasonal changes are being slowly erased from today's Japan. For example, in most cities it is standard practice in autumn to cut off the branches of trees lining the streets, in order to prevent falling leaves. To modern Japanese, falling leaves are not a thing of beauty; they are messy and to be avoided. This accounts for the stunted appearance of the trees which one encounters in most public places in Japan. Recently, a friend here told me, 'Just going to look at the mountain wilderness – what a bore! It is only when you have something to do that nature becomes interesting. You know, like golf or skiing.' This may explain why people feel compelled to bulldoze so many golf courses and ski slopes into the mountainsides. My wilderness remains that of the Chinese poets, my nature that of Basho's haiku. A frog jumps into an old pond; just that sound brings me joy. Nothing else is needed.

When Diane was living at Tenmangu, the house had almost nothing inside of it. However, in time, Tenmangu became the setting for my growing art collection. Japanese gold screens, Chinese carpets, Tibetan mandalas, Korean vases, Thai Buddhas, Burmese lacquer ware, Khmer sculpture – things Asian were crammed into every inch of the house. 'Crammed' is not, I realise, the most aesthetically pleasing of expressions; it hardly conjures up images of elegant refinement. But the art-works of every country and every historical period of Asia made up a jungle of such luxuriance inside Tenmangu that the foliage outside was almost outclassed: it was a greenhouse of beauty. One friend called it 'Aladdin's Cave'. On arrival, visitors would see a dilapidated old house which looked not much different from the Tenmangu I found in 1977. Then they would enter the foyer, and 'open sesame!' – colourful screen paintings, thick blue and yellow rugs, and the lustre of polished quince and rose-wood met the eye.

In recent years, the novelty of owning all these things has worn off a bit and I have cleared out Tenmangu considerably. The rugs and the furniture are still there, but taking a hint from old house-holds which used to store their possessions out of sight in the *kura*, I have loaned most of the screens, statues and paintings to museums. Now I keep just a few favourite things, and rotate them as the mood strikes me. I suppose I will keep removing more and more, until eventually the house will come full circle and there will be only a bare tatami room looking out onto an open garden.

In the meantime, even with a much smaller number of objects on display, Tenmangu still has an Aladdin's Cave feel about it. I think it has something to do with colour, one of the things I learned about from David Kidd in the days of my apprenticeship.

To digress slightly, I once read an account of life in Tibet before it was invaded by China, when Tibetan culture still flourished. One day, the author met a group of Tibet's high-ranking states-men travelling in a convoy across the steppe. They were a blaze of colour: even the horses were draped in gorgeous silk and hand-woven blankets. The statesmen wore garments of yellow brocade on which blue dragons, purple clouds and green waves danced wildly, and in their hair they wore beads of turquoise and coral.

In today's world, people's sense of colour has faded consider-ably. Just think of the drab suits of modern politicians and you'll see what I mean. This lack of colour is especially true of Japan, where all lighting is fluorescent, and most household items are made from aluminium and synthetic materials. However, Tenmangu is alive with rich, deep hues. It is a striking contrast to the ash grey colour of life in Tokyo. First, there is gold, a colour which, as Tanizaki pointed out in *In Praise of Shadows*, does not generally go well with a brightly lit room; this may be why gold is hardly seen in modern Japanese life. But in Tenmangu there is the gold leaf of screens, the gold of Buddhas, gold lacquer – many different kinds of gold. Within gold, there is green gold, red gold and alloyed gold, which tarnishes with time. In addition to gold, there are painting pigments, especially the vivid green seen in Tibetan mandalas. Then there is the deep red of lacquer ware, the pale blue of Chinese celadon, and the sombre and cloudy oranges and tea greens of Japanese brocade.

As a calligrapher, living in Tenmangu could not be more pro-pitious. I feel as though I receive direct inspiration from the deity of the shrine. Although I am not a Shinto convert, I have a secret belief in the god of Tenmangu, who has been worshipped since antiquity as the god of scholarship and calligraphy. Sometimes, I step out to the shrine, ring the bell and say a prayer. Actually, 'prayer' is too strong a word; it's more like an informal greeting. When high-school and college-entrance exam season rolls around, students come to pray at the shrine before class, and their prayers probably have a little more urgency than mine. The early-morning ringing of the bell often wakes me up, serving as Tenmangu's alarm clock.

There are many gods in Tenmangu. First of all, there is the household altar above the studio room. In the centre sits a figure of Michizane, and to the left and right of him are paper charms, talismans from shrines and temples, and rosary beads. Above the entryway there sits a small, blackened, wooden statue of Daikoku (god of prosperity). The statue is only about twelve centimetres high, but it radiates power as though it were carved by the sculptor Enku. Of all the things that were in the house when I first moved in, this is the only one I've kept, and I think of it as the true guardian of Tenmangu. On the central pillar is pasted a charm from Kuwayama Shrine, and a likeness of Marishi-Ten (god of contests) seated on a chariot of swiftly moving wild boars. In the living room, a *tanzaku* plaque by Onisaburo Deguchi hangs on the pillar of the *tokonoma*. In the innermost room is a Thai Buddha, and next to that a small altar to Shiva. This may seem an extreme sort of superstition, but I am only following the typical Japanese religious pattern: not wanting to be bound to a single religion, I subscribe to them all – Buddhist, Shinto, Hindu. Gods and Buddhas float ceaselessly in the air of Tenmangu, and their warm breathing fills the house.

Living in the countryside brings with it a number of inconveniences. Foremost among these are the insects. From the time of 'Squirming Insects' around the middle of March, legions of mosquitoes, moths, bees, ants, centipedes, spiders and helmet bugs sally forth. Doing battle with them is quite a chore. When Diane lived here, she had a thirteen-stringed *koto* which she kept on one side of the living room. Once, late at night, the sound of the instrument suddenly broke the silence. Strumming chords floated gently across the room – *chiri chiri chiri zuru zuru zuru* – but Diane and I were under the mosquito netting, alone in the house as far as we knew. Taking a candle, we went over to the *koto*, but there was nothing to be seen. Even as we watched, ghostly fingers continued to play and *chiri chiri chiri zuru zuru zuru* cascaded through the house, while Diane and I clung to each other in terror. Finally, I could bear it no longer and turned on all the lamps in the house, to find that a large moth had got itself trapped under the strings of the *koto*.

Ghost concerts I could live with, but mosquitoes were another matter. Mosquito netting is strange stuff: while not actually having any holes, it always seems to let some mosquitoes in. In the end, as a result of the mosquito problem, I finally put up glass doors against the garden, installed air-conditioning and effectively divided inside from outside. However, one hundred and fifty years have passed since Tenmangu was moved to its present spot, and as the result of a succession of typhoons and earthquakes, all the pillars lean and there is not a single right angle in the entire house. Insects manage to find a way through the gaps, and I don't think Tenmangu will ever be completely liberated from them.

Another problem is the length of the commute to Kyoto and Osaka. In truth it is not really all that long: twenty-five minutes to Kyoto by train, and one and a quarter hours to Osaka by car. But for city dwellers, the distance to the countryside feels wider than the Sahara, and it is not easy to get the courage to cross this desert. I once got a call from an art collector in Amsterdam. 'I'm going to Japan next month. I'd love to visit Tenmangu,' he said. A month later, when he arrived in Tokyo, he called again, 'I'm going to Kyoto tomorrow. I'll see you the day after.' The next day, a call came from Kyoto, 'I'm looking forward to seeing you tomorrow.' Then, on the morning of the appointed day, he called to say, 'I'm sorry. I can't go to Kameoka. It's just too far.'

At the turn of the century, the Comte de Montesquiou ruled the Parisian social world with an iron hand; nobody ever turned down an invitation to one of the Comte's soirees. But one day Montesquiou moved from the east side of the Bois de Boulogne to a larger palace on the west side. It meant only a two-kilometre drive through the park, but from the day the Comte moved, high society tossed him aside without a qualm, and Montesquiou lived out the remainder of his days in isolation.

Certainly visitors to Tenmangu are not numerous. It's bad for the art business, but I don't feel particularly lonely. On the contrary, the distance from Kyoto and Osaka screens me from casual visitors, so that most of my guests are good friends. As a result, having guests over to my house is always pleasantly relaxed and enjoyable.

Over the past eighteen years, Tenmangu has seen a stream of Japanese friends who have lived here with me or taken care of the house. They all shared one thing, which was not an interest in art, nor a love of nature, as you might think. Their aim was to escape from Japanese society. There are very few places in Japan where you can escape from the constraints of this society. It is nearly impossible to 'drop out' and live a hippie life in the countryside: the stranglehold of complex rules and relations is at its most severe in the rice-growing countryside. On the other hand, in the big cities life is so expensive that it is all one can do to just pay the rent. In Tokyo, people who want to work in an environment that is free of Japanese social constraints typically try to get a job with a foreign company; but working in one of these offices is a rat race which brings its own strains and hardships. So the relaxed life at Tenmangu seems like a peaceful haven for such people, at least until the next step, which usually involves leaving Japan.

A Japanese friend once said to me, 'I always associated old Japanese houses with an image of poverty. When I saw Tenmangu I realized for the first time that one could live well in an old house.' The key to the destruction of the city of Kyoto lies in this comment. In the eyes of the city administration, rows of old wooden houses look 'poor'; they are an embarrassment, and should be removed quickly. This is not only true of Kyoto – the same feeling lurks deep in the hearts of people all over Japan. If this were not so, the rampant destruction which has occurred here would have sparked a strong public outcry; but until recently there has been hardly a peep of protest.

Kameoka has already been completely transformed, for the wave of 'uglification' that threatens all of Japan is advancing here as well. Every year a few of the rice paddies surrounding Tenmangu are torn up to become parking lots or golf-driving ranges. Fortunately, the grounds of Tenmangu are spacious and the mountain behind the garden is shrine property, so for a while, at least, we should be safe.

There is a framed calligraphy in the foyer of Tenmangu which reads 'Nest of Peace and Happiness'. It was written by an Edo-period literati and harks back to the house of one of the Sung scholars who revived Confucianist philosophy in the twelfth century. Though he did not have much money, he surrounded himself with books and scrolls in his small cottage. He invited friends over to his 'nest', and there they laid the grounds for a revolution in thinking. For me, the true charm of Tenmangu lies in its air of relaxation. My friends and I may be plotting revolution, but due perhaps to the quiet surroundings, or to the 'black glistening' of its four-hundred-year-old pillars, whoever enters Tenmangu quickly succumbs to its relaxed atmosphere. The visiting businessman, the type who always rises punctually for breakfast meetings, inevitably oversleeps at Tenmangu, or forgets to fax or call his office. It is quite common for a guest who planned to stay only a single night to lose track of time and stay for several days.

The visitor to Tenmangu soon finds himself becoming inexplicably drowsy. It is not because I have put something in the wine, but because the pace of life has suddenly slowed down. While talking or listening to music, my guest gradually begins to slouch to one side. From a chair, he moves over to the soft silk cushions on the *kang*, and lies down. Soon he is unable to prop up his head any longer, his face sinks down onto the pillow and he slips off to sleep. The 'nest' has worked its magic again.

DINNER OF HERBS

CARLA GRISSMANN

CARLA GRISSMANN is American by birth but has spent most of her life elsewhere, including Morocco, Afghanistan, Pakistan and Sri Lanka. In the 1960s she lived in a village in Turkish Anatolia, which formed the basis of her only book, *Dinner of Herbs*.

Dinner of Herbs by Carla Grissmann, published by Arcadia 2001.

EVERY EVENING during Ramazan there was an invitation to a different house for the main evening meal. The first time Asiye Nedihe and Elif and the children went to join the women at a big party at the Muhtar's house, they didn't get home until nine-thirty, which is like rolling in at three o'clock in the morning. Asiye Nedihe was overexcited and she talked and wheezed and laughed in her bed-roll on the floor for almost an hour. She had brought me a piece of warm soft *lokum* in a little piece of cloth which she had kept all evening inside her shirts between her breasts.

The families who had sufficient food prepared big dinners and invited the poorer men of the village, and always the İmam, the head of the mosque, and Hacı İsmail, the Muhtar and Kâmuran, the Hoca, and now me, as guests. Three or four trays were set out on the floor and twenty-five or thirty men crowded around them. I was the only woman, and at the time I was not really aware of the magnitude of their courtesy and kindness. I was not a Muslim, I was a woman alone, and these two facts were enough to warrant suspicion, disapproval and exclusion.

People sat more or less as they came in, talking or not talking. There was always a radio, their own or a borrowed one, tuned to Radio Ankara, and as the room filled up it became more and more quiet under the chanting from the Ankara mosque. Then a clear, strong voice intoned the evening prayer. The fast was ended. Everyone moved up closer around the trays, pulling the cloth over their feet and knees and murmuring the blessing, '*Bismillah*', then picked up a folded piece of limp bread and took a swallow of water from a glass that was passed from hand to hand to open the meal. The head of the family, the host, stood to one side and he and his older son or sons, or sons from a neighbouring house,

CARLA GRISSMANN

passed the full dishes and placed them in the centre of each tray.
The first dish was always a wheat soup. The wheat is soaked in
water, handfuls are taken and rubbed together like a cloth being
washed, until the water is milky white, and then it is boiled and
sprinkled with dried mint. White beans in a hot red pepper sauce,
little balls of wheat in a pale soupy sauce, a sweet pudding of rice
and milk and water, then potatoes cut in small pieces simmered in
water and oil, a bowl of *pekmez*, the much-loved grape syrup
thick like molasses, then layers of bread dough cooked in fat.
Water. It was always the same menu with slight variations, a ban-
quet compared to the daily fare of the rest of the year. By the middle of winter not much was left of the small supply of sugar beets,
pickled tomatoes or dried grapes that each family put aside from
summer, and a single dish of potatoes, beans or boiled wheat was
the usual meal, or simply bread with a handful of chopped onions.

Everyone ate quickly and the dishes were taken away while
still half-full, to be given to the women in the next room. There
was hardly any conversation. Before the end of the meal, the
İmam abruptly began a prayer and the men dropped their bread
and raised both hands in front of them, palms upward, and murmured the words with him. His prayer was in Arabic, learned by
rote a long time ago, the words now unintelligible and their meaning lost, but no-one would think to wonder what it meant. When
the meal was finished, the trays were lifted away and the men got
to their feet and queued up to wash at a tin basin in a corner of the
room, where one of the sons held the soap and towel and poured
water over their hands. The men spread out and sat in a packed
line against three sides of the room. The father or his son swept
the floor clean with a short straw broom and went around dropping little tin ashtrays in front of every second person. For a few
minutes everyone shifted and moved to get comfortable on their
haunches and soon the room began to cloud with cigarette smoke.

Then again without warning the İmam rose and went to stand
at the wall facing south. The men rose and formed in lines. In one
gesture, they all turned their caps around so that the visor lay in
back. The first evening I didn't know what was happening and I
stood up too in confusion. Hacı İsmail said, 'You stay. There in

back, sit, sit.' There were three rows of eight or nine men and the room suddenly seemed very small. The İmam called out the beginning of the prayer, and instantly all the men in their dark anonymous clothing and matted wool socks full of holes were fused, their shoulders almost touching, into a single obedient body. The act of prayer is a prescribed ritual and the movements never vary. A man stands erect, his hands open at either side of his face and his thumbs on the lobes of his ears as he says the first words: 'Allah is most great'. Still standing, he continues to pray, then bows from the hips with his hands on his knees. He stands upright again, then sinks to his knees and puts his hands and his forehead to the ground. He sits up straight on his heels, then again puts his hands and his forehead to the ground. These movements are repeated several times. The prayer too does not change. It is of praise and gratitude, a simple act of worship, not a petition for favours or a personal dialogue with Allah.

All the things I had been reading began to take on meaning. In 1923 one of the dramatic reforms in Kemal Atatürk's secularisation of Turkey was the demand that Western hats be worn instead of the fez, which to him was the symbol of Muslim fanaticism. This caused great anguish amongst pious Muslims, who considered the hat an infidel execration, the brim rightly hiding the shameful pagan face from the sight of God. There were riots and defiance. Atatürk declared the wearing of the fez a criminal offence. Within three weeks, with thousands of Turks hung, beaten or imprisoned, this reform was complete. Besides the more Western appearance it produced, perhaps he hoped that a head under a European hat would think European thoughts. The hat, furthermore, might in an insidious way discourage prayer, as the brim made it difficult to touch the forehead to the ground. But the people got around this by adopting the visored cap, which could be swivelled front to back so the wearer, his head still covered, could easily touch his forehead to the ground while performing the ritual prayer.

CARLA GRISSMANN

Turkey had come so far. Much of the population after the First World War had been lost through battle, disease and starvation. No proper roads existed, only one railway from Istanbul with a few dead-end branches into Anatolia. Malaria and typhoid still broke out. There were no industries, no technicians or skilled workmen, in a country ninety per cent illiterate, with no established government. The heaviest liability, however, of Atatürk's derelict legacy from the Ottoman Empire was the great mass of benighted peasants, rooted in lethargy, living in remote poverty-stricken villages untouched by the outside world. Atatürk was determined to loosen the hold of Islam on the people, which he believed was the major obstacle to modernisation, and to awaken a sense of Turkish national pride. He fought fiercely for the emancipation of women, denouncing the veil, giving them the right to vote and to divorce. He had a consuming faith in the qualities and the character of the peasants. The élite of the cities should turn to the people, he said, as the living museums of Turkey's cultural heritage. The élite possessed civilisation, the people culture. 'Atatürk understood our country,' Kâmuran always said. 'He was a peasant himself.'

Whenever I quoted facts and figures about how much had been accomplished or still needed to be done, Kâmuran grew impatient. That there were only two taxis and one private car in the entire enormous province of Bingöl in 1963, that in 1962 only 5,000 out of 60,000 religious leaders could write the Latin alphabet, that now nearly six million students were registered instead of the 380,000 when his father was his age, that the GNP was rising at a steady seven per cent a year, did not interest him.

'I do not understand numbers like that, they are not important for us now, maybe later. Only the things that keep these people's minds closed are important now.'

The prayer ended and the men went back around the room and sat against the wall. On one of the first evenings I found myself sitting next to the İmam. He was an old man with only two large brown teeth, a big mottled nose, loose unshaven cheeks and a gruff manner. He was not from Uzak Köy and moved from house to house, spending two nights in each, and every family looked forward to their turn to receive him. I was rather afraid of him, as I knew that he, more than anyone in the village, must question my presence with mistrust. He had been very busy the week before talking about the astronauts and Apollo 12's trip to the moon. He had sermonised in his little mud mosque and told the men that they must not believe what was being said, none of it was true, and all the pictures were just fake pictures. He said that a while ago a man had tried to go to the moon, but had been eaten by the big fish that lived in the heavens and protected Allah's domain. If again someone had tried to enter this sacred region, they also would have been swallowed by this big fish, as big as the moon itself. All this was a wicked endeavour and could only result in terrible punishment.

Even Hacı İsmail, who was really open to the world, was made thoughtful by what the İmam said. We had long slow discussions in Hacı İsmail's house about it, with the older men emphatically agreeing for religious reasons and others agreeing for simple technological reasons. It was so clearly impossible to fly to the moon, all the stars and the big fish in the way were beside the point. Hacı Kadin poked me in the side and asked on her own if it were true that they had gone to the moon, and I uncertainly began to answer, 'Well, yes, I think they did . . . but . . .' She interrupted in a bewildered soft voice saying only, '*Why?*' I tried to say that they must not worry about these things, that in a few years they would all be a natural part of our lives. Had not electricity and the radio and automobiles been equally unbelievable and thought to be the works of the devil? Allah's world is bigger than anyone knows, and they agreed with this. Kâmuran was left alone to try to explain and he felt his way slowly, slowly, but there was no way to break through and I saw him turning into himself, discouragement on his face.

So I was feeling mindful of the İmam, and kept my eyes down and my feet under my skirts. When the little glasses of tea were passed around he waved his in my direction, and it was set down in front of me. He sniffed loudly when I thanked him. He was not accustomed to making small talk and, working the heavy folds of his face up into a quivering unaccustomed social smile, he reached out and pinched a corner of my skirts and loudly said, as if he were talking to a child, 'This?' I gave him the name in Turkish, and then the name for my shoe, my arm, my hand, my nose, as he pointed to each in turn, thankful that I had actually learned those words rather in the same way. He pointed to my cigarette. I said, '*Jarra*', which is the local slang name for cigarette, and he slapped his knee and laughed. From then on we were friends, although we never talked about anything complicated, and after he had looked through his Koran to make sure it wasn't a sin, he said I could take his picture if I wanted.

One morning during Ramazan, Asiye Nedihe came scuttling into Kâmuran's school in a very excited state. 'Come, come,' she panted, 'Duran's cow just died. He is selling the meat . . .' Kâmuran was alarmed and told her that, besides being forbidden by the Koran to eat meat that had not been ritually slaughtered, it was also dangerous to eat the meat of an animal that had died without reason like that; the animal could be sick and you would eat the sick meat and it could make you sick too. But she looked at him with a blank face. *Not* to eat this meat fallen from heaven was unthinkable. After she left, Kâmuran said darkly, 'You wait, we will eat this cow too, whether we want to or not.' It was, of course, a windfall, especially for the festive evening meals of Ramazan. And for seven days in a row, in seven different houses, we ate the cow in all its forms, the muzzle and brains one night, the stomach and intestines another, the liver, the meat and grizzle in stews, the tail, the feet, and at the end of the week we could reconstruct the entire animal as it had passed across our plates. Nobody got sick, and it was the only time in the village that we had meat, except during the great Kurban Bayramı feast which falls twelve weeks after the end of Ramazan, when every family that is able, kills a lamb or a sheep. This most important Muslim celebration is in commemoration of Abraham's sacrifice of his son İsmail. I asked Kâmuran to tell me his version of this sacred story and to my amazement he had nothing to say. He had watched for twenty-two years the ritual killing of a lamb and had never thought to question the origin of the ceremony. Later in New York, I asked a Turkish friend, from a wealthy Istanbul family, the same question. He looked rather vague and said, 'Oh, it's to celebrate when they found the little baby in the river. And then the Prophet Mohammad slaughtered a lamb.' I said, *'What!'* and he brusquely said, 'Well, history has never interested me very much.' I wondered if there were any Christians, even non-believers, who would not know the story behind Christmas or Easter.

Very early one morning, halfway through Ramazan, Emirel, Hacı İsmail's son, came into my room. It was still dark. I had heard a knock and pulled the heavy cotton quilt up over my head and moved over against the wall, which was the only way, I had learned, to keep from being disturbed. Most times, whoever it was would come up to the side of the bed and stand there for a few moments noisily shifting from foot to foot, sometimes lifting up a corner of the quilt hoping to find a shoulder or an arm to poke, but finding only an unresponsive back, would get discouraged and go away with a sigh. Emirel, though, nudged so insistently that I had to turn over and he said urgently, 'Come, come, my father wants to see you.'

Getting up for them was simply a matter of rolling over and getting up. Most of them slept half-dressed, in one or two layers of clothing, and had only to pull on a pair of extra trousers or another skirt, reach out for their cap or rewind a scarf around their uncombed hair. I told Emirel rather testily that I would come but he would have to wait, and he went outside. Then I got a little worried and wondered if anything serious was the matter.

When we got to the Muhtar's house, the kerosene lamp was brightly lit and Hacı İsmail was still in his bed, with his cap on, lying back on his bedding on the floor. He thought he had a fever, and he knew he had a very bad headache. I gave him two analgesic tablets, a supply of which I always carried in my pocket, and got him a glass of water from the bucket in the corner. He started to put the tablets under his pillow and I said, 'No, you must take them now, with a lot of water. In ten minutes your headache will go.' But it was Ramazan, and he was not allowed to take even a swallow of water. 'Tonight, I'll take them tonight, when I'm better,' he said, patting the pillow. Then he said, looking at me without blinking, 'Let's play cards.'

I smiled to myself the whole rest of the morning. It isn't against the Koran to take water during Ramazan if you are ill; it is against the Koran to play cards, but I guessed he knew all that much better than I did.

Everyone agreed that the hardest thing to do without was cigarettes. All the men smoked a great deal. Whenever you met someone or went into a house cigarettes were offered almost before the greetings were finished. One pack would be passed around the room and emptied before it got back to you, but since everyone contributed their share it always seemed to work out fairly enough. Hacı İsmail was an unconventional man, and he tossed cigarettes around the room willy-nilly into people's laps. In the poorer houses that had no carpets you flipped the butts into a corner, but where there were carpets, little tin ashtrays cut out of old tin cans were always spread around the floor by your feet.

The older women smoked too, and when there was a party or a gathering with all the women talking together in one of the rooms, Hacı İsmail would stick his face in and throw a pack of cigarettes into their midst. The women smoked deliberately and slowly, following the white curls of smoke with half-closed eyes, holding the cigarette pinched between the broken yellowed nails of their thumb and first finger in a very worldly fashion. They didn't know about inhaling, and when you lit their cigarettes there was always a flurry of sparks as they concentrated on blowing out. To get rid of the ash they gently pressed a finger against the end of the cigarette.

On a trip to Ankara I had obtained a huge brown glass ashtray from a friend who worked in one of the big hotels to bring back as a souvenir for Hacı İsmail. It had indentations around the edge for six cigarettes, and I thought it would be ideal for his card-playing hours. I gave it to him, explaining where it had come from and that I had more or less begged it for him. He laughed and turned it over, very pleased, several times in his hands, said that it was very beautiful, *çok güzel,* and then he looked at me with narrowed eyes and said, 'What is it?'

As Kâmuran and I had been invited every night to someone's house I asked him if he did not want in turn to offer a meal one evening before the end of Ramazan. He did not really know how to cook, and his room was too small to hold more than five or six people, but he loved the idea and I told him I would do all the cooking if he gave me a day's notice. We went over the menu and talked about the men he wanted to invite, and we set the day for when we had got together ten or more eggs. It was late November and the chickens had stopped laying, so this was a problem; also there was no yoghurt or milk any more, but I was determined to make my menu as I wanted to prepare things for them they had never tasted.

I told Asiye Nedihe and Elif about these plans and they were pleased and excited. They asked what pots I would need and offered their spoons, and said that everything must be neat and clean. Asiye Nedihe was all for it, and I woke up at night plotting out the various dishes and how I could get them cooked in the right order on just one little kerosene stove. I saw that synchronisation would take up most of the time. Every morning I said to Kâmuran, 'Eggs? The eggs?' and he answered, 'Maybe tomorrow.' He had made the announcement in his classroom and there was nothing to do except wait.

When the time came, I was going to buy a chicken for ten lira from Bekir next door, and I had the six remaining carrots and five leeks from a batch Kâmuran had bought in Çorak two weeks earlier. I was going to make a leek soup, a huge potato omelette, a chicken stew with carrots, rice pudding with walnuts and an apricot compote, and had figured out more or less exactly how and when to cook each thing during the day so they would all be ready by five o'clock. By Thursday only four eggs had come in and Kâmuran said the omelette was a bad idea as Ramazan would be over by the time we got the rest, but I said let's wait and who knows.

I was working in my room Friday afternoon and as usual at three o'clock the school let out and the children came running and shouting past the window. Suddenly Kâmuran appeared at the door. 'Come, come. They are coming tonight. You must cook.'

'Kâmuran! MY DINNER! It's three-thirty! I can't cook all those things by five o'clock! It can't be done, oh my God . . .' I wailed.

'Yes, come, come, don't worry, you can cook.'

I rushed to get Asiye Nedihe to tell her what had happened and she moaned, 'Aman . . . aman . . .'

Kâmuran was out the door, 'I put the table, you cook.'

Bahri was walking by and I yelled at him to go next door, find the chicken, kill it, and get its feathers off. Asiye Nedihe was already piling up pots and pans. I could hear Bahri running outside and the terrible squawking of a chicken vigorously trying to escape. He brought it to the school a few minutes later, a flesh-less, pale mauve little carcass with incredibly long thin legs and a long thin neck dangling from its puckered bony body. Elif came to the window of Kâmuran's room, looking upset. She went off to borrow another kerosene cooker and Bahri filled up the little tin stove in the middle of the room with wood and chunks of dried dung and lit it. Kâmuran's water buckets were empty. Halil and Yunus, left over from school and standing intensely by, grabbed them and ran out to the fountain on the other side of the village. I hacked away at the carrots and put them with the chicken on the kerosene stove and the apricots on top of the tin stove. Elif came back with the second kerosene cooker and we wordlessly got it going out in the hall on the floor. I put the rice on that. I hated to give up the omelette but with only four eggs it seemed out of the question, so I cut up the potatoes for the soup. It was getting dark and the room was stifling and full of steam. I had to use a torch when I went out into the hall to stir the rice and prime the stove every few minutes. Kâmuran had dragged out his wooden desk to set up in the schoolroom next door, with newspapers neatly spread over it as a tablecloth, and had pulled three school benches around it. Every time he looked into his room he laughed and said, 'Good, good. You see?' Once I caught a glimpse of Asiye Nedihe hovering in the dark hall outside wringing her hands.

It was quarter to five. The chicken suddenly smelled as if it were cooked, the apricots began to puff up and the rice started to look soupy. I felt a deep sigh well up from my lungs and a great wave of calm descend, as if the next thirty minutes were all the time in the world. The soup was also beginning to boil, and I blew on the hot chicken and on my fingers as I tore off the tough shreds of meat and put them back with the carrots. A boy came in with a load of bread wrapped in a towel. Halil came in walking carefully, balancing an old dented tray with tea glasses and saucers and little tin spoons, something I had not remembered. Kâmuran came to get his transistor radio from its nail over his desk and take it into the schoolroom. The table was ready and looked fine, with wooden spoons laid out and piles of bread at each place and in the centre a little saucer with salt in it. He had borrowed one of the big German kerosene lamps and had lit the stove and the room was bright and warm. The frenzy of cooking at my end had receded and one by one I could put the things in their big enamel bowls and line them up on the floor in the hallway.

A little before five o'clock the men began to arrive and their voices came muffled through the wall. Twelve men had come instead of five or six, and they laughed as they tried to fit onto the low teetering benches. Then there was silence and I knew the prayer had come over the radio and that they had begun to eat. Hacı İsmail had brought another chicken, which was a relief. I carried in all the other dishes and put them out on the table. They had left some soup in the bottom of the bowl, which was for me. They left a corner of food in every other dish too, and Hacı İsmail wrapped a chicken leg in a piece of bread and brought it out to me.

They sat for a long time, talking in the next room, and then came into Kâmuran's room one by one, stepping over the cooking debris, swivelling their caps front to back. They went into the corner, facing the wall, and began their prayer, as there was no space for this in the classroom.

Asiye Nedihe and Elif and the children were waiting for all the news, and when I got home we went over every detail from beginning to end, sitting in a heap together in front of the fire. Asiye Nedihe and I shared cigarettes as usual. She took my hands and, turning each one over near the light, began clucking and exclaiming. There were cuts and hacks and burn blisters over both hands, and dried bits of potato peel and carrot skin hanging all over my sweater sleeves. She pulled my head down on her lap and rocked me back and forth, laughing and sniffling.

A CO-OP BUILDING

FROM

NEW YORK

LILY BRETT

LILY BRETT is an internationalist, German-born, Australian-educated and now based in New York. She has published award-winning volumes of both fiction and poetry, as well as a couple of volumes of non-fiction from which the story published here is taken.

I LIVE IN A CO-OP building. In Manhattan, most residences are co-ops, co-operatives. A co-operative company owns the building. People own shares in the company. Shares which vary according to the size and value of their apartment.

I liked the sound of co-operative living when I first moved here. It sounded cosy and communal.

On the surface, this is true. Things seem smooth and co-operative. A civility is maintained, on a daily basis. People say good morning and good evening and sometimes exchange other greetings. No-one steals anyone else's newspapers, and most people are willing to sign for the delivery of a parcel if a neighbour is absent.

At meetings of the co-op, however, things can come unstuck. Can become not quite as civil. The most petty of grievances can be aired. There are unpleasant exchanges and unfair accusations. Strands of racism and bigotry frequently put in an appearance.

The people in my building are middle class. Artists, writers, scientists, bankers, businessmen and businesswomen. Individual popularity in the building rises and plummets. One minute you're in, the next moment you're out. The cause of the shift in status is usually unclear. The changing alliances and inexplicable rifts remind me of being a schoolgirl.

My husband and I had our fall from grace. Before then, I think we were reasonably well liked in the building. It was more of a crash than a fall, actually.

Two-and-a-half years ago, we let our apartment for two months. Letting your apartment is a common practice in New York, a city that commands exorbitant rentals.

I was persuaded to do this by a friend who rents out her town house every summer. In sixteen years, she told me, not even a glass had been broken.

The tenants we found had impeccable references. We gave the co-op board their share of the rental money, and left for Mexico. The idea was to paint – my husband is a painter – and write, in the sun, for two months during the New York winter.

While we were away, our home was burnt out. Over fifty per cent of the apartment was destroyed by fire. The Fire Marshall of New York City called us in Mexico. He was very nice. The cause of the fire, it was thought, was a faulty surge bar brought in by the tenants. Surge bars are supposed to cut out if they are overloaded. This one didn't.

I woke up in Mexico, the morning after I heard the news, and wondered if I still possessed a photograph of my late mother.

The toll was soon evident. Over a thousand of my husband's paintings had been destroyed. Thirty years of my diaries were gone. And so were my children's childhood photographs. And the photographs of my mother.

We came home to a mound of buckled and blackened rubble that used to be home. Fragments of years of photographs poked through the rubble. I'd been a zealous photographer and documenter of my children's lives. Both of my parents, separately, survived Auschwitz. We had no photographs or documents of their previous lives. No past we could lay our hands on.

I saw one of my mother's kitchen utensils, melted, in my kitchen and I wept.

The first thing the co-op did was ask my husband to resign from the board. The fire had grossly inconvenienced the building, they said. This was true. Smoke had entered other apartments. Someone's windows had been broken. The pungent stench of fire loitered and lingered in the building. The elevator was out of action for days.

Neighbours glared at us. A sense of neighbourliness was not really prevalent. No-one offered us a coat or a cup of tea. It took us a year to rebuild and get back into our apartment. It seemed interminable.

We're back now. And the civility has reappeared. In the building people nod and say good morning and good evening.

A HOUSE

IN THE CASBAH

JEFFREY TAYLER

JEFFREY TAYLER is the author of *Siberian Dawn: A Journey Across the New Russia* and *Facing the Congo*, and is currently at work on a book about his travels with Bedouin in the Moroccan Sahara. He is a correspondent for the *Atlantic Monthly* and has also written for *Harper's Magazine*, *Condé Nast Traveler*, *Salon* and *Spin*, among other publications. He lives in Russia with his wife, Tatyana.

SOMEWHERE AFTER Settat the landscape through which my train was creaking southward changed. Gone were the turbaned old farmers lashing bony-ribbed donkeys dragging carts; the scant grass and shrubs shrivelled and grew scanter, and then disappeared. The sun-baked plain of al-Haouz, edging out the last traces of green, announced the growing proximity of the Sahara, and adobe villages began rolling by against a flat horizon. Ahead was Marrakesh, the mud-walled city of 700,000 where I would spend the next two years as a Peace Corps volunteer. Marrakesh had a less-than-inviting reputation, being most renowned for Djemaa el-Fna (Assembly of the Dead), a square on which, until the French turned the country into a protectorate in 1912, heads were chopped off and slaves sold. Among Peace Corps volunteers, the city had garnered infamy as one of the most difficult places to live in Morocco, owing to the hustlers, con artists and pickpockets who swarmed on Djemaa el-Fna and the Medina (Old Town).

It was the summer of 1988, and I was twenty-seven. I was an Arabist and had chosen service with the Peace Corps in Morocco as a way to immerse myself in Arab culture. My decision to study Arabic (and come to Morocco) had roots in a burning romanticism that impelled me to learn the languages of cultures greatly different from my own, and search for a new life in remote countries. Since Arabic was the language of Islam, the tongue of revolutionaries, and the lingua franca of lands as storied as Iraq and Morocco, Egypt and Yemen, it promised me just what I wanted. Ahead now I faced the challenge born of my wanderlust: to make my life among people who knew nothing of my aspirations, but who had definite notions of what I, a Nasrani ('Nazarene', or Christian foreigner, as Moroccans say), was. To many Moroccans, Westerners were rich, dissolute smokers of hashish, drinkers of whisky, and frequenters of boy prostitutes; they were former colonisers; they were infidels. I would show them that I was none of those. I would forge a new identity for myself, with Arab culture as its basis.

The first palms of the oasis around Marrakesh slid into view, verdant evidence of the underground springs from which the city draws its water. I had heard that one could see the snowcapped peaks of the High Atlas from the oasis, but heat haze shrouded the horizon, blocky brick minarets cut into the blazing white sky, and there were no mountains.

We pulled into the station, where gaunt porters in tattered blue smocks were shoving their trolleys onto the platform and waiting. I joined the other passengers pressing towards the exit at the end of the carriage.

Joy, a Peace Corps volunteer who had already spent a couple of years in Marrakesh, met me at the station and took me by taxi to her home, which she shared with a couple of other female volunteers. I would stay with her until I rented my own place.

Joy lived in a house typical of the Medina near Bab (Gate) Doukkala, on a claustrophobic, winding *derb* (dirt alley) over-hung with the crumbling mud walls of windowless houses, rattling with boys on bicycles, resounding with the plaintive chants of hooded beggars. The curious eyes of loiterers and passers-by fell on us as we made our way down the *derb* to her house. Joy had been friendly at the station, but now she walked with lowered head and a stern expression – the expression Western women in Morocco adopt to discourage come-ons from men accustomed to viewing non-Muslim women as promiscuous.

A wooden door with a sluggish steel bolt permitted us entrance to her home. I followed her inside with some relief, and we shut the door on the alley. Orange trees gave shade to a broad but decaying tiled courtyard, around which stood high-ceilinged, cavernous rooms with glassless windows. Furniture consisted of dusty wicker tables, unsteady wicker chairs, and mattresses and cushions. A foot-high jar filled with dead scorpions that Joy and her housemates had caught in their kitchen occupied a table. I would probably be renting a house like theirs, she told me, as I examined the curled black stingers of the arachnids.

That evening we sat around the courtyard and talked about Marrakesh. In her mid-twenties, Joy was petite and wore glasses. Her dark brown hair was pulled back in a ponytail, exposing a wide brow and an intelligent face. Unlike most senior volunteers, she did not vaunt her knowledge of Morocco and did not preach about what I would find. Since I already believed I knew a lot, having learned Arabic and even having visited Morocco the previous year, her reticence set me at ease; we would not compete. If now and then in what she did say I detected hints of exasperation, traces of fatigue, I could see that Marrakesh had not damaged her trust in people or diminished her optimism.

'Mbarek will find you a house,' she said, propping her bare feet up on an opposing chair. 'Mbarek is a unique person, very kind, and he never pesters the women volunteers. The volunteer before you was teaching him to read Arabic. You'll probably want to keep that up.'

While in Rabat, I had heard about Mbarek. He had been the lover of this male volunteer. Sex between young men was not uncommon in Morocco, I'd been told, where Islamic custom made women (aside from prostitutes) largely unavailable before marriage. Moreover, I had heard accounts of Peace Corps parties in Marrakesh where men, both Moroccans and Americans, dressed as women, wore make-up, smoked hashish and had group sex. I didn't know whether Mbarek took part in these orgies, but I didn't want to find out.

'I think I'll find my own house,' I answered.

'It's up to you. But that can be a bit stressful. And those Arabic classes mean a lot to him.'

The next morning I set out alone onto the *derb,* which even early in the day was hot and smelled of dung, and followed it to where it met rue Doukkala. A short way down Doukkala, a hand-painted sign in Arabic hung crooked over a dark storefront: *wikalat al-amlak* (real-estate agency). I paused and peered inside, catching sight in the shadows of a yellowing portrait of King Hassan II, beneath which a fat man in white robes reclined on a couch. From the gloom he hailed me in a hoarse voice.

'Ahlan! Dkhul, aa khuya, dkhul!' (Welcome! Come on in, my brother, come on in!)

He gathered up the folds in his *djellaba* and came scuffling out of the shadows. He wore a white skullcap and a coarse beard. He was chewing something, and as he spoke he showered me with crumbs and spittle. I recoiled, but he grabbed my arm and yanked me inside.

'You need a house? To buy or rent?'

'I . . . well, I want . . . to rent.'

'You're married?'

'No.'

'Come! Come with me!'

He dragged me back onto rue Doukkala. Still feeling over-whelmed with the novelty of my surroundings, I let him lead me. We marched through the covered walkways of the Medina souks and entered the rising chaos of Djemaa el-Fna, wading through the acrobats, dentists and scorpion- and cobra-charmers who had long ago taken the place of slave traders and executioners. The man shoved his way through the crowd, pulling me along by the elbow. *'Yallah, aji! Aji!'* We left the square and slipped into another *derb*, and wound round and round into the maze, passing out of one alley into another.

With all our turns, the racket of Djemaa el-Fna faded, and we slowed down. Young and not-so-young women leant out of door-ways, wearing only nightgowns and slippers, taking deep drags on cigarettes, smiling and talking in low voices. *'Ahlan! Marhaba bik!'* (Welcome!) A couple addressed my real-estate agent as Si Hamid. I smelled a pungent melange of hashish and bad plumbing.

'Wait,' I protested. 'You're not taking me to a . . .'

He stopped and pounded on a great wooden door. 'Laila! Open up! Laila!'

The latch creaked, dust spilled over us from the clay bricks above. The door swung open and Si Hamid dragged me inside. Women in negligées lay about on divans; hashish smoke hung in the sultry air; there was a reek of unwashed feet and sweat.

'He's very young!' they remarked.

'This Nasrani's rich and he needs a room!' said Hamid.

'*Wallah?*' (Really?) one of the women exclaimed. No-one got up, but they kept their eyes on me and sucked on their cigarettes.

I wanted to leave, but for some reason I felt that it would be embarrassing to say so in front of the women. Hamid yanked me towards a dark corridor that seemed to lead to a pitch black staircase. The dark decided me. Excusing myself to the women, I pulled free and stumbled out of the brothel back onto the street.

Hamid came wheezing along behind me. I turned and faced him.

'Look, what kind of real-estate agent are you? I'm not renting a room in a brothel!'

'What's wrong? You said you have no wife!' He started yanking me back towards the door. 'What could be better for you than living with all these women?'

I pulled my arm free and walked, exasperated and dispirited, back towards Djemaa el-Fna and Joy's house.

Seated under the orange trees was a small man with a kind face. He was black, probably descended from the Africans the Moroccans had enslaved and dragged across the Sahara from the Sahel centuries ago. Despite the heat, he wore jeans and a flannel shirt. He was respectful in a way so many Marrakshi men, who tended towards brazenness, were not. Joy introduced him as Mbarek.

'I've found a house for you,' he said. 'It's in the Casbah.'

Casbah (*qasaba* in classical Arabic) means citadel, but in Marrakesh it refers to a district mostly ensconced within its own walls, beside the king's winter palace and the el-Badi Palace of sultans past. At the time, no other volunteers lived in the

Casbah. There, alone amidst the Moroccans, I could lead the native life I craved. Already inclined to rent the house, I agreed to take a look.

Ochreous and labyrinthine, the Casbah, beyond the Saadian Tombs and the palace portals, appeared to be a quarter like any other in Marrakesh. At the end of Derb Sidi Akerkour, Mbarek stopped at a small brick house painted ochre to resemble adobe. He knocked on the steel door. An old woman answered. Her arched nose extended over her veil, which, once we were inside, she pulled down to reveal sparse crooked teeth and a chin with a blue tribal tattoo. Geometrically patterned tiles covered the floors and the lower half of the walls; the upper half and ceiling were painted lime green. On the first floor, there was a squat toilet and a rudimentary kitchen – a sink and a counter. On the second floor there were two rooms, one with a small window on the street. Sunlight flooded in from an open-air stairway, which led up to a walled-in roof. The rent, the landlady said, would be seventy-five dollars a month – a sum I could afford on my three-hundred-dollar-a-month living allowance. I took it.

The next day I moved in, and Mbarek helped me set up house. He took me to a furniture shop to buy my bed and divans; he accompanied me to the wicker market outside town to get my chairs and tables; he showed me a souk where I bought kitchen utensils; he helped me buy a gas burner, and told me how to operate it. Most importantly, he introduced me to Fatima, the middle-aged woman whom I would hire as my maid.

Originally from a village in the foothills of the High Atlas, diminutive and motherly, with a quailing voice but gimlet eye, Fatima, more than anyone else, helped me feel at home. She cleaned and cooked for me, put my belongings in order, and attempted to instil in me the vigilant distrust that was, for her, the beginning of knowledge. My time in the Casbah, according to her, was not to be enjoyed but tolerated; each time we met she asked me if I had 'adjusted a little'. That I spoke Arabic mattered not at all. Moroccans would see me as a rich Nasrani and cheat me, try to trap me into marrying their daughters, and never keep their word to me. She had seen this before with other volunteers and it would be the same with me. Her cynicism aside, Fatima was a sad woman with a son who had run away and a husband long gone. Often in the months ahead I would come home to find her slumped on the floor (out of respect, she never would sit in my chairs, no matter what I said), her hands covering her weary eyes.

Despite Fatima's warnings, I got to know and like many of the people on Sidi Akerkour. There were two *hanuts*, or small grocer's shops, at the end of the *derb*. One was run by Ahmed, a lisping young Berber from the Souss Valley who resembled a Native American, with high, flat cheekbones and straight black hair. Ahmed always reminded me to get receipts from my landlady when I paid my rent, and distrusted his Arab countrymen. A curly-haired Marrakshi Arab operated the other *hanut*, and I could never pass by without having to exchange ten minutes' worth of greetings and inquiries about the health of our respective families. Farther down the *derb* was a tailor's shop, where for a few pennies I had clothes mended, and on occasion sipped tea with the proprietor. To be sure, these were acquaintanceships rather than friendships. But there was nothing wrong with acquaintanceships, superficial as they were.

There were some residents of Marrakesh, though, with whom neither I nor the denizens of my *derb* would ever share tea. Two or three times a month in the winter, as I was walking out of the Casbah at Bab Agnaou, policemen and soldiers would appear and close the street to traffic. Minutes later, a motorcade of black limousines would shoot past, stirring up trash, carrying the king, in his white-hooded *djellaba*, from his palace towards the road north to Rabat. As subjects of an absolute monarch, no-one in the Casbah ever objected to the inconveniences caused by these royal comings and goings. Veneration of the king was one thing I could not share with Moroccans, but I kept this thought to myself.

In October, rain fell and the sky turned gloomy. One day Mbarek knocked at my door.

'The volunteer before you was teaching me to read Arabic. Can you teach me, too?'

He had done so much for me that I didn't want to refuse him. He had made no advances towards me and I wondered if the rumours I had heard could have been false. I told him to wait and I would bring my Arabic textbook down from my room.

I walked upstairs. He followed me. I picked the book up off the shelf and he sat down on the chair. Furniture was so scarce downstairs that he could have thought it made sense to study up here. I sat down on the couch.

We began going over the letters. Two years of previous study had amounted to little. Showing meagre knowledge of *alif, ba'* or other letters, he slipped off the chair onto the couch beside me, and sat too close to me. I perceived that as I was reading the letters aloud he was looking at me, not at the page, and that he was edging his head close to mine.

I shut the book, and he looked up and stared at me.

'Our lesson's over,' I said, moving away. 'Sorry.'

He stood up and apologised, and left the house. I didn't regret his departure: there were some areas of the Moroccan 'experience' I had no desire to explore.

He visited me only a couple of times more during my time in the *derb*, politely inquiring from the doorway about how I was getting along, and never again asking to come inside.

Aside from the palaces, the Casbah was a *hay sha'bi* – a district inhabited by working-class folk. From what they had heard from past Peace Corps volunteers, most Casbah dwellers knew roughly how much money I made. My living allowance, small as it was, placed me well above them financially, and some looked upon me with envy. Being recognisably non-Moroccan didn't help, either. I found that I was rarely at ease walking down the street in the Casbah. At times children shouted 'Nasrani! Nasrani!' at me as I pedalled past on my bike.

One afternoon I was riding home. I turned down Sidi Akerkour and saw a group of boys nine or ten years old at the corner.

'Nasrani!' they called out. A couple raised their fists and made insulting gestures. I bumped down the *derb* towards them, determined to ignore their taunts.

One of the boys picked up an apple-sized rock and hurled it at me; it struck me on the knee and cut through my pants, leaving a bloody gash.

There was a round of laughter from the boys. I stopped and looked at my wound.

'Nasrani! Nasrani!'

If I was to be respected in the Casbah, I could not let this assault go unanswered. I aimed my bike at them and began pedalling hard. They panicked and scattered in all directions, but the culprit chose a dead-end street for escape. I quickly overtook him, jumped down from the bike and seized his arm.

'Don't you ever throw a rock at a grown-up again! Look what you did to my knee! Look!'

He twisted and screamed and tried to break free, and tears flooded his eyes. Wetness spread down his pant legs.

'Look at what you've done!'

He screamed so loudly I let him go, and he stumbled caterwauling back down the *derb*. I rode home.

Half an hour later there was a rapping on my door. I opened it to see a veiled woman holding the small culprit by the hand.

'How dare you frighten my son like that! *Hashuma! Hashuma!*' (Shame! Shame!)

'I'm sorry, but he hit me with a rock. Look at my leg.' I showed her the gash.

'Oh . . . well, if he does that again, take him in your house and whip him.'

At her words the boy began caterwauling again and she led him away.

The mother's words showed that in some way she had accepted me, but the children on the *derb* from then on regarded me with a mix of fear and hostility. I disliked the role of tyrant, but had to play it to avoid another stoning.

During my first year in Marrakesh I observed Islamic prohibitions, both because they accorded with the more ascetic life I was trying to lead, and because I wanted to fit in. I never drank alcohol, and when opportunities presented themselves to meet Moroccan women, I usually declined. But I gradually became aware of contradictions between the Islam about which I read and the habits of Marrakshis: drunks stumbled about in my *derb* at night; smashed beer cans littered the refuse heaps; men and women flirted on the main avenues during the evening promenade. Sometimes it seemed that I alone had been adhering to puritanical norms. As the months passed, I was coming to see that my idea of finding a new life here was flawed: life everywhere is filled with contradictions, with disappointments and falsities.

I decided to liberate myself, if not in the Casbah, then in the freer realms of Gueliz, the new town, where Marrakesh's more 'Westernised' residents lived.

One night in July, heat smothered my *derb*. Haze covered the stars; dust from passing donkey carts drifted through my windows. I had dragged my mattress to the roof, but even up there it was still too hot to sleep.

I gave up and got dressed, walked out to Bab Agnaou and caught a taxi to an air-conditioned nightclub on avenue de France, in Gueliz.

As I walked in, a wall of music hit me. 'I'VE GOT THE POWWA!'

I bought a beer and sat down, relishing the cool air. Across from the disc jockey sat a couple of young women. One had curly, shoulder-length black hair; she wore an olive green pantsuit and black pumps. She kept turning to look at me, and eventually, when a slow song came on, I asked her to dance.

It seemed marvellous to be dancing with a beautiful Moroccan woman. I lost myself in her musky hair, smelled her strong perfume, caught sight of her thickly polished green nails. Her name was Nadia. We talked for an hour, and then, feeling I had nothing to lose, I asked her home.

Half an hour later, after having showered together, we retired to my room. Within minutes we were drenched in sweat – more from the infernal heat than anything else – and locked in amorous exertions. I reached for the condoms.

'What are you doing?' she demanded, pushing away.

'Why, getting the *capotes*.'

'Oh, no, we don't need them!'

'But we do.'

'I'm not that kind of girl.' (In Morocco, men used condoms only with prostitutes, if at all.)

'I didn't say you were. But, haven't you heard of . . .' I paused. To mention disease would only cause further upset, even offence.

'Heard of what?' She pouted and turned away, tears in her eyes. But then she turned back to me.

'Habibi, habibi! (My love, my love!) I love you! I love you!' She pulled me onto her. 'Say it! Say you love me!'

'I . . . I . . .' I couldn't say those words so easily; I felt like a fool, trapped by my own preconceptions that one should be honest. She needed to hear those words to relax, but I kept an embarrassed silence.

She took the condoms from me and threw them into the corner. Sounding false, I did say the words, and she closed her eyes and thrust her mouth to mine, pulling me onto her.

We agreed to meet the next evening. Just after dawn she slipped out.

The next evening we sat at a restaurant on rue Menara as the sun sank behind the oasis palms. She had been quiet and I sensed something was wrong. I felt vulnerable, oddly guilty.

She clenched her hands and leaned towards me across the table.

'Habibi!'

Inwardly I began to shrink. 'Yes?'

'*Habibi,* while I was in your arms last night . . . while you embraced me, at the very moment we were tasting the pleasures God has ordained for man and woman . . .' She paused and swung her head away, addressing the wall. 'While I was tasting you, my beloved mother (May God have mercy on our parents!) suffered . . . a heart attack!'

'Oh my God!' I exclaimed. 'What do the doctors say?'

She choked on a sob and turned back to me, but I noticed her eyes were dry. 'Her final hour is nigh. Soon, she will appear before God for judgement. There is hope . . . a small hope. For her treatment, to save her life, she needs the sum of fifteen hundred dirhams [US$160], and fast.'

Her tearless eyes fixed me.

Had she come home with me only for money? If she had, she had followed a risky strategy that didn't match how hookers operated. More likely, she saw me as a rich Nasrani, young and exploitable, both sexually and financially. But I was living on my last dirhams, waiting for my next month's allowance. If I had wanted to give her the money – and to this, despite my doubts, I had no real objection, since maybe she *did* have a sick mother, or some other urgent need – I could not have.

'I'm sorry, but I don't have the money.'

She sobbed more tearless sobs, and said it was okay. Eventually, having promised to meet at the nightclub, we parted.

I never saw her again.

My Western notions that men and women could enjoy each other, either in sex or friendship or love, did not apply in Marrakesh, even among its 'Westernised' inhabitants. Marriage was usually an affair calculated to benefit the families of the betrothed; even sex outside of marriage could be turned to advantage. This for me was alienating and demanded a cynicism I would only gradually acquire – and, I now think, to my detriment.

As my second year in Marrakesh drew to a close and I readied myself for the return trip north across al-Haouz, I saw that I would never fit in – at least not in more than superficial ways. Because of my appearance and nationality and what they communicated to Marrakshis, I would always be both privileged as a guest and exploited as an outsider. By submitting outwardly to norms and religious laws, by professing beliefs I did not hold, I could have gained more acceptance, but this deception was not for me.

I had been born into a different world. This I could not change, and this, after leaving the Casbah, I would no longer deny.

THE VISIT

FROM

ON MEXICAN TIME

TONY COHAN

TONY COHAN is the author of eight books, including the best-selling travel narrative *On Mexican Time* and his memoir *Native State*. His articles, essays and reviews have appeared in a variety of newspapers and magazines in the United States and elsewhere.

From *On Mexican Time* by Tony Cohan, published by Bloomsbury 2000. Reprinted by permission of Bloomsbury and Bonnie Nadell Literary Agency.

SEPTEMBER. The crescendo of patriotic festivities gathers force. Fireworks shatter the dawn, explode in the midnight sky. School drum-and-bugle bands trudge noisily down the *calles*. Drunken youths stumble through the night streets singing and shouting '*Viva México!*' The toy sellers in the *jardín* have doubled in number, adding Mexican flags to their inventory, flags that now festoon nearly every building in town. Restaurants offer the seasonal delicacy *chiles en nogada*, with its colours of the national flag: whole green chilli peppers smothered in a white cream sauce of meats and fruits and spices and nuts, topped with red pomegranate seeds.

It was Colonel Ignacio Allende, born in the house facing the Parroquia I pass daily, who conspired with the priest Hidalgo from the nearby town of Dolores to ignite the revolt of 1810 against the Spanish Crown. Both paid dearly: hunted down and executed, their heads were hung from pikes in Guanajuato's granary as public rebuke. Their exploits and unhappy ends are endlessly memorialised in song and speech and mural, consecrating San Miguel de Allende as the 'Cradle of Mexican Independence'. Every September 16 the president of Mexico recites Hidalgo's cry of independence, the *grito de Dolores*, from the balcony of the National Palace, beamed to every corner of the country over radio and television. Our mayor follows this with a mini-*grito* from Allende's balcony to the throngs that pour into San Miguel from all over Mexico. Before the month is out there will be more music, marathon races, fireworks, a *pamplonada* (running of the bulls), bullfights, Indian *conchero* dancing – and, on the twenty-ninth, San Miguel Day, a celebration in honour of the Franciscan friar who established the town around 1542.

In the eighteenth century, San Miguel was formally charged by the Crown with the crime of having 'an excess of fiestas'. Citizens fought the charge and won. Now it seems there's a fiesta nearly every day in San Miguel – civic, Indian, religious, patriotic, pagan. I like the patriotic ones least, nationalistic fervour tending to be the same in every country – parades, bands, speeches, flag waving. Still I want to hear the famed *grito* spoken right here where the revolution began. At La Golondrina, Maruja and Billie regard my interest with benign amusement: they're closing up shop and going to Puerto Escondido. Billie counsels laying in provisions, staying off the streets, getting earplugs, and curling up with a good book. 'Why all the revelry?' she says irritably, fishing a fresh Marlboro from her shirt pocket. 'What has the Revolution done for anyone in a hundred seventy-five years? The same Spanish-descended families still hold most of the power.'

'It's better than being a colony,' Maruja says. 'And there've been changes. You exaggerate, Billie.'

Tomorrow our friends Janet and Richard arrive for five days. They'll stay through the festivities on the fifteenth and sixteenth, then return to Manhattan. We'll be leaving two days later for a few weeks: a novel of mine is coming out in England and France, and while I have no idea if it will help, it seems I should go. On the way back to Mexico we'll stop and see my daughter in New York. Rafael has promised to hold our rooms at the Ambos Mundos.

We've booked Janet and Richard, her new husband, into a complex of former colonial homes two blocks above the *jardín*. The rooms, at around fifty dollars, seem pricey in Mexico's flattened economy, but they can afford it; and we have some doubts about Richard's tolerance for humbler quarters.

Janet, a museum curator in Manhattan, is an old friend – open, ebullient, warm. We've met Richard, a professor of art, once. Older than Janet, he seems a cultivated, somewhat fastidious man who prides himself on his discernment in art, books, wines. What is it that draws fresh, exuberant Janet to these mentor types? We wonder how Richard will respond to Mexico's unruliness, its rough edges.

The evening before they arrive, Álvaro, a new friend, stops by to take us to a fiesta at a communal ranch outside of town. A thoughtful, delicate man with limpid brown eyes and a grey moustache, Álvaro grew up in the California lettuce fields and worked with César Chávez's farmworkers movement before coming to Mexico to teach printmaking at the Bellas Artes.

A few miles above town we turn onto a dirt road and pass through a low open gate. Álvaro parks in a clearing beside a barn. Stepping out, I smell hay, animal faeces. Horses are tethered to the barn, pigs and chickens roam free. Short, brown men mill about in clean cowboy outfits, women in bright dresses. A boy shoots off flares in the clearing, summoning people from the surrounding ranches. There is an open fire and a table with beer and *tamales*.

People arrive, greeting each other with quiet gentility and the soft handshake Mexican men use. 'The fiesta will go all night,' Álvaro says. 'This has nothing to do with the national celebrations. It's about the harvest. Most of these guys go to Texas or California twice a year to work, then come home for spring planting and fall harvest.'

'How do they cross the border so easily?' Masako asks.

'It's not easy. They pay a *coyote*, a smuggler, two or three hundred dollars. The *coyote* will try three times to get you across. If you don't make it you're out of luck. Even when you do, you often get caught and sent back, or beaten or jailed. Some die.'

'But they have land here. Why go?'

'These are *ejidos*, small plots given out to peasant farmers after the 1910–1920 Revolution broke up the big land holdings. It's below subsistence. Small farmers still can't get loans or decent machinery. So they make the trip. They're branded criminals for entering the States illegally, even though the American bosses welcome the cheap labour.'

The *campesinos* talk softly among themselves beside the barn. I visit their country by choice; they visit mine because they have to. Here in Mexico I come to know the places that fill their dreams when they're lying in a Texas bunkhouse, washing dishes in Chicago, bending over a hot central California strawberry field; the families they long for on the other end of the phone line in a *larga distancia* office.

On a wooden platform stage built against the back of the barn, young men and women begin a slow, circling dance to their own singing accompaniment. There are no instruments. The dancers repeat the lines of the song again and again, moving in the same shuffling circle. The singing is out of time, the dancing awkward; this is not the Ballet Folklórico. Yet everyone seems to know what to do. The near-tuneless, six-line Spanish ditty is oddly haunting, entering my head and lodging there. Something about corn and the moon, but so encoded in idiom I can't sort it out. Neither can Álvaro. It appears neither glad nor sad, this song, but empty of readable emotion entirely. The performers' expressions are blank, deadpan, as are the gathering audience's. When the performance stops or peters out from time to time, there is no applause or recognition. Yet Álvaro assures me this is a festival celebrating the corn harvest and everyone is happy.

I think of D. H. Lawrence's troubling description of Indian dancers at Lake Chapala, tamping the earth again and again, and his charge that the people had no developed consciousness and lacked the spark of reason. Mexico had overwhelmed the fussy, neurasthenic Lawrence, who deified the primordial but was terrified by the slightest encounter with it. In Mexico City he fled the bullfights in horror. He accused serene Indian babies of being flat-eyed and dull. Huxley's Mexican writings read similarly, as do Graham Greene's: full of distaste for the heat and dirt and dust, the untamed sights, smells and customs. Paul Bowles discerned in pre-Hispanic life the same maw of emptiness he finds in the Maghrebi deserts. Strange, the judgements of these Western writers about a people who've constructed ornate languages, vast cities, systems of mathematics and astronomy; who can be so graceful and sensitive in their human relations; whose extravagant, ironical arts speak volumes about existence. Cartesian 'reason' is confounded by what it finds here. Watching the ritual dance, I think how gringo commentators fail to grasp what Pascal surely meant when he said, 'The heart has its reasons that reason does not know.'

The celebrants carry on the tireless dance, undisturbed by sprinkles of rain that drive us under a pepper tree, a *pirul*. It will go like this until dawn, Álvaro says, only drunker. Finally we climb back in the Ford truck and leave the *ejido* ranch.

Back in town, Álvaro pulls up on Calle Insurgentes before a makeshift stand outside the Oratorio church where an aproned woman ladles hot corn *atole* drink from a metal pot into ceramic cups, hands us steamed chicken tamales on a paper plate.

At nine-thirty the next morning we meet Janet and Richard at their hotel. They'd arrived the night before in the American Express van from Mexico City. Walking them into town for breakfast, I notice how enraptured Janet is by the bright morning, the old buildings, the fountains. Richard seems wary. As Masako and Janet walk on ahead, he leans close.

'Digestively speaking,' he says, 'I'm, frankly, sensitive. So's Janet.' I happen to know she has a cast-iron stomach. 'Water, for instance. What do you advise?'

'Bottled water. And stick to the tourist restaurants.'

'Good. I brought a suitcase full of Evian. We brushed our teeth with it this morning. And one doesn't order the ice, I know.'

'Probably wise, Richard.'

After consulting various New York physicians, Richard has brought along a private pharmacopoeia worthy of a trip to remotest Borneo. It's easy to laugh; yet I think of Paul, who remains mysteriously ill from something we can only assume he contracted here eating or drinking.

'Kidnapping, rapes, murders,' Richard says.

'What?' I say, looking around.

'It's all we read about. How bad is it really?'

'I think you can feel safe in San Miguel. Most of Mexico, for that matter.'

At breakfast in La Mama's courtyard, among dappled light and birdsong, Janet feasts on *huevos rancheros* while Richard spills pills from vials into his palm. Masako and I trade glances: it's shaping up to be a long couple of days.

Richard, eager to start touring around, has already inquired about a driver at the hotel. We advise a day walking the town first to acclimate, reminding him that we're over a mile high. Well, then, what is there to see? he wants to know. I find it hard to answer. No Parthenon, no Louvre here. Richard is strung tight as a wire.

'Did you get some rest?' Masako asks.

'Hardly, with the fireworks at dawn,' Richard says. 'Don't they have laws?'

I explain that the patriotic holidays have begun. 'It's like our Fourth of July. Or July fourteenth in France. San Miguel is one of the old historical towns.'

That's possibly interesting, Richard concedes.

After breakfast we walk up to the plaza and find a seat on the benches facing the church. The sky frames the Parroquia's spires, casting its facetted surfaces into shadow. Pigeons flutter down from the bell towers to the forecourt to troll for crumbs.

'It's restful just to sit,' Janet says. 'We've been going like maniacs. Everything seems so vivid here, heightened . . .'

Richard spots the truck unloading newspapers onto the street. I walk him over to buy a copy of the *Mexico City News*, the English-language daily, from Rogelio, who sells them right off the pile. After a glance at the headlines to reassure himself that he hasn't fallen off the edge of the earth, Richard stuffs the paper in his pocket. With his salt-and-pepper beard, tweed jacket and fussy ways, Richard seems old, though he's younger than I am.

We head down Cuña de Allende, the street beside the church, passing La Fragua Bar where we'd celebrated Elenita's birthday, then the Posada Carmina with its towering, vine-latticed red walls and curling balconies. We march our guests through the Hotel Taboada lobby and up the stairs to the roof, which affords a rare view of the town. Every block of San Miguel, I realise, is textured with private associations to me now. Are these affinities communicable? Objectified through Richard's impatient, critical eyes, the place suddenly seems flimsy, without compelling attraction.

We drift down Calle Sollano toward the French Park. Willowy, athletic Janet delights in everything her eye falls upon. Richard, picking his way among the cobbles, pauses to consider the old buildings with their odd, extravagant doors.

'How do you get around without a car?' he asks.

'Like this. There are taxis, buses. Or friends give you rides. After California it's a relief not to drive.' I'm not about to tell Richard other reasons I don't enjoy driving in Mexico: old unsafe cars, two-lane roads travelled by speeding buses and trucks, predatory cops.

In the French Park, kids shoot hoops on the asphalt court, a tai chi practitioner parts the air like water. Banks of pink lilies spread down to the slightly malodorous stream. By the outdoor public wash area where women come to scrub their clothes, Richard asks, 'What interested the Spaniards in this region?'

'Silver. Over a quarter of the world's supply was mined around here.' We climb slowly up to the Chorro, the old waterworks. At the top we turn and look back over the trees. 'You'll see when we visit Guanajuato. Over there, beyond those mountains.'

Idling back toward the town centre, we pause by old walls, peer into courtyards, linger by fountains. The jerky, demanding quality of time we'd started out with untangles into a more human shape. In Carlos and Elenita's folk art store we wonder at a beautiful *quechquémitl* cape woven in Chiapas. Richard takes interest in a Huichol yarn painting showing the cycle of the seasons, and a riotous ceramic tableau of a truckload of skeletons. Janet tries on a Guatemalan blouse. Roaming the grand Bellas Artes building, once part of the nunnery, Richard becomes curious about an unfinished mural by Siqueiros.

We head for the market to gather ingredients for a lunch at our place. At El Infierno we select a barbecued chicken hot off the spit, then after promising Richard extreme acts of purification before ingestion, we select vegetables and fruits in the indoor market. Janet buys so many tuberoses, red roses and irises that we buy her a plaid plastic *bolsa* of her own to carry them in. 'In New York, a single rose would cost more than this entire bouquet,' she says.

We lug our *bolsas* to Lucha Contreras's pharmacy to buy disinfectant drops. Anxiously Richard pores over a *Physician's Desk Reference*, trying to find Mexican names for American drugs. He wants a list of local doctors in case he and Janet get ill or need more prescriptions. Most drugs are sold over the counter here, I tell him. In fact he could get a vitamin or flu shot in the back of Lucha's pharmacy. He's horrified.

'Without a doctor? What about infection?'

I start to tell him they use disposable plastic syringes, then think: What's the use?

At the hotel we immerse the vegetables and fruit in a bowl of water treated with disinfectant. Richard watches intently. Over lunch, Janet talks effusively of our morning walk and new places she'd like to see. Richard struggles mightily to get a verbal fix on San Miguel – 'I mean it's a bit like an Italian hill town. But then not. Southern Spain. Granada, say. Completely charming. Goes back to the Moorish . . .' – until finally he talks himself into silence, and there is only the sound of doves cooing in the stone walls, the clinking of silverware, the occasional bell from the nunnery. Sparkling fruit, mint tea, the afternoon's languor.

'Delicious,' I think I hear Richard murmur.

We walk them back to their hotel for siesta, arrange to meet for dinner.

The Nissan van bursts out of an underground tunnel into bright midday light. We pile out into Guanajuato's Jardín Unión, with its stately Indian laurel trees and kiosks. Posters advertise the yearly Festival Cervantino beginning in a few weeks: theatre troupes, string quartets and dancers will come from all over the world. We guide Janet and Richard through the dense, moody streets, the steep lanes that curve suddenly upward then come to dead ends, the cloistered alleyways that spread into little flower-filled squares called *plazuelas*. Dense, cultivated, mysterious, tucked in its narrow valley cleft, Guanajuato has all the *chiaroscuro* drama and interiority of a walk through an Arab medina.

We walk up the wide steps of the Teatro Juárez opera house. A velvet rope leads us through an ornate art nouveau lobby into the hushed, deserted theatre. A colossal curtain of plush red velvet falls to a hardwood stage floor. Soaring balconies overhang a sloping ocean of bright painted wood seats, silver and gilt filigree, brass fittings imported from France, Italy, Germany.

'It's like being inside a little music box,' Janet says breathlessly.

'Such extravagance, in these remote mountains,' muses Richard.

'The dictator Porfirio Díaz commissioned it at the turn of the century,' I say.

'They tried turning it into a movie theatre in the 1960s,' Masako says, 'but dirty jeans and popcorn and *chicharrones* were ruining the velvet seats.'

Back outside, billowy clouds, dark at the centre, prefigure afternoon rains. We climb twisting paths among stacked, brightly coloured houses. In the narrow, four-story house where Diego Rivera was born (only recently opened as a museum: for decades the painter was disowned by the conservative town for having been a communist), we take in a small collection of his early work. I imagine the gargantuan painter literally bursting out of the little house, the provincial city, into the larger world.

We eat lunch at El Retiro, a restaurant up from the opera house with an invariably good, fixed-price *comida corrida*.

'I can see why you like it here,' Janet says over dessert.

'What do you see?' I ask.

She laughs. 'This bite of flan. Here, in this place.' She looks across at Richard.

Richard puts his teacup down, a wild shine in his eyes. 'Okay, I admit it. It's great. What's the catch?'

We all burst out laughing – even Richard.

By the time we get back to San Miguel, the town is a madhouse. Horns honking, traffic is at a standstill. Most stores are already closed. '*Viva México!*' echoes off the walls and through the cantina doors. Climbing out of the van, we're drawn into the hotel bar by a group of celebrants from Mexico City. To resist is out of the question on this of all days. Tequilas are proffered, toasts raised, backs slapped. Richard tipples José Cuervos with the flush-faced, grinning *chilangos*. We leave Janet and Richard with their new friends, agree to meet later in the *jardín* for the chanting of the *grito*.

Working our way through the crowds on Calle Correo, Masako says, 'You were a little like that.'

'Like what?' I shout.

'Like Richard. Before we left L.A.'

'Thanks a lot.'

'How nice that you don't remember.'

Back at the Ambos Mundos, we close the hotel curtains against the noisy revellers in nearby rooms. Our suitcases lie open on the floor. What to take on our trip? Europe seems unimaginably distant.

Just after nine we work our way back to the *jardín*. The crowd has become a surging, shoulder-to-shoulder mass. From the second-floor window of the Allende house, above the white statue of the brave colonel in his cape, the words of Mexico's President Miguel de la Madrid – formal, lugubrious, carefully enunciated – spit from a loudspeaker, live from the balcony of the Presidential Palace in Mexico City. One by one he announces the names of Mexico's heroes, each answered by thunderous response in Mexico City's great square, and here in our little plaza. '*Viva Hidalgo! Viva Allende! Viva México! Viva! Viva! Viva!*'

We raise our fists and shout along with everyone else: '*Viva! Viva!*'

Feeling a hand on my shoulder, I turn around. It's Janet, looking dazed, worried.

'Where's Richard?'

'I don't know. He kept drinking with those Mexicans, then they wandered off somewhere.'

'I'm sure he's fine,' Masako says. 'How far can he go?'

Pinned in place, we can't possibly go looking for Richard in any event until the '*Vivas*' abate. Our mayor appears on the balcony of the Allende house and launches into a fulminating, over-long speech until finally the noise of the crowd drowns him out.

Slowly people disperse into restaurants and cantinas, houses and cars. We stand worriedly in the *jardín*, uncertain where to begin looking for Richard.

'Look,' Masako says.

Richard comes lurching up Calle Umarán, a Mexican flag in one hand, a plastic cup in the other. His jacket is off, and there's a bandage on his left temple. Janet rushes to meet him, with us in tow.

'Richard, what happened?'

He slumps onto a bench. Janet tries to dab at the bandage but he waves her away. 'They took me to a cantina,' he says woozily, his chest heaving. 'Afterward I fell down on the street.' He points to his bandaged head. 'Everybody stopped to help. They took me to a doctor – all of them. They patched me up for free, then helped me back to the hotel.' He starts to sob into his hands. 'As if they *cared*.'

Janet rubs his shoulder, looks helplessly at us.

We walk them back to their hotel, Richard singing snatches of a double-entendre song his Mexican friends taught him, and leave them at the entrance.

Walking back through town, Masako says, 'We should have thought of tequila earlier.'

The next morning we arrive at their hotel to see them off. Janet emerges trailed by Richard, doubled over with a hangover and a galloping case of *turista*.

'Oh, no,' Masako whispers.

'Montezuma's revenge!' Richard exclaims, hugging us each goodbye. 'Worth every miserable, dribbling bit of it!'

Janet says her goodbyes and thanks us.

Adiós, Richard. *Adiós*, Janet.

They wave out the back window as the van bounces off down the cobbles.

In the open entry of the Church of Santa Ana, on Calle Insurgentes next to the library, a lurid, bleeding, purple-robed Jesus greets passersby. Townsfolk always cross themselves and kiss their fingers when they pass. Humble by comparison to its neighbour churches, Santa Ana is a simple building with no niches or side chapels along its straight walls, no reliquary of particular value or art that would draw a price. Still there's something vibrant and welcoming about its mix of Catholic morbidity and pre-Hispanic playfulness. After picking up a gift for my daughter in the covered market, Masako and I veer into Santa Ana on the way back to the hotel.

It's cool and quiet inside, near empty. An old woman, her head covered in a rebozo, murmurs prayers up front. A caretaker on a ladder is changing a display. Birds chirp outside. We take a seat in the back.

In Mexico, where the invisible counts for so much, Masako and I, refugees from the techno-future, sometimes seem to gain glimpses of a wordless, sacral world. We don't understand it but feel its resonances continually, wending through Mexican Catholicism but not remotely contained by it. Maybe, as Carlos Fuentes has suggested: 'In the land of need that is Mexico . . . the impossible distance between desire and the thing desired has given both yearning and object an incandescent purity.'

'What were you thinking?' I ask Masako as we stand to leave.

'Just a wish for a good journey and a quick return.'

THE YEAR BRUNETTO IL PICCOLO FELL IN LOVE

FROM

LA BELLA VITA

VIDA ADAMOLI

VIDA ADAMOLI was brought up in London and lived for many years in Rome catering to the needs of an Italian husband and two sons. In Italy she spent every summer by the sea, at the place she calls Torre Saracena. She now lives in London, where her first novel, *Sons, Lovers, Etcetera,* was published in 1997.

La Bella Vita by Vida Adamoli, published by Summersdale 2002.

THE SUMMER SEASON proper started after the schools closed for the holidays in June. Torre Saracena aficionados arrived from America and Europe to join those of us who now came regularly from all over Italy. For several years there was even an Eskimo devotee, a girl called Taki, who made the yearly pilgrimage all the way from Northern Canada. By July the population had more than tripled – creating serious problems for the ancient sewage system. The apartments with purple bougainvillaea climbing the walls, with terraced gardens and balconies overlooking the sea were quickly snapped up by the rich. The less affluent rented dark, airless grottoes with walls that dripped condensation and turned bed linen and clothes green with creeping mould. The willingness – ardour even – with which visitors occupied what for centuries had accommodated mules or vats of oil and wine confirmed the Saracenesi's belief that foreigners were quite mad. It wasn't a wholly unwelcome madness, however. People began looking at their cellar space with new eyes and learned to describe cracked stone floors and rotting beams with the exotic term *caratteristico*. Suddenly opportunities for financial gain were wondrously expanded. Even those who had never thought they had anything of worth to sell were now poised to jump on the tourist bandwagon.

Brunetto il Piccolo, one of the first to take advantage of the new opportunities, was the most prominent presence on the apartment letting front. His friendship with many of the newcomers and his skill as property go-between had taken him from a lifetime's penury to a strutting new affluence. In the early years, except on the occasion of his aunt's funeral, I never saw him in anything other than a faded blue T-shirt and limp pink shorts. Now he was an immaculate and stylish dresser, regularly visiting the barbers in the main street for a shave, trim and manicure. It was the accessories, however, that defined his new style: the row of red and blue biros bristling in his shirt pocket, the green tinted sunglasses, the carton of contraband Marlboros cradled under one arm and, most importantly, the brown leather handbag.

This prized possession – of the type made popular when Italian men's trousers got too tight for anything larger than a slim-line Zippo – accompanied him everywhere. Signora Lucia, who had no extra space to let and had conducted a long and bitter feud with his mother, was one of the many not impressed by the transformation. 'Once a *cafone*, always a *cafone*,' she commented contemptuously as we watched him saunter past our communal stairs. 'You can put a pig in a silk suit but a pig he stays.'

Brunetto conducted his business in the piazza, positioned halfway between Giovanni's bar and the *tabaccheria*. For a large part of each day he stood in the same spot, receiving a steady stream of would-be leasers and lessees. His air of solemn dignity, and the impression he gave that the solution to any problem was in his hands, gave him the aura of a diminutive Godfather. His main rival, also called Brunetto, had his pitch on the opposite side of the piazza. Tall, stooped, crafty and in his sixties, he lost more than one commission for lunging at the breasts of foreign female clients. Brunetto il Piccolo, however, was far too astute to endanger his livelihood by such behaviour. Not that he was free from temptation. Sex, as I well knew from our many conversations, was a topic never far from his mind.

During the first year of our friendship, sitting in my kitchen chatting after he delivered Marcello back from the cinema, women and the bitter humiliations inflicted by the local girls was something he returned to again and again. On one occasion, talking about Silvia, a girl on whom he had had a passionate crush at fourteen, he even cried. According to Brunetto, Silvia had loved him too. Her father, however, who noticed the glances they exchanged, had threatened to disembowel Brunetto if he so much as looked in her direction again.

Brunetto's amorous problems were due to occupying the lowest rung in a desperately poor village. His father eked out a miserable living as a fisherman. The family had no land, no prospects, and seven of them shared a two-room apartment. His older brother was epileptic, indicating bad blood perpetuated by intermarriage, and confirmed by the fact they were all extremely short (that intermarriage and its consequences were common to the entire village was not taken into consideration). His one romantic success was a furtive affair with a much older widow. But she quickly dropped him when a man who had been an immigrant for twenty years in Marseille returned with a suitcase full of savings and started courting her.

Unmarried sex, particularly in the South of Italy, had never been easy. Men with good looks and charm took advantage of the summer influx of females who tripped off planes and tourist buses hot for suntans and Latin romance. The less fortunate took their libidinous needs to whores. What little money Brunetto il Piccolo managed to save was spent on hookers picked up in bars like the Splash B-Way in the nearby port town. Or on the fat, ageing women who warmed their bellies and billowing thighs at carefully tended bonfires strung out along the main road to Naples. For these occasions he borrowed one of the small, battered Vespa trucks used by local tomato growers, cruising slowly past tough-faced matrons who lazily lifted their skirts at approaching headlights to tempt prospective clients with a flash of the goods.

Because of his lack of money it was these *Belle di Notte* rather than the more expensive Splash B-Way girls that most often got his custom. Their business was mainly with the long-distance lorry drivers and travelling salesmen who were serviced for as little as five hundred lire. As Brunetto was always at pains to point out however, the size of the fee was not reflected in their skill – especially where a certain Concetta 'The Tongue' was concerned. He drew an analogy with roadside trattorias.

'If you see a line of trucks outside, you'll take that as a sign the food's good, won't you?' he said. 'Well, it's the same with whores. Truckers only go where there's value for money.'

Until Torre Saracena's Big Bang, Brunetto il Piccolo had resigned himself to making do with whores forever. But as an up-

VIDA ADAMOLI

and-coming entrepreneur his matrimonial prospects were no
longer so bleak. Although his emergence as a central player in
Saracena's new order was regarded with the same amazement as
the upgrading of dank cellars, several shrewd matriarchs were siz-
ing him up as a possible husband for their plainer daughters.

But Brunetto's requirements had changed along with his circumstances. The satisfaction he now anticipated from marriage
had as much to do with revenge as it did with anything else. With
his new and inflated self-regard he aspired to a dazzling match
that would be salve to his wounds and a lesson to all those who
had been stupid enough to reject him in the past. He now dis-
missed local girls as '*troppo semplice e ignorante*'. The wife he
fantasised about would be a 'Rose, a Diamond, a Shining Star'.

One evening in early July – after promising faithfully to produce a cheap, honest plumber to deal with the leak under our bathroom floor – he returned to the subject yet again. 'Nothing less than
the best will do for me,' he insisted, thumping his handbag for
emphasis. I was already irritable (because of the leak) and his arro-
gance annoyed me further. 'With that attitude sweet nothing is what
you'll get,' I snapped. But I was wrong. The following morning
two Germans arrived in a taxi from the station. And one of them
was the dream woman Brunetto il Piccolo had been waiting for.

Helga Schultz, somewhere in her late thirties, was a short
blonde, with knowing grey eyes and a very generously propor-
tioned backside. It was this part of her anatomy, shown to its best
advantage in tight white trousers, that Brunetto first noticed when
she approached him for accommodation. The elderly man with
her, in a state of near collapse from the heat, left her to sort out
the accommodation and disappeared into Giuseppe's to restore
himself with several beers. (He was later explained away as her
rich, industrialist uncle.)

The transaction, like all Brunetto's transactions with foreigners, was conducted mostly in sign language. What made it different this time was the unmistakably encouraging nature of her
body language. The flame of passion and love, Brunetto told
everyone later, was ignited there and then. From that moment on
anybody needing his services had a hard time finding him.

Professional obligations took second place to the demands of his first ever proper courtship.

Every morning at eight forty-five the three of them went down to the beach, Helga supporting the old man on her sturdy arm, Brunetto staggering behind under the weight of their collective beach paraphernalia. With 'uncle' comfortably parked in the shade of one of Rocco's umbrellas, he inflated the rubber dinghy (borrowed from a nine-year-old nephew) and paddled his sweetheart fifteen yards or so out to sea. For a blissful couple of hours they bobbed about on the gentle waves, eyes locked, hands entwined, totally oblivious to shrieking children or the curious, amused attention they attracted.

Communication in those early days posed no problem – a pocket German/Italian dictionary more than satisfied their verbal needs. And the success of their physical communion was such that an aura of charged contentment surrounded them at all times. Both blond, five foot and a bit, they looked as though they'd been especially crafted for each other – like bookends or matching jigsaw pieces. In the evening they joined the promenade of people strolling back and forth from the piazza to the bridge, arms around each other's waists, eating ice cream and graciously acknowledging greetings from Brunetto's many friends and acquaintances. Sometimes he took her for a ride on the back of the noisy second-hand *motorino* to which he had hung a precariously fixed sign advertising his professional calling. The 'uncle' was rarely seen and after two weeks returned alone to Germany. A week or so later Helga and Brunetto il Piccolo announced they were going to marry.

Brunetto did his best to ensure his romance inspired the envy and admiration he hungered for. He boasted about Helga's finesse, how sophisticated and well travelled she was and about the big factory 'uncle' owned on the outskirts of Essen. He carried around a photograph of her leaning against a Mercedes-Benz and another wearing a sequinned evening dress taken in a smart nightclub. But the response of the village was grudging. The general consensus was that she was 'shop-soiled' and 'second-hand goods'. Or, as Signora Luca put it, 'There's a worm in that apple somewhere.'

The 'worm' arrived at the end of October carrying a single shabby suitcase secured with a raincoat belt. She was a lanky fifteen-year-old introduced as Helga's little sister, Greta. Helga and Brunetto il Piccolo were now married and comfortably ensconced in the bottom half of one of the new villas built at the entrance to the village. With the end of the season and departure of the Summer People he was free to devote himself exclusively to his wife. Every morning they set off hand in hand to do the shopping, Helga pointing and Brunetto teaching her the name of the selected food item in Italian – or, rather, local dialect. And every evening they continued to promenade slowly up and down between the piazza and the bridge. But although they kept their smiles bright and their arms locked around each other's waists, it was clear that the sullen adolescent now trailing behind them was casting a dark shadow into their heaven.

Brunetto had not fulfilled his promise to find me an honest and reliable plumber. In mid-November he phoned Rome to say that the leak was worse and water was pouring into the bedroom of the old woman below. Exasperated and annoyed, I arranged for my mother-in-law to look after the boys and left for Torre Saracena prepared to stay for at least a week. It was unseasonably warm, almost summer-like. Alighting from the midday bus and seeing the sun glittering on a satin smooth sea I was tempted to forget the problem and go for a swim. Instead I dumped my bag in the flat and went to the bar for advice from Pina as to what could be done.

The reason I was having a problem getting a plumber was because I bought vegetables from Signora Rosalba's stall and not from Signora Annamaria. Signora Annamaria was married to the only plumber in the village and lived in the apartment below her mother's. Furthermore, it was on the mother's head that my bathroom was leaking. Despite the fact that she and her family were suffering the consequences, Annamaria refused to allow her husband to come to my aid. Not only was I her rival's customer, but I had once accused her of overcharging. I had rowed with her, reasoned with her, begged her. All to no avail. We were locked into a familiar village stalemate.

Pina did not need me to explain the situation. Like all village gossip she knew it already. 'You have two options,' she said. 'Either you get a plumber from Matia, or get somebody with influence to approach Signora Annamaria on your behalf. There's no other way.'

I carried my *latte macchiato* outside. Being off season there were no tables, and I sat on the broad stone ledge running along the wall coasting the steps. I wracked my brains trying to think of a possible mediator but to no avail. I was not on familiar terms with either the priest, the mayor or the head of the Elementary School. I was quite friendly with Signora Annamaria's second cousin, Rita, but as they had quarrelled over property and hardly spoke there was nothing to be gained there. As it happened, however, fate decided to intervene and the problem was resolved without my needing a mediator after all.

In the two short months she had been in the village Greta had done much to tarnish Brunetto's carefully nurtured image. She hung about the piazza looking pinched, defiant and neglected, soliciting cigarettes or a hundred lire from any man or foreign woman who happened to glance her way. Joining me on the wall she immediately indicated she wanted one of my Nazionale. After lighting up she exhaled noisily and muttered something in German that sounded like 'Torre Saracena stinks'. She said it with such venom that I burst out laughing. My reaction took her by surprise. 'American. Ya?'

'English.'

'Ah! Beatles! Rolling Stones! You like?'

I nodded, adding, 'And you'll like Torre Saracena better when spring comes. There are lots more people. Young people, your age.'

'You crazy?' She glared and tapped her forehead with a finger. 'I don't stay in this stinkhole for spring with them two stinking crazy shits. I split.'

I felt sorry for her and sorry for Brunetto il Piccolo, too. A ready-made teenage rebellion was never part of his plans.

The following day was spent asking everyone and anyone if they knew of a plumber who could come to my rescue. I was told long stories of outrageous overcharging, work left unfinished and old parts sneaked in instead of new. Salvatore the *pasticiere* said if I had come to him a week earlier he could have helped me but the man in question, who lived in Matia, had suffered a sudden heart attack and died. By then I was thoroughly fed up. It was late afternoon and I decided to cheer myself up with a walk on the beach and a bowl of Leone's mother's mussel soup.

For me mussel soup as made in Torre Saracena – although the recipe is simple and by no means unique – tastes better than any mussel soup anywhere else in the world. It is the village's one great culinary achievement. The fresh mussels are stewed with white wine, garlic and parsley and the resulting juice, sopped up with crusty hunks of pungent cassareccio bread, is pure ambrosia. Consequently, it was with salivating anticipation that I hurried down the broad stone-stepped path to the beach. The sun was setting when I arrived at Leone's and there seemed to be no-one around. Nosing around, however, I soon came across the mother dozing in a deck chair behind the kitchen. She awoke immediately and declared herself happy to serve me a plate of the mussels she had cooked that day for lunch.

I went to sit on the wooden veranda to wait. The sea was rose-tinted and the beach an empty silken sweep. The spacious silence, broken only by a gentle lapping of waves, was so numinously awesome I found myself holding my breath.

'It's so beautiful,' I murmured reverently when Leone's mother brought me the soup. '*E bella, si*,' the old lady replied smiling toothlessly. 'And once upon a time it was always like this. No umbrellas, no jukebox; no noise.'

It was dark when we said goodbye but I still wasn't ready to go home. Slipping off my shoes I continued barefoot towards the promontory at the far end of the beach. Suddenly the silence was shattered by a drunken voice booming from behind a clump of bushes. 'Oh, fuck her,' a man with a harsh American accent exclaimed. 'She's just a pain in the arse.'

Drawing closer I saw three marines from the American naval base sprawled around a crackling driftwood fire, bottles of wine and leftovers from a picnic littered everywhere. There were two young girls with them. The girl wearing just her knickers was Greta. She giggled happily while one man pawed her breasts and another kissed her. The other, small and slight with a waist-length dark plait of hair, was struggling to escape from a slobbering brute. It was Gianna, Signora Annamaria's thirteen-year-old daughter.

My arrival broke up the party. I informed the men that the girls were underage which meant if they didn't get court-martialled they would certainly be lynched. I also added that I was the wife of Sir Reginald Williams, the British Ambassador to Rome. This little lie had great effect and they couldn't get away fast enough. Greta was furious. She yanked on a T-shirt and ran off swearing at me in German and English for spoiling her fun. I put my arms around Gianna and held her until she stopped shaking. Then, with her clinging to my hand, we started the long climb back up to the village.

'Don't tell my parents,' she begged repeatedly. 'They'll kill me.'

I said I wouldn't if she faithfully promised to keep away from Greta in the future. How she was going to explain the torn blouse and scratches on her neck and arms, however, I didn't know.

Signora Annamaria, informed by at least ten people that her daughter had gone down to the beach with Greta, was waiting in a smouldering lather at the top of the steps. When we appeared she immediately seized Gianna by the hair, and began walloping her. Then she dragged her off screaming of worse retributions to follow.

The shouting and crying from their apartment went on late into the night. At some point Gianna must have confessed everything – including the part I had played – because at half past seven the next morning the plumber husband was at my door. Neither of us made any reference to recent dramatic events. All he said was that he now found he had time to attend to my problem. After a quick inspection he explained that the leak came from one of the pipes feeding the shower and to get at it some of the floor tiles would have to be broken. But I was not to worry. It would not be expensive and the job would be finished in a couple of days.

Later that morning I shopped as usual at Signora Rosalba's but I bought a kilo of tomatoes from Signore Annamaria's stall as well.

'Ah, children are such a trial, isn't that so, signora?' she said, picking out the best tomatoes for me. 'And boys can be as much of a worry in their way as girls.'

'You're so right,' I replied. 'And my boys get up to so much mischief I'm worried most of the time.' We shook our heads, shrugged heavily and gave a couple of long, weary sighs. Hostilities had ceased – although problems with our bathroom plumbing were to prove never-ending. And I was given not only a discount but also two lemons, an onion and a fist-sized bunch of basil free.

I didn't see Greta for the rest of my stay but Signora Lucia gave me a vivid account of the scene that occurred a few weeks later. A small travelling circus arrived in the village and a clown with a performing monkey turned up in the piazza to advertise the evening's performance. Among the crowd that gathered to watch its antics were Brunetto il Piccolo with Helga and Greta. The clown had a megaphone which he put down for a moment in order to better encourage the animal to walk on its hands. Suddenly Greta snatched it up and put it to her lips. Signora Lucia claimed her voice carried for miles. 'She stinking liar,' she bellowed pointing at a horror-struck Helga. 'Not sister – mother! *Madre*! My stupid idiot mother, you hear!'

Signora Lucia told me this while she prepared lunch in the cubby hole kitchen hung with bunches of dried herbs and black iron cooking pots by the front door. 'You see, I was right,' she declared with satisfaction. 'I said there was a worm in that apple somewhere.'

FROM

EXTRA VIRGIN

ANNIE HAWES

ANNIE HAWES suffered in London's Shepherd's Bush until she applied for a job to work on a rose farm in Liguria. Her experience of fifteen years in northern Italy, and of her acquisition of a house and garden, are the subject of her best-selling *Extra Virgin*.

WHEN IT'S NOT FIRE in late August and early
September, it's drought. This year the late tourists,
the ones with most money to spend, are leaving
waterless Diano Marina in droves. In theory, according to its
Comune, the town's taps are being supplied with water for one
hour in the morning and one in the evening. This would be bad
enough for the hoteliers' trade; but in practice water often
doesn't appear even at the official times. Residents are out-
raged, rebellion is close among what's left of the holiday-
makers, who now can't even rinse the salt off their skins at the
end of their day on the beach – no laughing matter at this time of
year, when the sea water is so concentratedly salty that it makes
you itch all night if you don't get it off. There are tales of taps
accidentally left on, spouting water at 3 a.m. Are you supposed
to stay up till dawn in case the water comes on? What kind of
resort is this, anyway? Diano Marina is dry as a bone, and facing
disaster. Great standing tanks of water have been put out by the
Comune on every street corner, but this has not noticeably
defused the situation; long queues mutter and fume at every one.
Fathers of holidaying families stand waiting impatiently
with sets of newly bought, sensible ten-litre containers, tapping
smartly casual feet and swearing under their breath on the many
and bestial variations of the Madonna, while they wait for some
local black-tube-clad old lady to fill, slowly and painstakingly,
dozens of carefully hoarded individual mineral-water bottles,
turning the tap off so as not to waste water once each is full,
while she screws on its lid, checks it for tightness, and packs it
into an ancient shopping bag before unscrewing the next
bottle, turning the tap back on, and starting the whole procedure
all over again . . .

Bankruptcy looms for the hoteliers, the beach owners and the tourist shops. And now, to make matters worse, the town is rocked by scandal. Money allocated to building water reservoirs after the last drought has vanished: in its place has been found a mere piece of paper, a document allowing Diano Marina to share in any spare water San Remo happens to have. This arrangement has passed unnoticed for years, while San Remo did have water to spare. But now the whole Riviera is facing disaster, and San Remo is certainly not prepared to share what little it has with a no-account, two-horse town like Diano. The deal was for spare water, not for a share of the water.

Our Diano friends gloat quietly; they have never been fond of the smug hotel and bar owners of their town, who are famous for never taking on enough staff for the summer season, meaning that half the youth of the town are worked to death, sixteen hours a day, seven days a week from May to September, while the other half are out of a job. Now, those who have grown fat from tourism are sunk. And so is this Comune, already disliked for caring more about tourists than locals; having failed so miserably in this self-appointed task, it is now forced to resign.

Inland in San Pietro there's not a lot to gloat about either; the entertainment value in the downfall of Diano Marina is heavily counterbalanced by the bans here on watering your *orto* with Comune water. Only people with a *vasca* or a well are managing to keep their gardens going; others are having to sit and watch their lovingly tended vegetable plots, vital not only to their emotional well-being but often to the family budget, shrivel and die.

San Pietro's Comune, like Diano's, is in the doghouse. Its own drought-protection project, an enormously deep and expensive well which has been started somewhere up by Franco's cow meadows to avoid just such a crisis, still isn't finished. Our Comune though comes up with a positively Machiavellian scheme for deflecting criticism from itself and saving its bacon. Drought instructions are posted up on the walls of the piazza as expected, giving everyone the dread news that it is forbidden to water vegetable gardens till further notice. But they go up in German as well as in Italian: the German version not only comes first, at the head of the poster, but is in slightly larger print than the Italian. It is never a hard job to foment bad feeling about German holiday-home owners, and there are certainly a lot more of them dotted around the place these days; but there still can't be more than a couple of dozen in the whole valley. The fact that the Germans don't even have vegetable gardens, only being here for a couple of summer months, and therefore certainly don't need this information, passes unnoticed. From Pompeo we hear that it's the Occupation all over again: this time, instead of killing villagers outright, the cunning *Tedeschi* have chosen the sneaky roundabout route of depriving them of their vegetables.

Meanwhile up in our mountain fastness, watering has become the main business in life. We may have our own water supply, but by now we have planted too many things for our poor well to handle in this emergency; not only all the stuff in the *orto,* but near the house a baby fig tree, two big bushes of marguerites, an oleander, a small palm tree, our big climbing plant with the salmon trumpet flowers. Then there are the cherry and the six lemon trees, which will lose their next crop's flowers before they set into fruit if they don't get a good couple of bucketfuls twice a week; the four grapevines we're trying to persuade to grow into a shady pergola like everyone else's; and all the geraniums and flowering rock plants in the crevices of our walls. Everything, apart from the cherry and the older Pompeo-planted lemon trees, is much too young to have established a decent root system yet in this poor stony earth, and our policeman's paradise will shrivel and die forever in this terrible heat if we can't keep up the watering till autumn comes. We are saving every drop of washing-up water, and have given up our lovely indoor shower, which drains on to the oleander and the new lemon trees outside the downstairs door. We can't allow them all the water so we are washing our selves and our clothes in an old tin bath contributed by Antonietta so as to be able to ration it. Thank God we don't have a water closet: think what precious resources that would waste!

Until now, even in high summer, the well has always filled itself back up slowly within a week or so after we pump up a tankful; but it's not filling at all any more. It's less than a third full, and distinctly pond-flavoured. Pompeo says that in all his life he's never seen it this low. And it's turned out to be our only resource. Our other waterhole thing, which might or might not have turned out to be a well if only we'd ever got round to clearing it out, has become a shrivelled brackish pond with a cake of cracked mud at the bottom. Our leafy salad bed is wilting horribly; our *trombette* are shrinking instead of fattening up. Domenico and Antonietta's well also contains nothing but a foot or so of smelly sludge. Nino says we can use his well if we want – he hasn't used it for years, he came by an easier, more accessible *orto* nearer home in his wife's dowry, but it's still there in a corner under the apple tree on the terrace just below ours. Antonietta and I find the spot with some difficulty, and disinter its mouth from under a pile of disintegrating mossy logs. No chance. It's as low as the others. We decide to abandon all thought of personal hygiene till the next rain comes – we may get a bit smelly but at least, unlike our garden, we won't die.

Another ray of hope breaks through when we bump into Carlo, the nice *nipote*, who is pottering about on one of the many bits of land his family owns, just round the corner and up the hill, amidst rows and rows of half-shrivelled drought-stricken bean plants climbing up twenty foot canes. He calls us over to look at an enormous snake a good three yards long and as thick as a well-built peasant's arm, which has come down from some more drought-stricken zone and is busy lumping and slithering about in the bowels of an extremely full well in a corner of his *campagna*. We aren't sure whether the snake or the water is the more exciting discovery. The snake, although it's not dangerous – just a *bicha,* a kind of enormous bird-eating grass snake – is still hair-raisingly horrible. The vast quantities of water in the well it is using for a swimming pool, on the other hand, are deeply attractive.

We can use as much as we want of it, anyway, says Carlo – it is lovely and clean, his father and Franco cleared it out this spring. Great, we say, if he's sure Franco and Signor Giacomasso won't mind. Carlo's somewhat perplexing response to this is to erupt into gales of laughter. What have we done now, then?

Giacomasso, it turns out, is not, as we've thought for years, the family's surname, but the father's nickname. Once you consider the matter, which we are now doing, you can tell it means something like 'Chunk-Jack' or 'Lump-Jack'; presumably a reference to the man's impressive girth. Their real surname, Carlo now tells us to avoid further embarrassment, is Saguato. Carlo and Nicola, meanwhile, are called 'the Giacomassi' because they are the sons of Giacomasso. Obvious. Still, it could have been worse – we might actually have addressed their father as 'Mister Lump-Jack' in some public forum.

How come your beans are all shrivelled up, we ask Carlo, when there's so much water in the well? Thereby, of course, hangs a tale.

His dad and Franco, says Carlo, both great bean fans, decided this spring to reactivate this bit of unused land for a family bean patch. Terrible mistake. They were utterly unable to agree on correct bean growing procedures, argued viciously for months about amounts of watering and types of fertiliser and how many shoots should be pinched out when, until eventually Franco, goaded beyond endurance, announced that he now realised he had made a terrible mistake in not opposing his sister's marriage to a man who understood nothing about beans, and should have nipped this relationship in the bud as firmly as he had put a stop to Evil Federico the taxi driver's pretensions. Brother-in-law Lump-Jack responded by telling Franco never to darken his door, or the bean patch, ever again . . . Now they are no longer on speaking terms, while the bean patch has gone to rack and ruin, both of them too proud to touch it. In fact, says Carlo, he was just wondering whether to try to salvage at least a bit of a bean harvest out of it, if there was enough water in the well, when he met the snake. Sadly, he has concluded that things are too far gone.

Even more sadly, from our standpoint, once we start thinking about how on earth we would carry any useful amount of water from here to our home, we realise that though the place may be very close as the crow flies, the trip on foot up and down terrace walls would be much harder work than the car ride to the public tap in the remnant of the outdoor public laundry in San Pietro, which is what we are doing at the moment for non-pond-flavoured water. Just to carry the canisters from car to house along the path is a killer, never mind going twice the distance over rough terrain. No use at all. So near and yet so far.

Down in the Sulking Café, everyone is waiting with bated breath for the weather to break, with chairs outside on the balcony so as not to miss a cloud, gazing in the direction of France and Spain, muttering horribly every time the sky darkens to the north, which it does regularly, to the accompaniment of many rolling oil drums. Down here, though, no water falls. The lazy good-for-nothing ignoramuses of the Pianùa get it all.

Giacò the Junkyard decides to cheer everyone up by reminding us that though the villages of the Pianùa may be stuffed with water, sunflowers, corn and meat, though its banks may be over-flowing with cash, there is a dark lining to their silver clouds: the chronic woman shortage. Up on the plains, according to Giacò, all the women run away as soon as they're old enough to leave home. They can't stand the idea of spending the rest of their life up there trudging muddily to and fro across the huge damp empty spaces, hectare upon hectare of unrelieved flatness, fogbound for half the year, rainbound the rest, no life, no neighbours, no sun, no fun; you can be as rich as you like up there, he says, but you still won't find yourself a wife. Not for love nor money.

The card-players all agree. Much nodding and *Ah, si, si*-ing. So desperate is the plight of the Plainsmen, they tell us, that nowadays they are reduced to importing wives, mail-order, through introduction agencies and small-ads – from Eastern Europe, from the Philippines, from all sorts of distant and poverty-stricken places. But as soon as these women pick up a bit of the language, realise they've got their right by marriage to a work permit, to civilisation, they won't stay on those miserable living-death farms any more than the local girls would.

Even in years gone by, pipes up one of the oldest bar-proppers, in the days before the olive net, when the women of the Pianùa used to come down here to work the olive harvest – there being nothing doing on the frozen farms of the plains in February, deep-est winter still up there – their menfolk would be lucky if half of them ever went back home: *Euh!* They'd arrive here all done up in their finery, ready to scratch the local girls' eyes out, desperate to catch themselves a good Ligurian boy with a few *piante*, a decent life and a place in the sun. Nowadays, though, he explains to us kindly, women don't have to get married to leave home. They can leave anyway, whenever they want, and leave they do.

It is a terrible plight the Plainsmen find themselves in, everyone agrees, much enlivened by having shared these reflections with us. Can it all be true? No idea: but it certainly makes everyone feel better about the water situation.

I'm sick of it. Why don't we just give up this stupid place for good? Something's always going wrong; it's just too hard to survive up here . . . I'm seriously demoralised by the no-water situation. Could we somehow deepen the well? No. You couldn't get the machinery along our horrible path to do it and even if you could, Domenico and Pompeo both agree that we might cause a catastrophe, maybe lose the whole thing, by breaking through the rock-base of the well. They both keep on and on telling me that this has never happened before, probably never will again, but I don't care. Besta de Zago just isn't liveable. I'm giving in, I say, it was a silly idea anyway, trying to make a home in a vile parched hovel on an eyeball-searing desert of a mountain.

In the nick of time Caterina and the Diano *compagnia* step in: they are taking us off for a cooling and cheering weekend trip to the mountain lakes above Triora. So serious is the heat and drought situation down here that, unusually for our tribe of Diano hunters and gatherers, there is no food collecting subtext to this outing. Nothing to collect anyway, they say, much too hot and dry. They just want to escape the water shortage, the sweaty itchy heat, the packed greasy bodies on the coast. They will show us a place where, though it is a mere thirty miles inland, all is coolness and greenness and space, and there is never any shortage of water. Extraordinarily hard to believe under present shrivelling conditions. Despite my grumpy scepticism, though, it turns out to be true. Three-quarters of an hour of slow uphill hairpin bends here doesn't just change landscape but apparently season too. As we drive up the narrow green gorge of the valley of the Argentino River, four valleys along towards France, it is like going from high summer in the Sahara to a pleasantly warm, green, shady springtime in the Black Forest. How sensible these Italians are. Or at least, how well they know their landscape.

Arriving at Molini di Triora, we stop at the village to shop for camp supplies: not as simple as you might think, not with a bunch of Italians. Still, at least there's a cool breeze up here. Our friends spend a good half-hour communing with the village butcher whose fine meat from his own herds in the high meadows is renowned throughout the area (knew there had to be a food sub-text in here somewhere); when we manage to drag Ciccio away from his blood-brother the butcher (Patrizia says we've done well – he was in there for over an hour last time), it is only to go and do the same thing at the baker's. Mills of Triora: of course, we are at the home of the famous bread-that-never-goes-stale. A mile up the hill is Triora itself, a tiny town with a peculiar mini tourist industry based on it being the location of the last witch-burning in Italy. The sister and I do our best not to stamp and snort in our impatient hot-foreigner manner, while everyone buys in their stock of the flat round loaves of Triora, a transaction which inevitably takes another half-hour, what with the low quality of modern yeast and the need to discuss in great depth the problem of getting decent flour these days.

At last we are back in our small fleet of cars, heading for open country. Park and walk for twenty minutes along a shady path, tall green leafy chestnut trees over us, hazels in amongst them, rich dark humus underfoot, ferns and wild strawberry leaves, and way below us, at the bottom of the steep banks to our right, yes, the sound of a river, a loud full-bodied healthy river, no trickling shrunken coastal *torrente*. The path runs level, clings to the side of the ravine, heading to meet the river at the high pools. If only we weren't loaded down with absurd numbers of carrier bags it would be perfect. Suddenly we are there, precious roaring rushing water, thousands of gallons of it, clear freezing mountain-spring stuff pouring down a dozen silver channels through the rocky hillside into a great blue mirror of a limestone lake. We put down our burdens and marvel.

Clothes off and into the water, splash about for hours, dust-free at last, clean and damp, ferns and verdure all around, dappled sunlight instead of the shimmering white heat of the coast. Up here with your feet in the cool ripples of shallow downstream pools, tiny trout slipping through your fingers, it's hard even to imagine our sad mud hole of a well, the tragic shrivelled hay which is all that's left of our once luscious green terraces, our taplessness and bathroomlessness.

One of Paletta's ingenious shelters is already going up in a clearing under the chestnuts, and we mess about making benches out of hazel saplings, wander about the woods, up and down ravines, finding new pools and tributaries to the main river and splashing in and out of them, full of unaccustomed energy now the heat can't get us. Lucy and I realise that this is our chance to collect the bendy twigs we need for our Antonietta-pizza-oven, and get ourselves a lovely big bundle.

We have brought an SAS survival guide with us, a present from a recent English guest who couldn't tell the difference between Liguria and the Mato Grosso: following its instructions, infected by the local hunting-and-gathering ethos in spite of ourselves, we make a very serious-looking fish-trap out of woven hazel wands, which so impresses Anna and Patrizia that they do one, too. We put them, as directed by the SAS, in a fast-flowing bit between two rocks, where everyone keeps prodding and poking at them all afternoon, much to Anna's despair, rattling them around and alarming any fish stupid enough to be poking its nose into the things. Unsurprisingly, we catch nothing. No-one cares: Italians don't think river fish are really worth eating anyway, not even trout. We grill some of the several tons of meat we've brought instead. As dusk falls a billion damp green frogs start to croak sexily on all sides of us, and we have to add lots of green leafy stuff to our bonfire to smoke the midges away.

By lunchtime next day one of those usual large crowds of friends and relations has gathered up here, bearing vast quantities of loaves and fishes (proper sea fish, that is), meat and vegetables, and even the only missing item for a home from home, a great cast-iron grill. Also a pair of four- and five-year-old girls Marila and Miki, who are as overwhelmed as us by the wetness and coolness of the place, not having been here before either. Miki and Marila speak Italian to about the same standard as us, even make the same mistakes, and all the humorous allusions of the grown-ups to Italian popular music and TV series of the last decade pass them by, too. Lovely not to be linguistically and culturally handicapped for a change. We bond immediately.

Soon an eating orgy is, as usual, under way. After weeks of stomach-shrinking heat and no appetite worth speaking of, after weeks of doing the absolute minimum to avoid melting into a puddle of sweat, we find that all the unaccustomed activity in this cool green place has left us famished. We have no trouble at all keeping up. But alas, after lunch our infant friends are forbidden to go in the water. Not for at least three hours, their anxious parents tell them. Kiddies cry; foreign females save the day. We bravely enter negotiations on their behalf; English children, we say, do not die from paddling after lunch. Can Italian kids be so much more fragile? Eventually, once we've promised under no circumstances to let the *bambine* get wet above the knees, we are permitted to leave together for the shallow pools down river to hunt for minnows. We find we have so much in common that we hang out together for the rest of the visit, to the exclusion of the adult company.

Time to go: misery. Time to face not only the dry despair on the coast, but the very irritating travelling behaviour of our friends. They are obsessed, for inexplicable Italian reasons, with travelling in close convoy. Nobody knows why, but it is vital that we all travel and arrive simultaneously: we often, or so it seems to me, spend as much time waiting by the side of the road as at our official destination. A market day in some hilltown, a concert, an asparagus hunt: it makes no difference. We are always in at least half a dozen cars, and have to keep stopping every ten minutes, waiting for the rest of the bunch to catch up, doubling back on our tracks to hunt for lost or straying members of the band who have stopped to use a loo or get a bottle of water or a snack or a coffee or do a spot of hunting and gathering or pop in to visit an old auntie or whatever.

Huge rows break out every time we are held up by someone vanishing, but this doesn't stop it happening: it just means that as well as the fifteen stops, there will be fifteen outbursts of rage. Of course this is all very healthy, you'll be saying. Latins are famous for doing it, steam is let off and soon all is joy again and you've saved all that money you would otherwise have had to spend on psychotherapists. Fine, in theory. We'd like to be able to do it ourselves, even. But you have to be brought up on it. We weren't, and the rowing sends us into stress-alert panic every time, neck muscles tied into anxious knots. And we can't get anyone simply to arrange to meet at the end of the journey, rather than trying to keep one another in sight all the way.

Don't the others know where we're going though? we ask plaintively.

Of course they do.

Why can't we just meet there, then?

Nobody knows why: we just can't, that's all. We are gazed at as if we were saying something incomprehensibly absurd and out-landish. Or made to suffer rude jokes about the unsociability of the English. And we really are unsociable compared to our Italian friends. They never seem to need to be alone. They find a group of less than half a dozen positively uncomfortable: if by some mischance you find that you're alone with just three or four of them – ideal for foreigners like us, who lose track of what's going on when groups get too big – they will wander restlessly around bars and telephones until they have added another few to the band. This doesn't mean they necessarily chat the whole time; any of them may decide to read a book for a bit, or have a nap, listen to their Walkman, play patience in a corner. But we haven't learnt to do this either; ignoring people we're with is just as unset-tling to us as having to be constantly in company.

In years to come, we will learn to reduce the cross-cultural trav-elling discomfort to a minimum by insisting eccentrically – all right, Englishly – on being shown on the map exactly where our destination is, and going in our own transport so as to have only one wait, in the place we're aiming for, rather than twenty pointless hangings around and shouting matches on empty brain-boilingly hot mountain roadsides or hair-raisingly busy crossroads. But for now we are still learning, and after gorging ourselves on coolness, dampness and billions of gallons of pure mountain water, we face the ardours of the trip back with all these extra Sunday lunchtime visitors and the usual incompetent military manoeuvre-style travelling behaviour. As we expected, it takes forever just to get our selves and all our luggage, including the massive grill, back along the path to the cars. Adding insult to injury, we are made to leave our bundle of twigs behind in case the Guardia Forestale stops us. Surely they won't care about a bundle of twigs, we ask, if they don't bother about bonfires and benches? Not to mention great hordes of people gathering forbidden narcissi?

You never know, says Alberto, whose car we are travelling in. Best not to give them any excuse to harass you.

As we travel gently downhill following the rushing water below in the gorges of the Argentino, heading for drought again, we begin to wonder where all this water goes to. Why can't the combined Comuni of these valleys just build a reservoir on this river, have all this stuff to hand when it's needed, instead of doing dodgy deals with San Remo and running low on water every summer? But of course, we are not the first to have thought of this. There have been several attempts, we are told, to build a dam across one of the high, wet valleys; our friends point out three of these false starts as we drive down enormous concatenations of abandoned concrete pillars and blocks on the steep tree-clad sides of the Argentino's high banks, already half-vanished into the undergrowth. But the problem is that no damable valley exists, which does not have fifteen or twenty villages dotted about lower down, below where the reservoir would be. Each time work gets started, the inhabitants of these places notice that, were the dam to burst, they and their homes and lands and olive trees would very likely be washed away in the flood.

They agitate against the scheme; work is halted while litigation goes on. And litigation taking the decades it does here means in practice that the dam is abandoned for good. Easier to look for another site.

I say something thoughtless and superior about the resistance of aged country folk to modernity and change. Mimmo, Alberto and Anna leap down my throat. Do I not remember the flat road to Imperia from Diano Marina? Indeed I do: the *Incompiuta*. And yes, now I see what they mean. If a dam was to be built to those standards of workmanship – and what innocent villager living in its shadow could tell how well-built it was until it was too late? – no-one below it would ever get a wink of sleep. I put my silly foreign attitudes away immediately.

Okay. We'll just have to wait for it to rain then. And, amazingly, as we travel down towards the sea – oh joy! – the sky suddenly darkens. Over towards France, too, no less. And yes, as we arrive at the coast and hit the Via Aurelia, it begins to rain. Rain! Next time we stop to wait for some lost car or other, we ring Diano: is it raining there as well? Yes, it is. And it goes on all night too, and all the next day. By the end of the week our well has begun, slowly but surely, to fill back up. We are saved.

WAITING FOR JUAN

FROM

A PARROT

IN THE PEPPER TREE

CHRIS STEWART

CHRIS STEWART was an early member of the rock band Genesis, but left them to shear sheep before they hit the big time. Farming remained his main activity until his first book, *Driving Over Lemons*, became an international bestseller. He still lives on his farm in Spanish Andalucia, which is also the subject of his second book, *A Parrot in the Pepper Tree*.

A Parrot in the Pepper Tree by Chris Stewart, published by Sort Of Books 2002.

WANDERING UP to the house for a morning break, Manolo has a habit of whistling some utterly tuneless tune about three seconds before he bursts through the fly-curtain of our kitchen. The tune is a considerate warning but it is not quite enough to prevent me from being caught in the act – *in flagrante fregantis*, Ana calls it – or, up to the elbows in the washing-up. Manolo pauses, a blush of embarrassment spreading across his face as he gazes first at Ana reading a newspaper on the sofa and then at me soaked in suds at the sink.

'*Tas fregando . . . ?*' he offers. 'You're washing up?'

'Yup,' I concur. '*Fregando . . .* washing up.'

He nods his head as if to register this anomaly.

Later at lunchtime, as often as not, Manolo will whistle again and arrive to find me standing at the stove.

'*Tas cocinando* – you're cooking?'

'Yup – *cocinando*,' I reply.

Now I love to cook. I consider it one of life's great pleasures, and one that can only be enhanced by constant practice, and I don't much mind washing a few plates and saucepans afterwards. Ana as it happens detests both jobs but has a peculiar tolerance towards tidying up, shopping and laundry, which I exploit to the full. And so we carve up the daily round in a reasonably equal manner.

This is not, however, the norm for Alpujarran men. When men work, they work like mules all day long, but when they finish that's it – they relax and have a drink and ease their aching limbs, while their wives, fresh from a round of chores, gardening and fieldwork, wait on them. Of course there are some men who might help out in the garden, do their bit with the childcare, or even try a few culinary ideas – witness Domingo's jam making. But this is fairly unusual stuff. It would take a brave man to interrupt talk of hunting or water rights in a village bar with a new recipe for chestnut soufflé.

To be honest, a part of me withers whenever Manolo catches me in the kitchen. There's a certain tone to his *tas fregando* that makes me question myself, wonder if all is as it should be in the masculinity stakes. Not that Manolo says anything specific, mind you, but his tone and slightly shamed look have a peculiarly crumpling effect. He reminds me, I fear, of my own reactions to Eduardo, a fundamentalist fruitarian who squats in a half-built house in the *vega* of Tíjolas. Eduardo is a fundamentalist in that he not only survives exclusively on fruit, but only eats windfalls; 'the tree must give its fruit without the duress of plucking,' as he puts it. As you might imagine, this is hardly a strengthening diet, and if the trees are unusually generous then he has to ferry his trawl home in small sacks like an ant carrying scraps from a leaf.

None of this should matter, except there are odd moments in life when a macho reputation does have some use. For instance, on the summer after my return from Sweden, when word got round that Juan Gallego, a local shepherd, had got it into his head to murder first his ex-lover and then me.

This episode began one July evening on the road outside Orgiva. I was standing by the car, talking to a cousin of Manolo's, when suddenly there was a yelling and shouting and a woman came stumbling round the corner in a state of hysteria.

'Please help,' she babbled in Spanish. 'He's going to kill her – he's gone really crazy – go now, please . . . !'

'Wait,' I said. 'Tell me what you want me to do and where and what's happening . . .'

'Just go, now, please, over there!' she implored.

So I got in the car and headed off in the direction the woman had indicated, wondering what on earth I was letting myself in for, but knowing I had to go anyway. After about a kilometre I came across two people standing by the side of the road. One was Petra, a slight Danish woman with long, light brown hair, which she had swept in front of her face in a vain attempt to hide behind it. The other was her lover Juan, a man I knew a little as a result of having sheared his sheep a few times. Though barely taller than Petra, Juan seemed somehow to be towering over her with a look of clenched menace.

Petra acknowledged my arrival with a terrified glance. 'Please don't leave me alone with him, Chris, he's going to kill me.'

'Cristóbal, what are you doing here?' demanded Juan with a look of fury.

I got out of the car and Petra explained as well as she could what was going on. 'I'm leaving him, Chris. I can't stand his moods and his wildness any more. And he can't accept that I'm leaving like this so he keeps grabbing me and shaking me and trying to make me say I'll stay. And now he says he's going to kill me – we've called the police but just please don't leave me alone with him. Stay till the police get here.'

Petra was crying now and rubbing her bruised arms. 'Okay,' I said. 'I'll stay until you tell me I can go.'

All this we said in English. It didn't seem necessary somehow to translate it for the benefit of Juan.

'What are you saying? Speak Spanish,' he shouted.

'Petra is telling me what's going on and I'm staying here until she says I can go,' I said to Juan.

'You can go now. I don't want you here.'

'No. Here I stay till Petra says I can go,' I repeated.

Juan bristled – a stocky man, with teeth mostly knocked out, nose well broken and a stubbly moustache. He muscled up to me. I held my ground.

'Cristóbal, a man does not get in the way of another man and his woman,' he snarled.

'He does, Juan, when there is violence, so here I stay.'

Little by little, as our group moved back and forth between the house, from which Petra was getting her belongings, and the van where she was stowing them, Juan began to get aggressive with me. He didn't hit me, but there was a lot of the pushing and shoving with chest puffed out that men do as a prelude to slamming their fists into each others' faces. 'We used to be friends, Cristóbal,' Juan growled. 'But now you have a serious enemy.'

Anyway, I did my stuff and stuck to Petra like glue, and after about half an hour a Guardia Civil patrol car appeared and two policemen got out. One was a pleasant-faced young man who was obviously a trainee, the other a little runt of a man with a thick grey moustache and a strut like a bantam-cock.

'Show me your papers, passport . . .' he snapped at Petra. 'And you,' he turned to me. 'What are you doing here?'

'I'm staying to make sure that my friend doesn't get hurt.'

'Well, you can clear off now,' he said, with a look of distaste.

'I'm staying until this woman says I can go,' I told him with what I hoped was an answering sneer. It was immediately obvious that this noble little custodian of the law thought that if Juan wanted to beat up his girlfriend then that was his own affair and none of us should be interfering.

The bantam disappeared into the house with Petra to check her papers, and Juan and I were left outside in the dark with the young apprentice. Juan was still being aggressive towards me. 'You're not going to arrive home alive tonight, Cristóbal,' he said. 'Juan,' I warned him. 'It's all very well to threaten a man, but to do it in front of the Señor Guardia here is surely foolishness, no?' I was a little emboldened by the young policeman's cosh and his gun and his silly green hat.

In the end the Guardia escorted Petra to the police station, and as she left she assured me that she had friends who would collect her and that she would be all right. 'Thanks, Chris,' she said. 'I'll be fine now.'

I drove home. Ana and I sat outside eating a late supper, as you do on hot summer nights, while Chloë dozed on the sofa. Halfway through the meal, the phone rang. Ana answered it. 'I want to speak to Cristóbal,' said an angry voice. Ana passed me the telephone. '*Diga* – speak,' I said, only to hear the phone slammed down. 'That'll be Juan,' I confided. 'Checking to see if I'm at home so he can come round and kill me.'

The call somehow put a damper on the rest of the meal. We lapsed into silence and you could hear the clinking of the cutlery and the burbling of wine being poured into glasses. At midnight, Ana rose from the table. 'I'm sure it'll be all right, Chris, but give me a shout if you hear anything worrying,' she said, as lightly as she could manage, then gave me a surprisingly tender goodnight kiss and took herself and Chloë off to bed. I repaired to the roof, where I often slept on hot summer nights, and placed a mattock beneath my bed.

Now, a mattock is a pretty uncompromising tool. A good blow to the head would be likely to end in serious injury or death. Still, I reckoned if Juan were going to make the effort to come all the way out here in the middle of the night, he was not just coming to bring me a bunch of flowers. He was going to fix me good. He had seemed just as much riled by my role in the evening's episode as over the loss of Petra. Pride was at stake.

One of the odd things about this event was that I felt a kind of guilt, as if I had offended some base animal instinct and that Juan was right to seek to duff me up or worse. I wondered how I would have felt had the situation been reversed. Surely I would have been glad to have someone there stopping me throwing punches – I mean, once I'd calmed down? Wouldn't I? I'd have given a lot to know at that moment whether Juan was of the same mind.

The roof I had chosen as summer bedroom has a sweeping view of all sides and is set a little higher than the rest of the house. Juan would not be able to see me in my bed unless he had decided to creep up from behind, but that would mean a very long, very deliberate tramp over the mountains. The moon was not far off the full so I would see my enemy long before he saw me – assuming, that is, that I didn't fall asleep.

What should you wear in bed when you're waiting for someone to come and kill you? It was a hot night and what I usually wear on a hot night is nothing. But it wouldn't do to have to pull on clothes as a prelude to defending myself, while a naked man wielding a mattock is a far from formidable looking opponent. I decided on a T-shirt and underpants as my battle costume, with a pair of sandals ready to slip on, under the bed by my weapon.

I lay down on my back and looked up at the bright sky. It was too light to sleep like that, so I rolled over and peered over the pillow at the moonlit rivers and valleys. I tried to breathe quietly so I could hear any furtive footfalls above the quiet swish of the river. Then I got fed up lying that way and rolled over again giving the mattock a quick fingering just to make sure.

It was a bad business, this. It seemed such unwarranted bad luck to find myself preparing to fight for my life in my underpants with a mattock on a rooftop in the moonlight. Life, which had hitherto seemed pretty good, suddenly seemed even sweeter. I fingered my mattock again and rolled over. There was a car creeping into the valley. I could see the lights in the dark rocks above La Herradura. This was it. It was late; who else would be coming in at this time of night? I had a good fifteen minutes till he got here, assuming that he left his car on the other side of the river – and he would do that because he would hardly drive all the way up to the farm and thus lose what he believed was the advantage of surprise.

I slipped into my trousers, buckled my sandals and grabbed the mattock, then I sat on the bed for a bit. All was silence now; the car had disappeared into the valley. I weighed up the mattock. Now, how do you hit a man with a mattock? Do you crack him over the head with the back of it? Or do you go for no holds barred, finish him off in one, cleave the bastard down through the middle with the blade?

I wasn't sure, but probably the technique would become clear as the combat heated up. I crept up the hill to look over to the river bridge. I just caught the lights heading off up the track to Carrasco. Not Juan at all, some midnight visitor for our neighbours across the river.

Back to bed. I thought about Petra and Juan. I had thought their affair was romantic – but maybe not. Petra was a generous soul, sexy and optimistic and always game for something interesting. She had come out to Orgiva after growing tired of an office job in Copenhagen, and fallen in with a Spanish-Moroccan bloke from Ceuta. Together they travelled back and forth to Morocco, trawling for artefacts which they would sell at a stall in the market. Then Paco, the partner, decided he was going to India to do some work on his karma, while Petra took up with an installation artist and part-time welder, whom she had met in Alicante. All seemed to go well for a while and she would return in high spirits with her new lover to stay with friends in the mountain villages. And then one day, I was out wandering in the hills of the Contraviesa when I found myself in the middle of a big flock of sheep. Standing at the back, tending them with a stick and a couple of scruffy-looking dogs, was Petra – the very same Petra who had once worked as a stationery buyer for a mobile phone company.

The sheep, she said, belonged to Juan. I knew Juan a little and had found him a quiet, reserved sort of a man. I liked him. Petra went on to tell me how she had cast her lot with him and moved into his ramshackle *cortijo* to share the shepherd's life. Sometimes I would come across her in town in her van, loading up with sacks of feed and shepherd's necessities. And then she told me how the two of them had left the flock in the charge of a cousin or two, and headed off round Spain in the van for a holiday – a thing Juan never would have dreamed of doing before.

So, all in all, it seemed that Petra enriched Juan's life, and Juan and his pastoral existence was really something of a revelation to Petra. 'Oh, it's wonderful, Chris,' she would tell me eagerly. 'It's opened out a whole new world for me. I can't tell you the pleasure I get from living up on the mountain with the sheep, getting to know this new way of life.' Her eyes would glisten with excitement as she said this, so I knew it was so.

And now here I was, alone in the moonlight with my mattock, waiting for Juan, who was on his way to kill me. I couldn't help but feel disillusioned about it all. I rolled over and listened to the sounds of the night. An insect hummed, another whined and stopped near my ear. A scops owl started its monotonous booping from the river – boop . . . boop . . . boop – a noise to drive you to distraction. Ana's Aunt Ruth from Brighton came to stay with us one weekend. 'Are you sure there's not a factory of some sort around here?' she had asked, peering fearfully into the unrelieved blackness of the mountain night. 'Not as far as we know,' said Ana acidly. 'But that noise,' said Ruth, 'it sounds so like people clocking off.'

I listened to the scops owl and thought a bit about Aunt Ruth's visit. She had enthused about the farm: 'How wonderful to live so wild and free in the mountains, drinking water from the spring, so far from the hurly-burly, the hustle and bustle, well out of the rat-race, and not stuck in the concrete jungle in an endless traffic jam.' She hooked one cliché after another. Later we discovered she had so feared the water from the spring that she had cleaned her teeth in lemonade.

I fell asleep for a while, but all of a sudden I was aware of the dogs barking furiously – the intruder-bark. Back into the trousers, grab the mattock, feel around for my glasses by the bed leg. The dogs were going crazy; somebody was lurking around the house. This was it. 'Right, you bastard! Come and get it!' I said out loud to myself, taking courage from the ring of these words and their sense of impending violence. I peered down from the roof. Nothing, not a sound. Still the dogs were at it, infuriated by some presence.

And then I heard it. It was the call of a fox in the valley, that little howl of feral yearning, the distillation of all the wildness, savagery and horror of the night, a call that thrills your very blood – and drives the dogs bonkers. It's the call of the wild and it makes the dogs feel guilty of a moral dereliction as they slumber on the rug by the fire. It reminds them of the way they should be – not consorting with cats, slurping dog food and biscuits for breakfast, and walking to heel on the end of a lead. 'Come to me,' the fox calls, 'this is how life should be lived, racing through the woods on starlit nights, massacring runs of obese hens, delighting in their cries of terror. Come on, you unfit, mollycoddled slobs, come and get it.' Of course it drives the dogs to distraction.

I returned to my bed, almost regretful at the lack of action. And sleep did not come easily. The night was just too exciting and, besides, if Juan did succeed in sticking me with his knife, then this might be the last night I would ever see. It seemed a pity to waste it in sleep.

The moon moved on down and slipped behind Cerro Negro, 'Black Hill', and the sky filled with stars. I gazed up at the Milky Way, and remembered when I was a child lying awake and listening to the terrors of night, the shifts and cracks made by my parents' old house, or more probably by fearful fiends and things too horrible to name who were inching their way out from under the bed. I was always a little surprised to see the sun shining through the curtains in the morning, and to know I had made it through yet another night. But over the years I became accustomed to surviving, and this was the first night for a long time that I had been unsure of.

As I considered the stars in those dark hours that come before dawn, I began to feel a little more confident of making it through to morning. And then I heard him – of course, he would choose the darkest hour. He was creeping through the bushes on the hill above me. He could see me from there before I saw him. I froze with fear, fished again for my glasses and waited shivering by the bed, hefting the mattock. I could hear his breath, he was that close. Then a careful footfall and the breaking of a bush. I gripped the mattock hard. I heard him cough – and then an enormous fart. No man could fart that loud, not even the formidable Juan. It was Lola, the horse, and now I could hear her munching happily amongst the rosemary.

A distant cock crowed and then another, and the scops owl stopped booping. The sunlight filtered through, a fly settled on my nose, and I knew it was morning. Juan wouldn't come now. He didn't come the next night either.

I told Manolo about the business and he looked earnestly at me. 'Juan?' he said. 'Juan! You don't want to mess with Juan – he's a maniac. He kills people for fun! You know he killed old Pepe Diáz, don't you? He's known for fighting – even the Guardia Civil are frightened of him – well, they're frightened of everybody but they're particularly frightened of Juan. He carries a *navajón* – a ten-inch knife – in his boot. He's bad news. Cristóbal, you're in real trouble now.'

'Thanks,' I replied. 'That's very reassuring. How do you know all this, anyway?'

Manolo rolled his eyes. 'I worked for Juan last year, mucking the dung out of his sheep stables. He's a strong bastard. He could lift a mule up with one hand. And he has a terrible temper – I'd sooner mess with a wild boar than with that Juan.'

'Still,' I replied, keeping a front of optimism. 'He didn't come and get me last night, nor the night before. I don't think he'll bother to come and kill me now. I may have got away with it . . .'

'Oh, I wouldn't count on that. He'll probably get you at the Feria – the summer fair. That's when these things are done here. He'll be drunk and spoiling for a fight and he'll be furious about losing his blonde. Yes, Feria's when he'll get you.' Manolo smiled happily at me.

Orgiva Feria – the town's big festival – was the following week. The business with Juan might make it a little more interesting than usual. Feria is a time of unbelievable cacophony, when the towns-folk go overboard indulging their passion for noise. There's a fair-ground where each and every ride has its own sound system, each more ear-splitting than the last. The streets are lined with brightly lit sweet stalls and lottery stalls where you can win polyester Day-Glo cuddly toys, and these too have their own music, pumped out at about ten times the decibel level that strikes you stone deaf. The bars in the plaza, meanwhile, have sound systems the size of small houses, which thunder and rattle day and night, making it impos-sible to hold the faintest trace of conversation. Yet the locals just sit there chatting away as though nothing were happening. It's my belief that the Spanish have better evolved ears than the rest of us.

As if the noise isn't enough, Feria is also the time of year when the wind gets up. It comes trickling over the top of the Contraviesa, building up speed as it races through the gullies and canyons, then roars uphill from the Seven-Eye Bridge and howls into town, carrying plastic bags and beer cans before it. It moans and wails round every corner, thick with grit and gravel which stings your eyes and gets in your nose and sets your teeth on edge as you eat the public paella in the plaza.

The only saving grace of the Orgiva Feria is the *pinchito* stall in the funfair, where you can lean against the tin bar hour after hour, munching your way through spicy skewers of pork and drinking warm dry sherry from a paper cup. It's the thought of this – and the fact that Chloë enjoys hanging out at the fair with her schoolfriends – that keeps me going back each year. And besides, this Feria I had to show my face. I wasn't going to let myself be bullied into missing the festive delights by some homicidal shepherd . . . even if he could lift a mule with one hand, and even if he did carry a ten-inch *navajón*.

Almost as soon as Ana, Chloë and I arrived in town, I spotted Juan chatting with a couple of friends in the street. I was all for stepping over to him straight away and giving my masculinity an airing, but Ana made this impossible by walking off and leaving me with Chloë. A smart move. She knew I wouldn't consider a brawl the most edifying spectacle for my six-year-old daughter.

After Chloë had gone off with her friends, I settled down for a stint at the *pinchito* stall, and waited to run into Juan. Manolo and Domingo were both at the bar, and Domingo comfortingly assured me that Juan reckoned I had been Petra's lover – why else would I interfere? – and that his anger was still festering.

Juan, however, didn't show up again.

In the town a few weeks after Feria I ran into Petra for the first time since the night of violence. She embraced me warmly.

'For Chrissake lay off, Petra!' I said, backing off. 'You want to try and get me killed again?'

'No, don't worry about it, Chris. I just wanted to thank you for being so wonderful that night.'

'It's all very well to say "Don't worry", but there's a dangerous maniac out there with a big knife and if he sees his blonde all over me in the high street then I'm meat.'

'Oh, Juan is all right. He's not a dangerous maniac at all. In fact I must rush because I'm just going to pick him up and take him to hospital . . .'

'You what?!'

'He's got kidney stones and the pain makes him crazy. That was partly what made him so aggressive that night; he was crazy with pain and I had refused to take him to hospital.'

'Petra, why on earth didn't you say any of this then?' I asked, appalled.

'Perhaps I was wrong that night. Juan is usually as gentle as a lamb. Anyway I must fly. Bye!'

I told Manolo what Petra had said. 'Oh – Juan is all right,' he said. 'He wouldn't hurt a fly. He didn't actually kill Pepe Diáz either, it was a heart attack. No, there's no doubt about it, Juan wouldn't have harmed you.'

I looked at him sideways.

'And what about the *navajón* he keeps in his boots?' I asked.

'I wouldn't know about that,' he answered with a smile. 'I've never had any cause to look inside them.'

LATAIFA

FROM

IN AN ANTIQUE LAND

AMITAV GHOSH

AMITAV GHOSH was born in Calcutta in 1956. As well as *In an Antique Land*, he is the author of three novels, *The Circle of Reason*, *The Shadow Lines* and *The Calcutta Chromosome*.

I OFTEN THOUGHT of telling Shaikh Musa that I wanted to move out of Abu-'Ali's house; for a while I even considered asking him to help me make some other arrangement. I had always felt secure in his friendship, from the moment of our first meeting: there was a gentleness and a good humour about him that inspired trust, something about the way he rocked his short, portly frame from side to side as we talked, the way he shook my hand every time we met, his round, weathered face crinkling into a smile, and cried: 'Where have you been all this while? Why haven't you come to see me?'

There were times when I had the distinct impression that Shaikh Musa was trying to warn me about Abu-'Ali. The two of them were of the same age after all, in their mid-fifties; they had grown up together, and Shaikh Musa probably knew him as well as anyone in the hamlet. Once, while dining with Shaikh Musa and his family, I had the feeling that he was cautioning me, in an oblique and roundabout way, telling me to be careful with Abu-'Ali. It was only because of a series of unfortunate interruptions that I didn't beg him right then to find me some other house to live in.

We were sitting in his bedroom that evening. Shaikh Musa, his son Ahmed, his two grandsons and I were eating out of one tray, while the women of the household were sharing another, at the other end of the room. It was something of a special occasion for I had just crossed an invisible barrier. Whenever I had eaten at Shaikh Musa's house before, it had been in the *mandara*, the guest-room on the outside of the house, facing the lane; every house had one, for this was the room where male guests were usually received. But on this occasion, after saying his evening prayers, Shaikh Musa had risen to his feet and led me out of the guest-room, into the lamplit interior of the house.

We had gone directly to his bedroom, pushing past a nuzzling sheep tethered by the door. Shaikh Musa chased a brood of chickens off an old sheepskin, sending them scuttling under his bed, and we seated ourselves on the floor and played with Ahmed's two young sons while waiting for the rest of the family. After Ahmed returned from the mosque, two women came into the room carrying a pair of trays loaded with food. The trays were set out on the floor, and the women gathered around one, while we seated ourselves at the other; each tray was as big as a cartwheel, and there was plenty of room for all of us.

There were three women in the room now, all of them young, one in the first bloom of her adolescence with a gentle, innocent face and a rosy complexion – a family inheritance shared by many of the inhabitants of Lataifa. From the strong resemblance she bore to Ahmed, I knew at once that she was his sister. The other two women were a good deal older, perhaps in their mid-twenties. One was a pale, pretty, self-possessed young woman, dressed in a long, printed skirt. The other was dark and thickset, and she was wearing a black *fustân*, a heavy, shapeless robe that was the customary garb of a *fellah* woman.

I had encountered all of them before, occasionally at the doorway to Shaikh Musa's house and sometimes in the guest-room when they came in to hand out tea. There were times when I had the impression that I had passed them in the lanes of the hamlet, but I was never quite sure. The fault for this lay entirely with me, for neither they nor anyone else in Lataifa wore veils (nor indeed did anyone in the region), but at that time, early in my stay, I was so cowed by everything I had read about Arab traditions of shame and modesty that I barely glanced at them, for fear of giving offence. Later it was I who was shame-stricken, thinking of the astonishment and laughter I must have provoked, walking past them, eyes lowered, never uttering so much as a word of greeting. Shaking hands with them now, as we sat down to dinner, I tried to work out the connections between them and the rest of the family. The pretty woman in the printed dress was Ahmed's wife, I decided: her clothes and her bearing spoke of a college, or at least a high-school, education. Since Ahmed had been through school and college too, I had every reason to assume that they were a couple. As for the other woman, the dark one in the black dress, it took me no more than a moment's thought to reach a conclusion about her: she was the wife of Shaikh Musa's other son, I decided, Ahmed's younger brother, Hasan.

I had never met Hasan, for he was away, serving his draft in the army, but I had heard a great deal about him. Shaikh Musa spoke of him often, and with something more than the usual warmth of a father remembering a son long absent. He had shown me a picture of him once: he was a strikingly good-looking young man, with a broad, strong face and clear-cut features; in fact, he bore a marked resemblance to a picture of Shaikh Musa that hung on the wall of his guest-room, a photograph taken in his youth, in army uniform.

Unlike Ahmed, who had been through school and college, Hasan had not had an education. He had been taken out of school at a fairly early age; Shaikh Musa had brought him up as a *fellah*, so that at least one of his sons would profit from the land their ancestors had left them. It was that shared background perhaps that lent Shaikh Musa's voice a special note of affection when he spoke of Hasan: Ahmed was the most dutiful of sons and he helped Shaikh Musa on the land as often as he could, but there was an unbridgeable gap between them now because of his education. Ahmed worked as a clerk, in a factory near Damanhour, and he was thus counted as a *mowazzaf*, an educated, salaried man, and like all such people in the village, his clothes, his speech, his amusements and concerns, were markedly different from those of the *fellaheen*. Hasan, on the other hand, fell on his father's side of that divide, and it was easy to see that their shared view of the world formed a special bond between them.

I was soon sure that the woman in the black dress was Hasan's wife. I overheard Shaikh Musa saying a few words to her and, detecting a note of familiarity in his voice, I attributed it to his special closeness to his younger son. But now I began to wonder where his own wife was and why she had not joined us at our meal.

The meal that was set out on the tray in front of us was a very good one: arranged around a large pile of rice were dishes of fried potatoes, cheese preserved in brine, salads of chopped tomatoes and fresh dill, plates of cooked vegetables, large discs of corn-meal bread, and bowls of young Nile perch, baked with tomatoes and garlic. Everything was fresh and full of flavour, touched with that unname-able quality which makes anything grown in the soil of Egypt taste richer, more distinctively of itself, than it does anywhere else.

It was when I complimented him on the food that Shaikh Musa suddenly raised his head, as though a thought had just struck him.

'Things are cheap in the countryside,' he said, 'much cheaper than they are in the city. In the city people have to buy everything in the market, for cash, but here it isn't like that; we get every-thing from the fields. You should not expect to pay as much here as you would in the city. This is just a little hamlet not – even a big village like Nashawy.'

I was taken aback for a moment, and then I realised that he was referring obliquely to Abu-'Ali: he had asked me once how much I paid him and had sunk into an amazed silence when I quoted the sum. But before I could say anything, Shaikh Musa changed the subject: resorting to one of his favourite ploys he began to talk about agriculture.

'And these,' he said, pointing at the cucumbers on the tray, 'are called *khiyâr*. The best are those that are sown early, in spring, in the month of Amshîr by the Coptic calendar.'

Not one to be left behind in a conversation of that kind, Ahmed immediately added: 'Amshîr follows the month of Tûba, when the earth awakes, as we say, and after it comes Barmahât . . .'

Later, after dinner, when Shaikh Musa and I were alone in the room for a while, he began to wax expansive, talking about his boyhood in Lataifa and about Abu-'Ali as a child. But once the family returned he cut himself short, and there was no opportunity to discuss the matter again for shortly afterwards he got up and left the room.

No sooner had Shaikh Musa left than Ahmed began to tell me how cotton was rotated with the fodder crop *berseem*. 'Write it down,' he said, handing me my notebook, 'or else you'll forget.'

I scribbled desultorily for a while, and then, searching desper-ately for something else to talk about, I happened to ask him if his mother was away from the hamlet.

A hush immediately descended upon the room. At length, Ahmed cleared his throat and said: 'My mother, God have mercy on her, died a year ago.'

There was a brief silence, and then he leaned over to me. 'Do you see Sakkina there?' he asked, gesturing at the woman in the black *fustân*. 'My father married her this year.'

For a moment I was speechless: in my mind Shaikh Musa was very old and very venerable, and I was oddly unsettled by the thought of his marrying a woman a fraction his age.

His wife noticed me staring and smiled shyly. Then, Ahmed's wife, the self-possessed young woman in the cotton dress, turned to me and said: 'She's heard about you from her family. You have met her uncle, haven't you? Ustaz Mustafa?'

Again I was taken completely by surprise. But now things began to fall into place.

Jabir, Abu-'Ali's young relative, had woken me one morning, soon after I arrived in Lataifa. 'Get up, ya mister,' he said, shaking me. 'Get up and meet my uncle.'

I sat up bleary-eyed and found myself looking at a short, plump man who bore a strong family resemblance to Jabir; he had the same rosy complexion, blunt features and bright, black eyes. He also had a little clipped moustache, and the moment I saw it I knew it was the kind of moustache that Jabir was sure to aspire to once his feathery adolescent whiskers had matured.

At that time, I was still innocent of some of the finer distinctions between salaried people and *fellaheen* but I could tell at once, from his starchy blue *jallabeyya* and white net skullcap, that Jabir's uncle did not make his living from ploughing the land. Jabir's introduction made things clearer, for he added the word Ustaz, 'Teacher', to his uncle's name – a title usually given to men who had been educated in modern, rather than traditional, forms of learning.

'This is Ustaz Mustafa,' said Jabir. 'My uncle. He studied law at the University of Alexandria.'

Ustaz Mustafa smiled and, nodding vigorously, he addressed me in classical, literary Arabic. 'We are honoured,' he said, 'to have Your Presence amongst us.'

I was dismayed to be spoken to in this way, for in concentrating on learning the dialect of the village I had allowed my studies of classical Arabic to fall into neglect. I stuttered, unsure of how to respond, but then, unexpectedly, Jabir came to my rescue. Clapping me on the back, he told his uncle: 'He is learning to talk just like us.'

Ustaz Mustafa's face lit up. '*Insha'allah*,' he cried, 'God willing, he will soon be one of us.'

I noticed that he had a habit of flicking back the cuff of his *jallabeyya* every few minutes or so to steal a quick look at his watch. I was to discover later that this gesture was rooted in an anxiety that had long haunted his everyday existence: the fear that he might inadvertently miss one of the day's five required prayers. That was why he looked much busier than anyone else in Lataifa – he was always in a hurry to get to the mosque. 'I have read all about India,' said Ustaz Mustafa, smiling serenely. 'There is a lot of chilli in the food and when a man dies his wife is dragged away and burnt alive.'

'Not always,' I protested, 'my grandmother for example . . .'

Jabir was drinking this in, wide-eyed.

'And of course,' Ustaz Mustafa continued, 'you have Indira Gandhi, and her son Sanjay Gandhi, who used to sterilise the Muslims . . .'

'No, no, he sterilised everyone,' I said.

His eyes widened and I added hastily: 'No, not me of course, but . . .'

'Yes,' he said, nodding sagely. 'I know. I read all about India when I was in college in Alexandria.'

He had spent several years in Alexandria as a student, he said; he had specialised in civil and religious law and now practised in a court in Damanhour. He talked at length about his time at university, the room he had lived in and the books he had read, and in the meanwhile two of Abu-'Ali's sons came up to join us, carrying a tray of tea.

Soon, the conversation turned to village gossip and for a while, to my relief, I was forgotten. But Jabir was not going to allow me so easy an escape: he had noticed that Ustaz Mustafa's questions had unsettled me and he was impatient for more entertainment.

'Ask him more about his country,' he whispered to his uncle. 'Ask him about his religion.'

The reminder was superfluous for, as I later discovered, religion was a subject never very far from Ustaz Mustafa's mind. 'All right then,' he said to me, motioning to the boys to be quiet. 'Tell me, are you Muslim?'

'No,' I said, but he didn't really need an answer since everyone in the hamlet knew that already.

'So then what are you?'

'I was born a Hindu,' I said reluctantly, for if I had a religious identity at all it was largely by default.

There was a long silence during which I tried hard to think of an arresting opening line that would lead the conversation towards some bucolic, agricultural subject. But the moment passed, and in a troubled voice Ustaz Mustafa said: 'What is this "Hinduki" thing? I have heard of it before and I don't understand it. If it is not Christianity nor Judaism nor Islam what can it be? Who are its prophets?'

'It's not like that,' I said. 'There aren't any prophets . . .'

'So you are like the Magi?' he said, bright-eyed. 'You worship fire then?'

I shook my head vaguely, but before I could answer, he tapped my arm with his forefinger. 'No,' he said, smiling coquettishly. 'I know – it's cows you worship – isn't that so?'

There was a sharp, collective intake of breath as Jabir and the other boys recoiled, calling upon God, in whispers, to protect them from the Devil.

I cleared my throat; I knew a lot depended on my answers. 'It's not like that,' I said. 'In my country some people don't eat beef because . . . because cows give milk and plough the fields and so on, and so they're very useful.'

Ustaz Mustafa was not to be bought off by this spurious ecological argument. 'That can't be the reason,' he began, but then his eyes fell on his watch and a shadow of alarm descended on his face. He edged forward until he was balanced precariously on the rim of the bed.

'You still haven't told me about this "Hinduki" business,' he said. 'What is your God like?'

I tried to stutter out an answer of some kind, but fortunately for me Ustaz Mustafa wasn't really paying attention to me any more.

'Well thanks be to Allah,' he said quickly, eyeing his watch. 'Now that you are here among us you can understand and learn about Islam, and then you can make up your mind whether you want to stay within that religion of yours.'

He jumped to his feet and stretched out his hand. 'Come with me to the mosque right now,' he said. 'That is where we are going – for the noon prayers. You don't have to do anything. Just watch us pray, and soon you will understand what Islam is.'

I hesitated for a moment, and then I shook my head. 'No,' I said. 'I can't. I have many things to do.'

'Things to do?' cried Ustaz Mustafa. 'What is there to do here that you can't do later? Come with us – it's very important. Nothing could be more important.'

'No,' I said. 'I can't.'

'Why not?' he insisted quietly. 'Just come and watch – that's all I'm asking of you.'

And just then the voice of the muezzin floated over from a nearby mosque, singing the call to prayer, and before I could say another word Ustaz Mustafa and the boys had vanished from the room.

But I couldn't go back to work even after I was alone again. I began to wonder why I had not accepted Ustaz Mustafa's invitation to visit the mosque and watch him at his prayers; he had meant well, after all, had only wanted to introduce me to the most important element of his imaginative life. A part of me had wanted to go – not merely that part which told me that it was, in a sense, my duty, part of my job. But when the moment had come, I'd known that I wouldn't be able to do it: I had been too afraid, and for the life of me I could not understand why.

But soon enough, Ustaz Mustafa came back to talk to me again. This time he had a child in his arms. 'This is my son,' he said, tweaking the child's cheeks. He glowed with love as he looked at the boy.

'Say *salâm* to the mister,' he said, and the child, alarmed, hid his face in his father's shoulder.

Ustaz Mustafa laughed. 'I missed you the last few days,' he said to me. 'I was busy in the evenings – I had to go and meet someone in Nashawy, so I couldn't come to talk to you. But today I decided that I would come over as soon as I got back from work.'

I was better prepared for him this time, and I began to talk at length about the hamlet's history and his family's genealogy. But Ustaz Mustafa had little time for matters of that kind, and soon he began to steal anxious glances at his watch over his son's back.

Eventually he brushed my patter aside and began to ask questions, first about my family and then about Indian politics – what I thought of Indira Gandhi, was I for her or against her, and so on. Then, with a wry, derisory smile he began to ask me about 'The Man from Menoufiyya' – the current nickname for the president, the Raïs – phrasing his questions in elaborately allusive, elliptical forms, like riddles, as though he were mocking the Raïs' habit of spreading surrogate ears everywhere. My answers left him a little disappointed however, for many of his riddles had stock responses with which I was not then familiar.

Suddenly the bantering note went out of his voice.

'Tell me something,' he said, 'tell me, are you a communist?'

He used a word, *shiyu'eyya*, which could mean anything from 'communist' to 'atheist' and 'adulterer' in the village dialect; my understanding of it was that it referred to people who rejected all moral and ethical laws.

'No,' I said.

'All right then,' he said, 'if you're not a communist, tell me this: who made the world, and who were the first man and woman if not Âdam and Hawâ?'

I was taken aback by the abruptness of this transition. Later I came to expect elisions of this kind in conversations with people like Ustaz Mustafa, for I soon discovered that salaried people like him, rural *mowazzafeen*, were almost without exception absorbed in a concern which, despite its plural appearance, was actually single and indivisible – religion and politics – so that the mention of the one always led to the other. But at the time I was nonplussed. I mumbled something innocuous about how, in my country, people thought the world had always existed.

My answer made him flinch. He hugged his sleeping son hard against his chest and said, 'They don't think of Our Lord at all, do they? They live only for the present and have no thought for the hereafter.'

I began to protest but Ustaz Mustafa was not interested in my answers any more. His eyes had fallen on his watch, and he rose hurriedly to his feet. 'Tomorrow,' he said, 'I will take you with me to the graveyard, and you can watch me reciting the Quran over my father's grave. You will see then how much better Islam is than this "Hinduki" of yours.'

At the door he turned back for a moment. 'I am hoping,' he said, 'that you will convert and become a Muslim. You must not disappoint me.'

Then he was gone. A moment later I heard the distant voice of a muezzin, chanting the call to prayer.

He had meant what he said.

He came back the next evening, his Quran in his hands, and said: 'Come, let's go to the graveyard.'

'I can't,' I said quickly. 'I have to go out to the fields.'

He hesitated, and then, not without some reluctance, decided to accompany me. The truth was that walking in the fields was something of a trial for Ustaz Mustafa: it demanded ceaseless vigilance on his part to keep particles of impure matter, like goat's droppings and cow dung, from touching his *jallabeyya*, since he would otherwise be obliged to change his clothes before going to the mosque again. This meant that he had to walk with extreme care in those liberally manured fields, with his hem plucked high above his ankles, very much in the manner that women hitch up their saris during the monsoons in Calcutta.

Before we had gone very far we came upon some of his relatives, working in a vegetable patch. They invited us to sit with them and began to ask me questions about the soil and the crops in India. Ustaz Mustafa soon grew impatient with this and led me away.

'They are *fellaheen*,' he said apologetically. 'They don't have much interest in religion or anything important.'

'I am just like that myself,' I said quickly.

'Really?' said Ustaz Mustafa, aghast. We walked in silence for a while, and then he said: 'I am giving up hope that you will become a Muslim.' Then an idea occurred to him and he turned to face me. 'Tell me,' he said, 'would your father be upset if you were to change your religion?'

'Maybe,' I said.

He relapsed into thoughtful silence for a few minutes. 'Has your father read the holy books of Islam?' he asked, eagerly.

'I don't know,' I answered.

'He must read them,' said Ustaz Mustafa. 'If he did he would surely convert himself.'

'I don't know,' I said. 'He is accustomed to his own ways.'

He mulled the issue over in his mind, and when we turned back towards Lataifa he said: 'Well, it would not be right for you to upset your father. That is true.'

After that the heart went out of his efforts to convert me: he had a son himself and it went against his deepest instincts to urge a man to turn against his father. And so, as the rival moralities of religion and kinship gradually played themselves to a standstill within him, Ustaz Mustafa and I came to an understanding.

A connection was already beginning to form in my mind now, as I turned towards Shaikh Musa's wife. 'Is Ustaz Mustafa really your uncle?' I asked her, uncertain of whether she was using the word in a specific or general sense. 'Your father's real brother, your "*amm shagîg*"?'

She was too shy to address me directly, at least in Ahmed's presence, so he spoke for her. 'Ustaz Mustafa is her real uncle,' he said. 'Her father and he were carried in the same belly. They still live in the same house.'

'But then Jabir must be her cousin,' I said in astonishment. 'They must have grown up in the same house.'

'Yes,' said Ahmed, 'she is Jabir's *bint 'amm*, his father's brother's daughter.'

He could have added: 'If Jabir were older he could have married her himself.' Certainly Jabir's parents and relatives would probably have wished for nothing better, since a marriage between first cousins, the children of brothers, was traditionally regarded as an ideal sort of union – a strengthening of an already existing bond.

'So she is of Abu-'Ali's lineage then?' I asked Ahmed.

'Yes,' said Ahmed, 'Abu-'Ali is her father's first cousin. His half-sister is her grandmother as well as Jabir's. She still lives in their house: you've met her.'

And so I had, a portly matriarch dressed in black, with fine features and delicate papery skin: she bore not the remotest resemblance to Abu-'Ali. I remembered her because of the posture of command she had assumed, perfectly naturally, with one knee flat on the floor and the other drawn up to support her arm and clenched fist. A glance from her had been enough to keep even Jabir quiet.

'Yes,' said Ahmed, 'Abu-'Ali's father was her great-grandfather's brother. And of course, his father, Abu-'Ali's grandfather, was my great-great-grandfather's brother.'

By this time I had lost my way in this labyrinth of relationships. It was only much later, when Shaikh Musa helped me draw up a complete genealogy of the hamlet of Lataifa (all of whose inhabitants belonged ultimately to a single family called Latîf) that I finally began to see why he was always so careful never to voice a word of criticism about Abu-'Ali: his wife, Sakkina, was Abu-'Ali's great-grandniece. The lines of the genealogy led inexorably to the conclusion that Abu-'Ali had played a crucial part in arranging the marriage.

It became clear to me then that there were complexities in Shaikh Musa's relationship with Abu-'Ali that I did not understand, and probably never would; that it would be deeply embarrassing for him if I were to ask him to help me find some other house, or family, to live in.

I realised then that my deliverance from Abu-'Ali would not come as easily as the dreams that took me to Cairo.

ALOFT

IN PARIS

KARL TARO GREENFELD

KARL TARO GREENFELD is the editor of the Asian edition of *Time* magazine and the author of the recently published *Standard Deviations: Growing Up and Coming Down in the New Asia* and *Speed Tribes: Days and Nights with Japan's Next Generation*. A former staff writer for *Time* and correspondent for *The Nation*, he has also contributed to *GQ*, *Condé Nast Traveler*, *Outside*, *Men's Journal*, *Vogue* and the *New York Times Magazine*, among other publications. He currently lives in Hong Kong with his wife and two daughters.

BEFORE US, there had been a brooding, aristocratic Russian artist who worked in the tenth *arrondissement* loft constructing abstract sculptures out of neon. And after us, there would be a German open wheel driver new to the Formula 5000 series who used the spacious, sky-lit apartment as a crash pad between circuit stops. Downstairs there lived a French TV star whose beautiful brunette wife sometimes vacuumed topless.

Chronologically and geographically, we were an aberration. Yet the basketball court-sized atelier had fallen into our hands through that angry Russian artist, who had become fed up with Paris' gentility and moved to Berlin. Even then, our tenancy would have been impossible had not the strongest U.S. dollar of the post-war era enabled American college students to live like French TV stars.

Thomas had known Dmitri, the Russian artist, through the Parsons School of Painting and Design, where Dmitri had taught a sculpture class and Thomas hung around playing backgammon. When Dmitri announced he was moving, Thomas convinced me I should take the flat with him, which I did, sight unseen. When I walked in with my suitcases, I was stunned. The main room was immense, with thirty-foot ceilings and vast skylights with tarpaulin curtains that were controlled by a mechanism of winches and pulleys which looked capable of hoisting a sail. There was a small shower and sink in an adjacent dressing area and a spiral staircase ascending to a bedroom upstairs, but the overwhelming feature was this main chamber. It was spacious enough, we would discover, to set up a skateboard ramp with plenty of takeoff, or a basketball hoop . . . or to leave a cantaloupe rotting in one corner for a month without the stench making the place uninhabitable.

There was one drawback. It was instantly apparent to anyone who entered the loft that Thomas could not paint. His works were vast canvases that wavered uncomfortably between the abstract and figurative. His brushwork was erratic. His sense of colour was disastrous. His choice of subject matter was always unfortunate. And, as if to make up for the smallness of his talent, Thomas worked his bizarrely deformed and badly tinted renderings of famous moments in Saint Louis Cardinal baseball history as gigantic twenty-by-twenty epics. Jack Clark's National League championship-winning home run. Don Denkinger's blown World Series call. They were embarrassments.

Despite the oppressive baseball imagery, the apartment quickly became a hub for a few of us who spent most of our downtime gambling: rummy five hundred, pitching francs and, most time-consuming of all, Nerf basketball. The Nerf hoop had been installed by Thomas between the entrance and a *Battle for the Planet of the Apes* poster after the TV star downstairs complained about the noise we were making shooting on a real basket. Brian and Trey, two friends who hung around the American College in Paris without actually attending classes, moved in and we became, economically and socially, almost a closed society. It wasn't so odd that American males in Paris tended to mingle primarily with each other. The American girls at the ACP, which I attended, found it easy to hook up with French dudes. For the boys – still unfinished products and, compared to our French counterparts, practically feral when it came to how we ate and dressed – finding a local companion was much harder.

The gambling on Nerf basketball quickly became ferocious. Thousands of francs changed hands in Nerf HORSE tournaments in which the shots grew increasingly complex: *from the corner, scraping the ceiling, bank shot, no rim* was a common call. And we were hitting these shots. Regularly. I believe, for that brief period, we were the best Nerf basketball players in the world. Occasionally, one of us would get hot, win big, and withdraw a few hundred francs from the loft economy to head out on a bender or, very occasionally, a date. But then more money would arrive via my monthly allowance from my parents or Thomas' trust fund, the economy would reinflate and the gambling would recommence in earnest. Once in a while, a female would show up in the apartment and the Nerf shooting would halt until it became clear whether any of us would get to sleep with her, and which of us that would be. Then we'd get back to business.

Though the loft was spacious, living there was a communal affair. I slept downstairs, along with Trey and Brian, albeit in opposite corners. There used to be a cavern beneath New York's Grand Central Station where if you stood in one corner and spoke in a normal voice, the listener in the opposite corner could hear you as if you were standing next to him. This loft had a similar auditory quirk, hence when any of us had a girl over for the night, our mates on the opposite side of the loft could hear everything.

Most females soon grew weary of the oppressively male environment of overhearing every fart and burp, Nerf basketball and lousy baseball paintings, but Francesca, for some reason, seemed to thrive there. An Argentine who had attended the American College for three semesters before dropping out to bum around Paris, she had short, curly brown hair and a cherubic, almost boyish face that was just cruel enough to make her pretty. Standing five foot three inches, she usually wore faded Levi's and an old pair of roller skates with bubble-gum pink urethane wheels. Her parents worked for the United Nations in some capacity, and Francesca had attended high school in three different countries, leaving her one of those cultural refugees who seem to come from nowhere and everywhere at once. Her only overtly Argentine trait was a fondness for *empanadas*, which she could find in one joint down in the fifth.

I had seen her around the American College café and at a few parties. Sometimes we played pinball together, and Francesca would flit around on her skates while I was hitting the flippers. It confused me a little why a girl as pretty as Francesca wouldn't be mobbed by competing suitors. Had I not spent all my time shooting a foam ball at a plastic cylinder and devoted a little more time to studying in the tiled hallways and panelled classrooms of the ACP, I would have known that she had what in a previous era would have been called a 'bad reputation'. She'd dated a procession of boys, and for a few months had regularly left parties in the arms of different males.

Francesca, to her credit, would never have been self-conscious about this, nor was she making any sort of statement with her sexual libertinism. That's just how she was. Impetuous. Eager to have a good time. Yet by the time she met me, I think she'd realised that a reputation as somewhat dissolute made her seem less dateable, at least among those guys who had already slept with her.

When Franny first came over to our apartment, even though she'd roller-skated along the sidewalks beside me to get there, it took an hour for me to clearly assert she was with me. I had to jovially fend off Brian, who insisted not that he was a better lover than me, but that he was less intrusive. 'I pride myself in my brevity,' he explained.

'I'm faster,' I assured her.

Thomas, because of his lousy paintings, never had a chance.

Franny found in our gang of blissfully oblivious boys gambling in our immense apartment a sort of refuge, from her somewhat seedy past, from needing to figure out what she wanted to do with her life, from having to think about anything more than the hash and tobacco spliffs she rolled whenever she had the dope and papers.

The weather that fall was dreary. Paris' best-kept secret may be its terrible climate. It rained most days, the water pooling and running in impressionistic puddles on our skylight – like Monet's water lilies without the flora. The loft was heated by banks of radiators along two walls. Whoever decided when to run the heat – presumably a landlord somewhere kept tabs – would wait until nightfall before stoking the boilers, which meant we wore jackets or sweaters indoors most of the day. At night, we slept like we were drugged. We could sleep for days, months if necessary. College-age boys are like that, able to consume entire seasons with slumber. Since we were up until dawn most nights, we crashed until late afternoon, sleeping bags pulled tight around us, the grey light of day kept at bay by those vast curtains. Franny always woke a few hours before me. She'd slip on her jeans, bomber jacket and roller skates and clomp down the stairs, taking heavy, careful steps with her rubber wheels, before rolling away on her missions of larceny. She was a thief.

At the time I thought it was just a hobby. Later, I would realise she was a kleptomaniac, a habitual swiper who made the rounds of grocery stores, stationers, pharmacies and department stores making off with whatever was laxly monitored and caught her fancy. Over the course of the first week she was with us, she returned with a Serrano ham, three cashmere scarfs, complicated and ill-fitting new lingerie, four Casio watches (one for each of us guys), a pilot's band radio, a box of chocolate-covered strawberries, a protractor and compass set, a dozen bottles of shampoo and three black-haired wigs of varying lengths. Trey, Brian, Thomas and I would look at each other and shrug. Okay, so she was a bit of a crook. We'd all been known to break a few rules now and then. Franny never offered any explanation. But at night sometimes, when we were lying on the mattress on the floor – she in a black wig and antique lingerie looking like a cross between Natalie Wood and a drag queen – she'd ask me what she could steal for me.

'Tell me anything, baby,' she'd whisper, 'anything and I'll take it.'

I didn't know what to say, so I'd shush her and we'd go back to our murky, dank sex.

How long can a lifestyle like that last? We barely interacted with the real world, relying on outside contributions to sustain ourselves. Eventually Thomas, whose trust fund was the well-spring for most of this little economy, accused Trey and Brian of taking money off the table when they won. He wouldn't play any more Nerf hoops unless Brian and Trey would make wagers large enough for him to win back what he'd lost. Brian, a gifted natural athlete, had become a frighteningly efficient shooter. During one streak he'd won several thousand francs from Thomas and then refused to keep shooting for double-or-nothing, insisting they go back to the fifty-franc stakes at which they'd started. Thomas, realising it would take days for him to win back the money at that rate, fumed, stomped around the apartment and accused Brian of not being a gentleman and misunderstanding the fundamentals of friendly wagering.

Their argument would recommence whenever we'd be shooting around.

'Game of HORSE?' Brian would ask.

Thomas would shake his head. 'Double or nothing?'

'Around the world?'

'You know the score.' And then the inevitable of Brian calling Thomas chicken and Thomas explaining the unwritten code of collegiate gambling. The disputes would last until I would intervene or we'd see the TV star's wife vacuuming topless across the courtyard and we'd all rush over to the window to watch her.

One evening she caught us spying. We ducked behind curtains and beneath window sills. She just shook her head and went back to her vacuuming.

It turned out Nerf basketball was the cornerstone of our community. Without that we were left with Thomas' lousy paintings and a lot of cheap Kronenbourg. Final exams were coming up and I had to cram to make up for a misspent semester. Franny continued her shoplifting, keeping us supplied with wine, steaks and the occasional oddity – like that melon we tossed around for a while and then abandoned in the corner. We had spent so much time in the apartment it no longer seemed so large or magnificent; in fact, the scale and immensity of it had come to seem tedious, especially as we all sat by ourselves in various corners. I read my Nietzsche and Marx. Brian and Trey listened to their Motörhead cassettes. Thomas worked on his awful canvases. Once in a while a new visitor would show up and marvel at the place: it really was one of those apartments you seldom see before you are older and know people who've made millions.

I found that without the static of endless gambling and macho posturing, I was able to tune in on my relationship with Franny enough to wonder if we really liked each other. The sex had a decent rhythm to it and as twenty-year-olds we took the appropriate delight in each other's bodies. But through the acrid beer and spliff haze, we struggled to make conversation. It annoyed me that Franny never minded these silences. She'd wade through the long breaks in conversation with a deep exhalation and then a craning pan around the room, her round, brown eyes seeming for those vacant moments as pretty and dumb as a cow's. After fifteen minutes or so she'd shrug and slide on her roller skates.

'I'm going out,' she'd explain, and it would never occur to me to stop her.

Or she would discuss these bizarre episodes from her past. It was in Franny's nature never to be surprised by what went on around her. Her own past she found so banal that she would lay out astonishing stories of old boyfriends and bad relationships as if every twenty-year-old could reel off a litany of nasty affairs. Franny was the tenth girl with whom I'd had sex – I didn't have a long list of lovers. So I found myself listening to her tales and nodding as she slid on jeans or tried on a silk shawl she'd lifted. There had been so many lovers, and she would let slip these peculiar details of her relationships with them. The boyfriend who'd dripped wax on her. The French guy who got off watching her stuff tropical fruit down the front of her jeans as she ripped off Arab groceries. The Dutch guy who stole her panties. And the Brit who would only let her suck him off and stick her fingers up his arse; other than that, he'd never touch her. What did I think of that?

I'd never broken up with anyone before. Girls usually dumped me. So I didn't know how to break it to Franny that I thought this wasn't working. I couldn't tell her at the loft. Our lives there were too public – and somehow, Thomas' paintings precluded any sort of serious conversation. How could I break up with someone beneath a gaping, smudged, stick-figure painting of Vince Coleman sliding back to first on a pick-off play? Instead, we arranged to meet after classes at a café near the Gare de Lyon. I don't remember why we picked that café to meet, except that it was close to a metro station and near a Printemps department store she had identified as an easy mark. I arrived first, set my backpack down and ordered an Orangina.

She was late.

Finally, after an hour and another Orangina, I gave up and took the Metro home. Perhaps she knew what I'd intended.

When I walked in, I noticed the little trash bag of swag she kept in the corner was still there. The wigs and lingerie, shampoo bottles and tube socks – a monument to petty thievery. Why would she just abandon that? Other than that bag, however, she'd never left many signs of her presence. She always used my tooth-brush and even shaved her legs with my razor. I explained the situation to Brian.

'I've done that,' Brian said.

'What?'

'Not show up for a break-up meeting,' he said as he drained twenty-five-footers. So that he wouldn't have to chase down the ball after every shot, he was shooting rolled-up pairs of socks. He had a half-dozen piled on the chair beside him.

'But how did she know it was a break up-meeting?'

'They know,' Brian explained. 'Don't you always know?'

I nodded, pointing to her gear. 'What about all this crap?'

'She stole it anyway.'

'So I'll just see her some day around the ACP café and that will be it?'

Brian nodded. 'Something like that.'

I was surprised that I felt a little bit sad. Or was I just disap-pointed I didn't get my break-up moment? At any rate, that night, instead of playing Nerf basketball, we went back to playing rummy five hundred and I found myself winning huge pots, scor-ing on fast, easy runs and catching the other players with rich points still in their hands. I was shuffling to deal another hand when the phone rang.

A man with a scratchy voice introduced himself as Franny's brother. He spoke with a slight Spanish accent, saying her whole name, Francesca, instead of Franny. She'd been detained, he told me: Francesca had been busted stealing a sweater from Printemps.

'For you, I believe,' he said, 'she tells me she was taking it for you.'

What did he want me to do? She had parents. Her own resources. I was this college kid. How was I going to intervene on her behalf?

'I'm not requesting you do anything,' Gregor said. 'She wanted me to tell you.' He explained she would be sentenced in a few days, would probably plead guilty and serve her time rather than tell her parents. It would be a three-month sentence. If she behaved, she'd be out in a month.

'A month?' I was shocked. 'For shoplifting?'

'It was a very expensive sweater.'

What I couldn't tell him was that I had been planning to break up with her, so technically, this was out of my jurisdiction. If I told him, I'd sound like some kind of cad. After hanging up I discussed it with the rest of the guys and the consensus was it would be bad form to break up with a girl on her way to jail.

'But I was going to break up with her anyway,' I kept saying.

It didn't matter. The right thing to do was stay by her during her hitch.

That Saturday, I took the train from the Gare de Nord out to a leafless, windswept suburb where along with a dozen Arab and African families I caught a shabby, creaking bus whose only stop was the prison at Fleury Merogis. Outside the prison, we sat holding laminated numbers in groups of ten on plastic chairs in a corrugated metal shed. Wind whistled through the badly joined walls; there was no heater. I caught the eye of an Arab boy in a light blue-and-white wool cap as we simultaneously pulled our jackets tight around us. I'd never been so cold.

Finally, a guard wearing a short, wide tie with a dull silver tiepin and asymmetrical badge came out and told our group we could enter the prison. He stood by the door and waited as we handed him our laminated numbers on our way up the short hill to the visitors' entrance.

There was no glass between us. Franny sat with arms folded sullenly behind a table in a narrow, rectangular room open on both ends. There were eight such visiting rooms. Female guards paced behind the prisoners and male guards behind the visitors. Signs in French and Arabic reminded us there was to be no touching.

Franny looked tiny in her light blue jump suit like a hospital gown. I was used to seeing her outside of the loft on roller skates.

Without them, she seemed shorter but also tougher, her boyish-ness coming to the fore. Her cheekbones looked lower. The line of her jaw heavy. Wearily she stared back at me with blank eyes and forced herself to smile. I had expected her to be happy to see me. Instead, she brooded, answering my questions with short, sharp replies. She didn't want to talk about prison, she explained, it was just boring; for example, these Senegalese women, they get so sad they eat bark.

'Bark?' I asked her. 'You mean from trees?'

She nodded.

'Why?'

'Because that's what they do when they're sad,' she told me. She found these details as tedious as those of her past boyfriends. It was just more information, stuff that happened to her, nowhere near as interesting as ripping off a department store. They got chicory instead of coffee to drink. The bread was always a little stale. The Arab and African girls went to French lessons and were given daily dictation. Franny helped them cheat on their homework.

After her sentence, she would probably be deported. She'd go back to New York, she told me, and stay with her parents, who still didn't know where she was. The only time she smiled was when she asked about life at the loft, about the Nerf basketball and what Thomas, Brian and Trey were doing. Were we still shooting hoops and gambling all day? Were Thomas and Brian still arguing? Had we seen the topless neighbour again?

I didn't tell her that Brian and Trey were planning to return home to New Jersey. Brian had spent the money he'd won from Thomas. Trey had been living off a thin wallet anyway that was finally depleted. Most days, rather than hang around the loft, I'd head to the library or the study lounge on Avenue Bosquet to work on my term papers and prepare for finals. At night, when I got home, Brian and Trey were usually out and Thomas was often at one of the cafés looking for a backgammon game. I'd boil some pasta, which I ate with butter and salt, read more Nietzsche and Marx and then go to sleep. The apartment, which had once been the centre of our community, began to seem cold and impersonal

– a vast hangar from which our fraternal bond had long since taken off.

I didn't explain all this to Franny. Would it even make sense to her? Did I even understand at the time that the whole episode by its very nature was ephemeral? None of us had jobs. I was the only one who was even a student. Only Thomas and I paid rent. And any collection of early twenty-something males was bound to be eminently fragile. Our hormones and interests were tugging us in dozens of different directions.

So I let Franny imagine our lives were going on back at the loft just as she remembered it. The loft became for her, I think, the symbolic opposite of the bottom bunk bed she now inhabited in a cramped twenty-inmate ward. Our expansive apartment came to represent freedom – enough space to do whatever she wanted whenever she chose. She could roller skate away as she pleased. Boys all around her. What more could she want?

When Franny got out, she stopped by the loft one last time before heading to the airport the next day and a flight back to New York. Brian and Trey were already gone. I was planning to move out in a few months and return to New York myself. She brought hundreds of francs worth of ham, salami, chicken, cheese, chocolate, wine, coffee and three baguettes, boasting she'd actually paid for everything. I'd never seen a woman eat as much as Franny did that night, ripping huge chunks of bread, butter and ham, chewing with her mouth open. She'd been skinny before her conviction, and had lost more weight in the joint. As she chewed, she talked about what she was going to do now that she was out; how happy she was to be leaving Paris. I'd come see her when I was in New York, right?

Definitely, I told her.

The day I moved out of the loft, the German racing driver had already begun arranging his sectional leather sofas and expensive sound system. He was going to remake the place as the sort of upscale bachelor pad it really deserved to be. Thomas' paintings

KARL TARO GREENFELD

were all shoved in a corner, their backs to the apartment. Our old mattresses and jerry-rigged tables were piled in another corner, soon to be trashed. The Nerf hoop, however, was still nailed to the wall. I remember dragging my suitcases down the stairs and wondering how many hours it would be before the German racing driver tore down that orange, plastic cylinder.

CHINESE LIFE

FROM

RIVER TOWN

PETER HESSLER

PETER HESSLER graduated from Princeton and Oxford before travelling to Fuling on the Yangtze River to teach English. He has written for a number of publications and described his China experiences in his first book, *River Town*. He now lives in Beijing.

EVERYTHING in Fuling was new that second year. I had new students – all of last year's seniors had graduated, and most of them were teaching in the countryside. My own Chinese tutors were as good as new; they were real people now, and we could talk comfortably about anything. The city didn't seem as dirty and loud as last year, and the people were friendlier. When they spoke, it made sense. The only thing that hadn't changed was my job; I still taught literature, but now it was easier because I had last year's notes. I spent most of my spare time in the city, wandering around and talking to people.

I had city routines for every day of the week, every time of the day. Sometimes in the mornings I went down to South Mountain Gate and sat in the park, watching the city come to life. Tuesday afternoons I talked to the photographer and went to Wangzhou Park. Monday evenings I walked along the busy streets of Mid-Mountain Road. On Sundays, I went to church, and afterwards I sat and talked with Father Li, who served me bad coffee. I did not like good coffee but I drank the priest's coffee out of respect, just as he served it to me out of respect for the *waiguoren* tendency to prefer coffee to tea.

After talking with Father Li, I would wander through the old city and watch the blacksmiths at work near the river. Then I would walk up to the teahouse in the middle of town, because on Sundays a group of middle-aged and older men brought their pet birds there, hanging the cages from the rafters. They were always happy to see me, especially Zhang Xiaolong, who was the Luckiest Man in All of Fuling. Ten years ago he had been injured in a motorcycle accident, shortening one leg, and now he walked with a limp. It was a wonderful injury because it meant that he was officially classified as disabled, and thus he could never be fired from his job at the Hailing factory. It was a state-owned enterprise, and reforms were leading to layoffs, but none of this concerned Zhang Xiaolong, whose job was completely secure. It was more luck than one could expect from a motorcycle accident, but Zhang Xiaolong had beaten the odds again when his wife became pregnant and gave birth – not to a daughter, or to a son, but to *twin* sons. To be slightly but certifiably disabled, and to have twin sons – that was fantasy; it didn't happen in real life; people wrote books about good fortune of that sort.

Every Sunday, Zhang Xiaolong limped proudly to the tea-house, carrying his birdcage, and he sat beaming in the sunshine as he drank his tea. He was the Happiest Man in All of Fuling, as well as the Luckiest, and I liked talking with him – not because he was particularly interesting, but simply because he was always pleasant. And he reminded me that my own life in Fuling was also charmed. Almost everywhere I went, people knew who I was, and I could follow my routines and be assured that regulars would be happy to see me. There were still plenty of young men who shouted a mocking 'Hah-loooo!' when I walked down the street, but it was less of a problem than last year, and in any case the harassment was drowned out by the kindness of most people. It was the same paradox that I had realised during the summer – the Chinese could be hard on foreigners, but at the same time they could be incredibly patient, generous and curious about where you had come from. I felt I had spent my first year coping with the hard part of being a *waiguoren*, and now I enjoyed all the benefits.

In many ways the city had turned full circle for me, but of course I was the one who had really changed. I was a new person, He Wei, or as the Sichuanese pronounced it, Ho Wei. That was the name I had been given during Peace Corps training, and it was common in China: the given name, Wei, meant 'great' and was as run-of-the-mill as John in America. The family name was also prevalent; there were plenty of Hos wherever I went in Sichuan, and when I introduced myself they always said that we were *jia-menr*, family. There was even another Ho Wei at the college, who taught in the physical education department.

It was different from living in most countries, where you could use your real name or something similar to it, which was a clear link to who you had originally been. My Chinese name had no connection to my American name, and the person who became Ho Wei had no real connection to my American self. There was an enormous freedom in that – at the age of twenty-eight, I suddenly had a completely new identity.

And you could tinker with that identity, starting with changing your name itself. Adam had done this at the end of our first year, because his original name, Mei Erkang, sounded too much like a foreigner's name (it also sounded a lot like a popular Sichuanese brand of pig feed). Looking for something that was more authentically Chinese and less agricultural, Adam asked his students to propose new names, complete with explanations, and after several rounds they came up with Mei Zhiyuan. The given name, Zhiyuan, meant 'Motivated by Lofty Goals', and it was shared by Ma Zhiyuan, a Yuan Dynasty poet who seven centuries ago had written a famous verse on homesickness. Virtually all educated Chinese recognised the allusion, and there were subsequent writers who had used the two characters in other poems. Suddenly, Adam went from pig feed to a noble-sounding classical allusion – that was how easily a *waiguoren* could redefine himself in China.

I never changed my Chinese name, but I sensed the ease with which my Chinese identity became distinct from my American self. Eventually, I came to think of myself as two people, Ho Wei and Peter Hessler. Ho Wei wasn't really a person until my second year in Fuling, but as time passed I realised that he was becoming most of my identity: apart from my students, colleagues and the other foreigners, everybody knew me strictly as Ho Wei, and they knew me strictly in Chinese. Ho Wei was completely different from my American self: he was friendlier, he was eager to talk with anybody, and he took great pleasure in even the most inane conversations. In a simple way he was funny; by saying a few words in the local dialect he could be endlessly entertaining to the people in Fuling. Also Ho Wei was stupid, which was what I liked the most about him. He spoke with an accent; he had lousy grammar; and he laughed at the simple mistakes that he made.

People were comfortable with somebody that stupid, and they found it easy to talk with Ho Wei, even though they often had to say things twice or write new words in his notebook. Ho Wei always carried his notebook in his pocket, using it to study the new words, as well as to jot down notes from conversations. And when Ho Wei returned home he left the notebook on the desk of Peter Hessler, who typed everything into his computer.

I had two desks in my apartment. One was for studying Chinese, and the other was for writing; one desk was Ho Wei's and the other belonged to Peter Hessler. Sometimes this relationship unnerved me – it seemed wrong that behind Ho Wei's stupidity there was another person watching everything intently and taking notes. But I could think of no easy resolution to this divide; I had my Chinese life and my American life, and even if they occupied similar territory, they were completely different. My apartment was big and I kept the desks in separate rooms. Ho Wei and Peter Hessler never met each other. The notebook was the only thing they truly shared.

One Sunday there was a funeral at the church. Noreen was sick that day and I sat alone, trying to follow the service in my missal. I always liked doing that, because it was good Chinese practice and it reminded me of boyhood, when some of my earliest reading had been done during Mass.

People milled around the courtyard after the service and I could see that it was a special event. Father Li and I sat in the rectory, where he called for coffee and cookies, and one of the old women who lived there brought them on a tray. The coffee was even worse than usual. I thanked the woman and drank as much as I could bear, eating cookies to dull the taste. Father Li and I asked about each other's health, and then he mentioned that today's service had been a funeral.

'Oh, I'm very sorry,' I said. 'Who was it for?'

He said a woman's name that I didn't recognise. 'How old was she?' I asked.

'Eighty years old.'

'She had a very long life.'

'Yes,' the priest said. 'And she was very good for our church. She was here every Sunday.'

'What was her job?'

'She was retired, of course. But before that she worked at the Hailing factory.'

There was a small number of parishioners who went to Mass every week, and I asked some more questions to see if I could remember the woman. Father Li answered patiently, and then finally he pointed behind me and said, 'She's right there.'

I turned around and saw the woman laid out ten feet behind me, on a table at the back of the room. The place was dimly lit and I hadn't noticed her when we came in. A white sheet was pulled up to her chin. She was a small woman with grey hair and her mouth was pinched shut. I remembered seeing her in church. I was in the middle of eating a cookie and now I put it down on the tray.

'Oh,' I said. 'There she is.'

'Yes,' said Father Li. 'That's her.'

'Well,' I said. 'I think I'll go outside now.'

It was sunny in the courtyard and the parishioners were writing memorials on long strips of white paper. A number of big funeral wreaths, made of white tissue and bamboo, were set against the wall of the church. In the sunshine I recovered quickly from the shock of seeing the body on the table, and I watched the people as they went about the business of mourning. All of the old ladies had been waiting patiently for me to finish my coffee, and now they entered the room to pay their respects to the body.

The woman's son was there, a man in his fifties, and he was thrilled that a *waiguoren* had come to his mother's funeral. I told him that his mother had always been very kind to me, which made him even happier. It was a tradition for the family to give small gifts at a funeral, and the son gave me some fruit and a box of Magnificent Sound cigarettes. I thanked him and accepted the cigarettes. It was hard to imagine a more appropriate funeral gift.

Later I went to the teahouse, where Zhang Xiaolong, the Luckiest Man in Fuling, grinned and waved. He was with some of the other old men and I took an empty table nearby. The waitress came over, smiling, and asked me what I wanted.

'The *yangguizi* wants a cup of tea,' I said. Calling myself *yangguizi*, 'foreign devil', was one of the easiest and most disarming jokes in Fuling. I had started using that word to describe myself during the summer, and people often didn't know how to react; sometimes they were embarrassed and tried to persuade me to call myself something different. But I always responded by proudly saying something like 'We foreign devils have a long history' or 'We foreign devils have a great culture.'

At the teahouse it was an old joke between me and the *xiaojie*, the young woman who worked there. She covered her mouth and laughed, and then she poured me a cup of tea. I had bought a newspaper on the street and now I read it while the tea cooled.

It was a typical day at the teahouse and a few people came up and talked with me. At the end of the morning, a young woman whom I had never met came and sat at my table. We talked for perhaps ten minutes. It was slightly unusual for a woman to approach me, but not so unusual that I thought anything of it. Her name was Li Jiali, and she asked for my phone number. This was also common – I always gave my number to people in Fuling. The only problem was that some of them had a tendency to call between the hours of five and seven o'clock in the morning, so I often took my phone off the hook when I was sleeping. I gave my number to Li Jiali and thought no more about it.

A week later I returned to the teahouse, and once again she sat at my table. She was dressed in a very short skirt and tights and she wore a great deal of make-up. She was not pretty, but she had successfully adopted a number of the habits that you saw in a certain type of *xiaojie*, who smiled too much and talked in a cutesy way, drawing out her words at the end of sentences. The woman who worked at the teahouse was not like this, and I saw her shaking her head as Li Jiali sat posing at my table. The old men were staring; even their birds seemed stunned into silence. I could see that something was happening that I didn't understand, and so I excused myself, paid for the tea, and left.

Li Jiali followed me out of the teahouse. 'Where are you going?' she asked.

'I have to go now,' I said. 'I'm going to eat and then I'm going home.'

We passed a noodle restaurant where I often ate. Suddenly I had a great fear of this woman following me home and being seen with me on campus. 'I'm leaving now,' I said. 'I must eat at this restaurant. Goodbye.'

'Oh, I'll eat with you,' said Li Jiali.

The owner of the restaurant cleared a table and I found myself sitting there with the woman. That was how everything always went in Fuling – things happened to me. Usually I liked the passive unpredictability but today I was suspicious of her intentions, and yet I had no idea what to do. She sat there chattering about something and I asked her where she worked.

'That's not important,' she said, and suddenly it became very important.

'Do you work here in Fuling?'

'It's not a good job,' she said, shrugging. 'But my uncle is getting me a better job in Chongqing. He owns a big restaurant – he's very rich! He's giving me a job there as a *xiaojie*. The *xiaojie* at my uncle's restaurant wear fine clothes – I'll have to wear a *qipao* like this' – she showed me how it would look: no shoulders, tight around the neck, slit high up her thigh.

'Oh,' I said.

'But it's very expensive,' she said. 'I'll have to buy the *qipao* myself.'

'That's too bad,' I said.

'Do you like to sing karaoke?'

'No,' I said. 'I do not like to sing karaoke. Most Americans do not like to sing.'

'We should go to a karaoke bar sometime. I'll teach you how to sing.'

'Sorry, but I'm not interested in karaoke.'

'That's okay,' she said, smiling. 'I'm very interested in your America.'

'What about my America interests you?'

'Everything. I would like to go there.'

I did not like the way this conversation was going. 'It's very difficult to do that,' I said.

'I would like to live in your America,' she said. 'People there have more money than here.'

'There are many poor people in my America.'

'Not as many as there are here in Fuling.'

She had a point and I tried a different tack. I talked about how difficult visas were to obtain, and then our noodles arrived. I ate quickly and tried to think of what to do next.

'Ho Wei,' she said. 'You are very *ke'aide*' – adorable. She said it in the best *xiaojie* manner and I was certain that the others in the restaurant were listening now.

'Your eyes are very pretty,' she said. 'I think you *waiguoren* have prettier eyes than us Chinese.'

'It's not true,' I said dumbly. 'Chinese are much prettier than *waiguoren*. *Waiguoren* are very hard to look at.' She took this as a compliment, smiling and trying to blush. I thought: Ho Wei, you are a jackass.

'I like to hear you speak our Chinese language, Ho Wei,' she said. 'It sounds very funny!'

I remembered how guys in college used to hit on the local au pair girls from Sweden with their accents and cluelessness. It was not a pleasant comparison, and I tried not to think about it.

We were leaving the restaurant now and the owner grinned knowingly as I paid. On the street Li Jiali took my arm and I stood there in passive disbelief. A Fuling woman was touching me and we were right near the intersection of South Mountain Gate; everybody was honking at us, or so it seemed.

'I have to go now,' I stammered. 'You can't come with me. I am very busy today.'

'Next week is my birthday,' Li Jiali said.

'That's nice,' I said.

'I'll see you next week,' she said.

A cab swung by, horn blaring, and I smelled the hot breath of its exhaust. The sun was warm and now I was sweating. 'Goodbye,' I said, and at last she let me go.

Two days later, Li Jiali called and Ho Wei answered the phone. She asked if he would be at the teahouse on Sunday and he replied that he would. He was there every Sunday and there was no reason to lie about that.

After the phone call, I began to think once more about the possible complications of this particular aspect of my Chinese life, as well as the many ways in which Ho Wei was not capable of dealing with them. The simplest solution was to avoid going to the teahouse, but she knew I worked at the college and I did not want her to track me down there.

I knew that Li Jiali was trouble – she was far too forward for a Chinese woman, and either she wanted money or she was crazy. Adam and I had both had experiences with this in the first year. A freshman girl student had spent a couple of weeks lurking outside of Adam's apartment, and there was a middle-aged woman named Miss Ou who had pursued me more or less throughout my time in Fuling. Both of these women were clearly unbalanced, and undoubtedly they turned to us because we were outside the loop, just like them. That was at once the most interesting and most disturbing aspect of living in Fuling – as a *waiguoren* you tended to attract a certain fringe element. It was possible to have a Chinese life, but that didn't mean it was a normal Chinese life.

Last year those complications had at least been in English, which gave us a certain degree of control over the interactions. But now it was strictly in Chinese – I met the people on their terms. And I knew that Li Jiali's terms would be difficult to deal with; somehow I would have to convince her that she would not get whatever it was that she wanted. It was all Ho Wei's show and I didn't have much confidence in his ability to handle the problem.

The next Sunday, I delayed my trip to the teahouse as long as possible. I spent a long time chatting with Father Li, and then I wandered down to the blacksmith's shop and watched them make chisels. It was nearly noon by the time I made it to the teahouse.

The *xiaojie* brought me tea; I was too nervous to make any foreign-devil jokes. She smiled and said that Li Jiali had been looking for me. I asked her if she knew the woman.

'I know her, but she's not my friend.'

'Where does she work?'

'She works across the street, at the *meifating*.' It meant 'beauty parlour', but it also meant something else, and the *xiaojie*, like everybody in Fuling, spoke the word with distinct scorn. Most of the city's prostitutes worked in beauty parlours and now I knew for certain what Li Jiali did for a living.

I sat there and waited for her. One of the teahouse regulars came over and talked with me. Usually he was annoying, because he was a fanatical disciple of Falun Gong, which was a mixture of Buddhism, Taoism and *qigong*-style deep-breathing exercises. At first I had been interested in hearing him talk about Falun Gong, simply because I had never heard of it and the local followers seemed to believe with religious intensity, which was a rare passion in Fuling. But soon the man came to see me as a potential convert, and he often telephoned and gave me long lectures on the benefits of Falun Gong. He especially liked to call at five o'clock in the morning, because it showed how little sleep he needed now that Falun Gong had entered his life.

It was another mess of Ho Wei's. I had no interest in any sort of *qigong* – I was a runner and I disliked the idea of an exercise regimen that involved moving as slowly as possible. Of course, I might have been more interested in talking with the man if I had known that in 1999 the Communist Party would ban Falun Gong as a cult, persecuting its followers. But in Fuling I had no idea that the practice would someday become such a political issue, and I never would have imagined that the government would consider it to be a threat. As far as I was concerned, the main problem with Falun Gong was that it woke me up at five o'clock in the morning.

But today I was happy for any distraction and I listened to the man's lecture. A major sticking point between us was alcohol –

his personal interpretation of Falun Gong stressed no smoking or drinking, and in a moment of desperation I had latched onto this as a way of discouraging him, explaining that there was no way I could ever give up beer. Like so many of Ho Wei's solutions, this was a serious miscalculation. It resulted in the man's making a full-fledged assault on the dangers of alcohol, week after week, in mind-numbing detail. His lectures began with the way alcohol settles in your cells, whereas Falun Gong seeks to bring every-thing into balance at the cellular level. There was more to this explanation, but I always lost the thread and sat there nodding as if I understood.

Li Jiali arrived while the man was lecturing. She smiled and sat down at our table. I didn't acknowledge her, and the man contin-ued lecturing about alcohol and Falun Gong. All of the old bird men were watching.

She was dressed brightly again and she put on her make-up at our table. She dabbed rouge onto her cheeks, looking into a tiny mirror, and then she put on eye shadow. In Fuling, few women wore much make-up, and even fewer painted their faces in pub-lic, which was a sign of loose morals. There were many signs like that – the clearest was for a *xiaojie* to smoke a cigarette in public, because when a Fuling woman did that you could be almost cer-tain that she was a prostitute. Li Jiali was not smoking but the show of painting her face was bad enough.

She tried several times to get my attention until at last I looked.

'Ho Wei,' she said, 'your American name is Pete, isn't it?'

'Yes.' She had asked me this the first time we met, and now I regretted telling her.

'Pete,' she said. She pronounced it 'Bee-do' and I didn't like hearing her say it; I saw no reason to bring that name into Ho Wei's mess. 'Bee-do,' she said again, 'did you bring me a gift?'

'No.'

'I told you it was my birthday!' Again this was the flirty *xiao-jie* voice and I felt my anger rise.

'In America we don't have that tradition,' I said.

'You don't give presents on birthdays?'

'We don't ask people to give us presents.'

It was one of the sharpest things Ho Wei had ever said, but it didn't faze her. I could bring her a present next week, she said. She asked if I would take her to lunch today, and I decided that I had had enough.

'I already have a girlfriend,' I lied. 'At the college I have a *waiguoren* girlfriend – the tall one with red hair.' I figured that Noreen was the best choice, because she was tall and her height sometimes intimidated the Chinese. The Falun Gong man was listening carefully now.

'That's okay,' Li Jiali said. 'It doesn't matter if you have a girlfriend.'

'I have to go now,' I said. 'I don't want to eat lunch.'

'I'll go with you,' the man said.

We stood up and Li Jiali said something to him. They were talking quickly in the dialect, and I walked out of the teahouse. On the street they caught up with me. The Falun Gong man was on my left, and Li Jiali started tugging at my right arm. 'Bee-do,' she said, 'where are you going?'

'Please leave me alone,' I said.

I pulled away, slipping into the crowd, and the Falun Gong man whispered in my ear, 'What's your *guanxi* with her?'

'There's no *guanxi*. I don't know who she is. She bothers me.'

'You don't have any interest in her?'

'No, not at all.'

Li Jiali had caught us again, and she came between me and the man. He said something to her and she responded sharply, and now he turned and faced her. He shouted at the woman and she shouted back, calling him a *gui'erzi*, a Sichuanese obscenity meaning 'son of a turtle'. All of the *xiaojie* cuteness was gone, and it was as if a mask had been stripped away; she spat at him and shouted obscenely like a whore. People stopped to watch. The man stood his ground, shouting back, and in a minute it was over. Li Jiali tossed her head and stormed down the street.

The crowd dispersed and I walked to the bus stop with the Falun Gong man. I looked back over my shoulder and I could feel my heart beating. For once I was glad that I had tolerated so many of the man's phone calls and lectures about alcohol. I promised myself that I would always be polite with him, and that at least once I would try his exercises.

'She was asking me to leave you alone with her,' he said.

'Is she a prostitute?'

'Perhaps,' he said, but it was the Chinese perhaps that meant: Certainly.

We came to the bus and I thanked him.

'You need to be more careful,' he said. 'Often people like that will want you for your money, or because you're a *waiguoren*. You shouldn't give your phone number to everybody. And remember that I don't want your money – I only want to teach you Falun Gong. I'm different from her.'

I nodded and got on the bus. For the next three weeks I shifted my routines to avoid the teahouse. Li Jiali moved to Chongqing, and later that fall she sent me a series of love letters, which I ignored. I never saw her again. I never tried Falun Gong. In the early mornings I kept my phone off the hook. I realised that complications were an inevitable result of my Chinese life, but I also realised that even at his worst Ho Wei could find a way to bumble out of problems. I had allowed him this much freedom, and in the end it was like an adult watching a child grow up – there was only so much control that I could take over that part of my life, and its unpredictability, although risky, was much of its charm. All I could do was let Ho Wei go his own way and hope for the best.

A LOVE-SCENE AFTER WORK:

WRITING IN THE TROPICS

FROM

SUNRISE

WITH SEAMONSTERS

PAUL THEROUX

PAUL THEROUX is the author of many works of fiction and non-fiction. *The Great Railway Bazaar*, his account of a train journey from London to Tokyo, was credited with reinventing the travel book when it first appeared in 1975. His most recent works include the novel *Hotel Honolulu* and *Fresh-Air Fiend*, an anthology.

ONE OF THE MOST pathetic illustrations in all literature about the difficulty of holding a job and writing a novel at the same time occurs in Anthony Trollope's *Autobiography*. He has been sent to Scotland 'to revise the Glasgow Post Office', and in order to assess the labours of the letter carriers he must trudge alongside them all day as they deliver. He is determined to do a good job; when a letter carrier goes to the top floor of a house, Trollope follows. It is mid-summer and hot. 'The men would grumble,' Trollope says, 'and then I would think how it would be with them if they had to go home afterwards and write a love-scene.'

Any person who has tried to work and write understands that remark. Trollope knew a further difficulty: writing in the tropics. *The West Indies and the Spanish Main* was written in Trinidad, Jamaica, Costa Rica and Cuba, on board ship, in stuffy hotel rooms, in terrible heat. And he was working in the West Indies – surveying the postal service. Trollope was an unusual man, a great whist player, an avid horseman, a curious and observant traveller, a devoted civil servant (framer of postal treaties, inventor of the pillar box). He was a prolific novelist and a hard-working editor. Trollope's energy is a rare thing, and so is his candour: 'But the love-scenes written in Glasgow, all belonging to *The Bertrams*, are not good.'

A job, especially one that requires alertness, always menaces the novel. A job overseas is different; there are many advantages in being an expatriate worker, but there are more disadvantages, and after working abroad for nine years as a teacher in the season-less monotony of three tropical countries I have decided to chuck the whole business and never take a job again. I have to admit that some of my objections are petty. I am made unreasonably angry when one of my unsmiling superiors, summoning me through his secretary, bites on his pipe, and mispronouncing my name, demands that I must do this or that. I suppose the rudeness angers me; it is the Singaporean's least endearing quality. But it is a Chinese rule. The most powerful are the least polite; a promotion means a diminution in civility, which is a quality – not a virtue – of the very low. The weak have no choice but to be polite.

'Excuse me, sir,' says a student. 'Eddie Fang says you are a novelist. Are you going to write a novel about Singapore?'

'No thanks,' I reply. 'But you've lived here your whole life – why don't you write one?'

'Can't.' He flinches and adds: 'There's nothing to write about.'

There have been excellent English schools in Singapore for a hundred years. Singapore claims to have the best school system in Asia. English is the official language. No Singaporean has ever written a novel in English. Once there was a girl here who wrote poetry, but she went to Iowa and never came back. The highlight of the UNESCO-sponsored Festival of Books in Singapore was a children's fancy-dress contest; Raffles, Cinderella, Robin Hood and Lord Krishna were winners.

'Well, if there's nothing to write about, then how am I supposed to write a novel about Singapore?'

'Eddie Fang said you used to live in Africa. And you wrote some books about Africa. So I thought –'

Sometimes during a conversation like this (I am asked the question twice a week) I say, 'I'm writing a novel about a writer in Singapore who wants to write a novel about Singapore and can't.' No-one laughs at that.

No-one laughs at much. The Singapore government, which is a mixture of paranoia and paternalism – inspiring the fearfulness of childhood, when authority always seems irrefragable in its strength – exhorts her citizens to be busy. The Singaporeans' play looks like work; people made into children are fearful about breaking rules, and very tense they become very humourless. They don't want to be caught laughing – anyway, what's so funny? Humour is the sort of independent mimicry that requires the same rebelliousness writing does. Humour also emphasises differences in people, in their speech and habits; it has a tendency to distort gleefully in order to express a truth. At Morning Coffee, which is a tropical ritual observed as thoroughly as Afternoon Tea is in a temperate climate, I tell a joke. The several Chinese at the table fall silent, although the joke is quite harmless. If it was about physical deformity or race they might laugh. Then one says, 'That's very interesting,' and looks grave. My Indian friend giggles; like me, he's an expatriate. He offers a joke of his own. The Chinese stare at him.

A few days later the Indian asks me if I plan to stay in Singapore. I tell him I intend to leave, to quit teaching entirely and take up writing full time.

'So you vant to be another Faith Baldvin?' he says, and titters into his coffee cup. But he is not mocking. He also reads Oliver Goldsmith for pleasure.

Conrad said (in 'A Glance at Two Books', *Last Essays*): '... a book is a deed ... the writing of it is an enterprise as much as the conquest of a colony.' This means a daily effort of laborious concentration. It cannot be haphazard, weekend flurries of composition, and who can get up as early in the morning as Trollope? By stages one encloses oneself in one's novel, erects a barrier that shuts out the real world to duplicate it. Obviously, if one is married and has a job and children and friends, one can't write one's book as if one is serving a prison sentence, going into isolation and emerging when the work is done. On the other hand, one doesn't write a book by observing a landscape or hearing a phrase at a party and then going home and scribbling the observation in the margin of the text. 'Are you writing a book about Singapore?' the student asks. I'm not; if I do it will be elsewhere.

Mornings in the tropics – an hour or two – are for teaching, afternoons for sleeping; the lighted pause of early evening is spent in a bar or drinking on a verandah. Writing at night is out because of the heat, and the desk lamp attracts insects that make shadows as they strafe the pages. But also, teaching in the tropics is undemanding, hours are fewer, classes smaller, and I've given all my lectures before. I can dig out last year's lecture on *The White Devil* or Middleton's comedies and with a little planning I can free myself during the best hours of the day, the glittering spring-like morning, from seven to ten or eleven. I write in long-hand so I can memorise everything I've written; committing a novel to memory makes it possible to think about it, extend it, and correct it in any idle hour.

I consider myself to have been very lucky. Both in Uganda and Singapore my bosses were writers themselves; they were interested in my work, and I think they made some allowances for me. Mr Moore used to ask me how my poems were coming along, and Mr Enright and I used to commiserate in the Staff Club; he would look around at the drinkers, when we were talking about writing, and say, 'They think it's easy!'

The best job for a writer, a job with the fewest hours, is in the tropics. But books are hard to write in the tropics. It is not only the heat; it is the lack of privacy, the open windows, the noise. Tropical cities are deafening. In Lagos and Accra and Kampala two people walking down a city street will find they are shouting to each other to be heard over the sound of traffic and the howls of residents and radios. V. S. Naipaul is the only writer I know of who has mentioned the abrading of the nerves by tropical noise (the chapter on Trinidad in *The Middle Passage*). Shouting is the Singaporean's expression of friendliness; the Chinese shout is like a bark, sharp enough to make you jump. And if you are unfortunate enough to live near a Chinese cemetery – only foreigners live near cemeteries, the Chinese consider it unlucky to occupy those houses – you will hear them mourning with firecrackers, scattering cherrybombs over the gravestones.

Sit in a room in Singapore and try to write. Every sound is an interruption, and your mind blurs each time a motorcycle or a plane or a funeral passes. If you live near a main road, as I do, there will be three funerals a day (Chinese funerals are truckloads of gong-orchestras and brass bands playing familiar songs like 'It's a Long Way to Tipperary'). The day the Bengali gardener mows the grass is a day wasted. Hawkers cycle or drive by and each stops; you learn their individual yells, the bean-curd man with his transistor and sidecar, the fish-ball man on his bike, the ice-cream seller with his town crier's bell (a mid-afternoon interruption), the breadman in his Austin van, leaning on the horn; the elderly Chinese lady crouching in her *sam foo* and crying 'Yeggs!' through the door, the Tamil newsboy, a toddy alcoholic, muttering 'Baybah, baybah.' Before the British forces left there was a fish-and-chip van; it didn't beep, but there were yells. The Singaporean doesn't stir from his house. He waits in the coolness of his parlour for the deliverers to arrive. The yells and gongs, at first far off, then closer, console him. It is four-thirty, and here comes the coconut-seller ringing his bicycle bell. He has a monkey, a macaque the size of a four-year-old, on the crossbar. The coconut-seller is crazy; the buyers make him linger and they laugh at him. A crowd gathers to jeer him; he chases some children and then goes away. After dark the grocery truck parks in front of your house; the grocer has a basket of fish, a slaughtered pig, and the whole range of Ma-Ling canned goods ('Tripe in Duck Grease', 'Chicken Feet', 'Lychees in Syrup') and for an hour you will hear the yelp and gargle of bartering. You have written nothing.

The heat and light; you asked for those in coming so far, but it is hotter, though less bright than you imagined – Singapore is usually cloudy, averaging only six hours of sunshine a day. That persistent banging and screeching is an annoyance that makes you hotter still. You are squinting at the pen which is slipping out of your slick fingers and wondering why you bothered to come.

Slowly, it happens, a phrase, a sentence, a paragraph. Nothing comes out right the first time, and you are not so much writing as learning a language, inching along in what seems at times like another tongue. A characteristic of writing in the tropics is this recopying, rewriting, beginning again, and understanding that it will take a long time, whatever you write: it has taken me a week to get this far with this little essay. It is not impossible to finish, just hard, because many things have to be in your favour: it can't be too hot, it must be quiet, two or three hours have to be totally free of interruption; your health must be good and your mood fairly bright – a late night, an argument or a hangover means a lost day.

But the fact of being in a foreign place has made you small. You are not a public figure (public figures who are habitually vocal are deported), simply an English teacher. The bookstores do not stock your novels, or anyone's. No-one is going to ask you to lecture at the National Library on 'The Future of the Novel'; the worst that can happen, if it is known you are a writer, is that you'll be asked to edit the church newsletter. You are unaware of any sense of celebrity or reputation. That happened last year, in another country, when your novel appeared; and there hasn't been a murmur since. Everything has to be proven anew, and if you need humility, look at the bookshelf behind you where your novels, even last year's, have become mildewed and discoloured in the humidity: they could be the books of a dead man. No-one where you live has the slightest idea of what you are doing. To write you have withdrawn, like any conscientious hobbyist; and ceasing to live in the place you may be lonelier: your world is your house, your family, your desk; abroad is a bar.

It is a form of eccentricity, but in the tropics the eccentric is common, and far from being held in contempt, he is regarded as rather special and left alone. At Makerere University in Uganda, one head of department was never seen. He didn't teach his classes; he was never sober; he was said to be a great character. He had many defenders. There was a professor of philosophy in Singapore who used to saunter down the street in his pyjamas, reading difficult books. This was his uniqueness. He was watched but never pestered. Expatriates by the very fact of their having come to the tropics are considered by the locals to be somewhat crazed, and the expatriate who fails to be a person in any subtle sense can still, with a little effort, succeed as 'a character'. This requires a specific obsession, a singular tic of personality. Your distinguishing mark might be your continual absence ('Oh, *him* – he's *never* around'), and if not doing your job is your affectation, then you may proceed with other things. What does it matter if anyone sees this as dereliction? You are an expatriate on contract, not an exile; you intend to go home eventually. Gain a modest reputation for being unreliable and you will never be asked to do a thing. The students will become used to receiving their essays late.

The students demand less than American ones; the system, Oxbridge in equatorial decline, forces them to work alone. They are as insular as their parents and subservient to the government; their civic-mindedness takes the form of fashion shows for charity. They are intelligent, nervous, inexperienced and poorly read. Many would like to emigrate to Australia (Singaporeans talk reverently about Australia, the way people from Massachusetts used to talk about California: 'Plenty of opportunities there, and a really nice climate'). Like students in developing countries everywhere their speech is a mixture of the bookish and the political ('whilst we go from strength to strength', 'timorous Claudio is part and parcel . . .'). Some in essays sound like Jacobeans. One discovers Irving Ribner and tears him to shreds; another who has never heard of the First World War writes about Wilfred Owen. There is no American literature. 'Richard Cory' is said to be an old English ballad, and Herman Woo and Heidi Chin think the eponymous hero's name 'ridiculous and comic'. Except for the archaic phrases the students write clearly, in mission school copperplate; they speak less well, and in a tutorial sometimes spell out the word they want to say. Lady Macbeth is 'roofless' or 'rootless', and Dickens is very good at 'crating a crackter'. It is easy to laugh at such lapses, until one reminds oneself of the émigré scientists in the States – brilliant men in their fields – pronouncing their original sentences all wrong. Chinese students are plagued by glottal stops and certain consonants, and they always speak very fast. In a tutorial a girl holding a leatherbound book reads aloud to prove a point she has just made:

> *Must dow esplain da ting I hate most on erf,*
> *Da treason, da shame, da assident of my berf?*

In a lecture on *Tamburlaine* I repeat the line, 'Holla, ye pampered jades of Asia!' They smile earnestly in recognition. What will become of them? It is a foreigner's question. Their parents have saluted four different flags, some more; in twenty-five years, when these students are middle-aged, what flag will be flying over the Singapore City Hall? It is futile to speculate, but not less worrying for the person who has spent three years among them, who knows many as friends and who has come to understand that the student who says, 'Must dow esplain . . .' is no fool.

I never travelled much in the United States, but I remember my two older brothers making a train journey from Boston to Ohio when I was seven or eight – in the late forties. Somehow we had the idea that people in Ohio suffered from a lack of iodine because of the scarcity of fish. The Ohioans were afflicted by goitres, and people walked around Cleveland with bulbous growths on their necks. I was too young to go to Ohio, but I remember my brothers' stories: about their meal on the train, how the waiter brought their change back on a plate (a *plate*!), the flatness of Ohio, and they *had* seen some people with goitres, and one elderly lady called my brothers 'Yankees'. They had their rolls of film developed; the results were blurred and banal, every one was a disappointment: Ohio, which sounded so foreign, looked like Massachusetts.

Growing up, I mistrusted anyone who had not travelled. I thought of becoming a White Father, not out of any piety but from a desire to be sent to Africa. I thought of becoming a doctor: then I could have a useful occupation overseas. When I was nineteen or twenty I applied for a job in a Lebanese university, and having fabricated much of the application, was called for an interview in a Boston hotel. The interviewer was kind, asked me my age, then smiled and said I wouldn't do: Beirut was a rough city, and 'there is always some kind of trouble in the Arab quarter'. I finally left in the spring of 1963, and I have not been back in the States for more than a few weeks at a time, a total of about four months in nine years. Now I want to go back for good, not because it is too difficult to live abroad – only writing is hard in the tropics – but perhaps because it is too easy. Africa, for all its mystery and strangeness, unquote, is really a very simple place to live.

Africans are candid and hospitable, and make it easy for you to live among them. The Chinese in Singapore appear not to see you; the students do not greet you or each other. Anonymity is simple.

Living among strangers in a foreign place I am like an unexpected guest waiting in a tropical parlour. My mind is especially alert to differences of smell and sound, the shape of objects, and I am apprehensive about what is going to happen next. I sit with my knees together in the heat, observing the surfaces of things. At the same time, the place is so different I can indulge myself in long unbroken reflections, for the moments of observation are still enough to allow the mind to travel in two directions: recording mentally the highly coloured things one sees is simple; the mind then wanders. The reflection may be a reminiscence of early youth, a piecing-together of an episode out of the distant past; it is not contradicted or interrupted by anything near. In a foreign country I can live in two zones of time, the immediate and apprehensible, and in that vaguer zone I thought I had forgotten. Since I do not write autobiographically, I am able to see the past more clearly; I haven't altered it in fiction. That detail of the goitres in Ohio, the forsythia bush behind our Medford house, our large family; slowly, in a foreign place, the memory whirrs and gives back the past. It is momentarily a reassurance, the delay of any daydream, but juxtaposed with the vivid present it is an acute reminder of my estrangement.

And it may be wasteful and near senility, this reaching back that living abroad allows. Certainly trivial details can be strongly visualised: twenty-five years ago I pulled myself up the side of my grandfather's rainbarrel and looked in and saw mosquito larvae twitching near the surface like tiny seahorses. I had not thought of it until yesterday, in a suburb of Singapore. I wonder at its importance.

Most of a writer's life is spent in pure idleness, not writing a thing. Up to now I have used this idleness to poke in places with bewitching names, Sicily, the Congo, Malaya, Burma, Singapore, Java; this distraction could be a form of indulgence, but I can't think what else I should have done. I know it is a mistake to stay away from home too long, and it is foolish if one calls oneself a writer to go on teaching. The professions are separate; I admire the people who can write love-scenes after work. I can't, and it is unprofitable to pose as if I can. I told a colleague I was leaving. She was concerned. She believes my subjects are little countries. She said, 'But if you live in Europe or America, what will you write about?' We'll see.

FROM

A HOUSE IN CORFU

E M M A   T E N N A N T

EMMA TENNANT has written more than twenty novels and, most recently, three volumes of memoirs. There is a strong element of memoir about *A House in Corfu*, her latest work of non-fiction, which describes her parents' move to Greece in the 1960s.

LES JOURS *se suivent et se ressemblent tous.'* This Racinian declaration, denoting an intolerable passage of time, can be translated into an expression of contentment at Rovinia. Days – and indeed years – have passed; and if they are not all exactly the same, they are alike enough to provide a sense of time passing as seen and felt in the antique world. Dominated by seasons, spring planting, late-summer harvests of olive and grape, and in months punctuated by celebrations and farewells, we come and go (though I more frequently than others) to this place that has mysteriously become home.

It's the late 1980s, and five years since my father died here, on October fourth 1983. He had suffered from the family heart disease (for which he'd undergone an operation seven years earlier, at the age of seventy-five) and had gone on with the rhythm of life at Rovinia as if nothing had happened. The sea and the bright sunlight continued to dominate his paintings; and the artist Ghika, coming to visit on a day when bay and point were swept by rain and lowering cloud, picked out a dark view of mountain and livid ocean as the best of the lot.

But it was Mathraki, the magical repository of fossils and flints, the low-lying island we visited in the big caique, with its health-infusing mud and white cluster of simple buildings, that my father most loved to paint. In those pale oils he did somehow capture the faintness of the blue in a sea that, unlike ours here on the deeply shelving west coast, lies shallow for miles, over sand; and the softly yellow promontory, crumbling down to its mirror image in the water below, is as much of an apparent illusion when approached in real life as in one of my father's many representations of Mathraki. At the time of his operation in London, the picture hung on the wall at the end of his bed. I saw him lie there and stare at it, as if the tubes that drained from his side and the rumble of traffic on a grey London day simply vanished in the presence of the island and its relics of a time that long pre-dated Odysseus' landing at the bay south of the palace of King Alcinous.

Because of the sense of one day blending into the next, here, there is also a strong sense of my father's continued occupation at Rovinia. The pride he took in the exactness of proportion comes back each time one steps out on to the terrace, or looks out through the width of the door into the room where he sat at the desk (another victim of the otherwise excellent Corfu carpenter, leading to squashed-knee syndrome) writing in longhand on the blue airmail pad that he and my mother bought at the stationer's before a quick drink at the Corfu Bar, and then home. The lightness of the house at every season of the year brings to mind his dislike – perhaps after a childhood in a fake Jacobean manor and then in an imitation Gothic castle – of the old, the dark, the fusty. Here, of course, my mother's own love of the 'nothing' of their bedroom, where the sea provides a violently blue and ever-changing wallpaper and there is otherwise on the walls only the whiteness of the light, joins my father's preference for the unpretentious and the plain.

I was in London with my two young daughters when news came of my father's last illness. It was quick – but there had been anguish; and the kindness and selflessness of the doctor and heart specialist, who came at night across an autumnal sea all the way from Paleocastritsa to our bay, was typical of the generosity of the Corfiot people. There was nothing, in fact, that could be done. My father, stretchered up the path by strong young men, spoke in a way that was as typical of him as the efforts by the doctor to help him had been of a Greek to a suffering stranger: this was the first time, the prone figure announced, that the landscape of groves and olives had been seen while lying supine. He declared his delight in seeing the land he had come to nearly twenty years before, from a stretcher – not many, my mother and I had to agree much later, would see their transportation to the clinic while seriously ill in quite this debonair and dispassionate light. Yet I understood, too, that this was not after all the very last journey for my father. His will stipulated that he be buried at Traquair in Scotland, and there, in a grave overlooking the hills of his youth, he was finally laid to rest. Marie Aspioti sent wild cyclamen, from the other hills he had come to love.

Since I'd been coming here, it had seemed to me that my parents grew younger and I – children, work, money all heavily engraved on my face and soul – had grown considerably older. The feeling of freedom enjoyed after a quarter of a century of office life was of course most evident in my father: but together, and with new friends (Michael and Mirabel Osler, who had been teachers in Asia and were now living in an old house beyond Gastouri on the cliffs overlooking the sea), he and my mother enjoyed trips and explorations on the island with the fervour of much younger people. The Greek sun, too, played its part: even in his eighties my father looked rakish and handsome in his straw hat, leading a middle-aged couple, siblings of an English writer friend, to mistake him on arrival by taxi-boat on our beach for – as my mother recounted – 'a dashing beach bum in need of a tip'. ('But where,' said my father, on being told this intriguing compliment, 'where then *was* this tip?') His continuing presence, a reminder of his practical abilities, his humour and his love of a mystical past, lives on at Rovinia without any sense of a gloomy 'haunting'.

On this occasion, half a decade on from my father's death, we're on our way up to Liapades, to attend a christening. Yorgos of the Nikterida, the small taverna halfway down the steep hill on the outskirts of the village, has invited us to his house, not so far as the crow flies, but so high in a narrow cobbled street above the houses and courtyards shuttered and bolted against prying eyes that to arrive there is to feel oneself permitted to enter the secret upper floor of an intricate doll's house.

On the way there we pass the pretty church where it seems only funerals take place – for all other functions are presided over by the *papas* in the church in the main square. This church, with its banana yellow distempered walls and picturesque cypresses, may make a picture suitable for a tourist camera – but the cemetery, only half-screened from the road by a low wall, is, quite literally, the last place anyone would want to be. There is clearly no tradition of seeing to the upkeep of graves: weeds trail the chipped and mildewed slabs of stone, which lean at perilous angles. It would come as no surprise, when one hasty glance over the wall is rewarded by the sight of oblong piles of earth long neglected and refusing even a crop of grass to cover the incumbent, to discover that corpses lay there, coffinless and waiting for the next downpour, with the coming of the autumn equinox, to wash away the thin counterpane of soil. 'Not here,' my mother says as we fall into the silence that walking down the long stretch of road beside the cemetery invariably produces. 'I did see that once – it wasn't here in Liapades, but in Turkey. Dead people's toes were sticking up out of the graves.'

We all fall into an even deeper silence, a picture of the ancient Alexandros and his motionless white feet on our beach below the house springing instantly to mind. Birth, marriage and death are also never far from the surface in a Greek community such as this; and we do not voice the thought that today's celebration of a birth is an occasion we're grateful to be asked to join.

Not that a christening here can be expected to take place at all near the birth of the child. A good year or so can go by while the infant, still unnamed, grows into a lusty toddler – and I can't help admiring this slowness, similar to the long wait during betrothal for the day when a wedding can be planned, which appears to characterise Greek family life. After all, a couple can always decide *not* to marry, if they find each other's company uncongenial. And why does a child, unable to speak in its first year or so, actually need a name until fairly late on, if it comes to it?

The answer, as so often, turns out to be pragmatic. The infant, who must be plunged in cold water and be seen to be totally immersed, will not thrive if this rite is performed in the winter months. So a child born in spring must wait until the following spring or summer; and a winter birth will go a whole year and a half before the requisite conditions for baptism can be shown to exist. Today, a day when the sun seems set in the sky, fixed and without any intention of finding a cloud to obscure it, is clearly perfect for the christening of Yorgos' little granddaughter.

'What have you?' We remember the answers we were told, when we first came here, that are given to questions regarding the gender of a newborn. 'A son? *Tou Theou*' (from God). But if a daughter had been born, the hapless parent had but one answer: 'Excuse me!' We wonder if this remains the practice, in a community where, gradually, the modern world is being introduced. Do they say 'Excuse me' still, on the birth of a daughter? It seems unlikely, certainly, that the good-natured Yorgos will do anything other than welcome his female grandchild with open arms.

Of course I know the reasons here are pragmatic also. A daughter must provide a dowry: often, if a succession of bad harvests or misfortunes descends on the family, it is impossible to come up with the trees, the inch of land in the patchwork surrounding the village, the chest with its consignment of sheets and embroidered blankets. A daughter may not be able to afford to leave home and become the slave of another woman, her mother-in-law: she must upset the balance determined by nature and stay a slave at home. I think of the young Scottish – and English – girls who fall in love with the local lads out here, and goggle in amazement at what would have been expected of them, if they had been Greek. For they bring with them nothing at all; and are not loved by their elders here, for it.

Strips of intensely cultivated earth begin to appear, once we have left behind the misleadingly pretty yellow church and the cemetery. These are the allotments of the villagers: each strip no more than three or four feet wide and six feet long, as neat and well tended as the burial plots of similar dimensions are ignored. Onions grow here, the green fronds bright against the red-brown earth of the region. Carrots show feathery plumes. Spinach – essential for the popular and delicious dish *spanakopita*, the flaky pastry spinach tart served on special occasions – looks like a succession of dark bundles in the meticulously weeded ground. Soon, we think to ourselves as we trudge on, calves aching from the walk up from the house (and the fact that we've come on a road nearly all the way, albeit an unmade road, the all-important new way down to the sea at Yefira, doesn't prevent us from feeling that we're engaged in a marathon, if we're to climb all the way to the top of Liapades), soon we'll be enjoying the food and drink Yorgos and his wife will provide for the guests to the christening. 'Expect a lot of sugared almonds,' says my mother, who has participated in one of these events before. 'Very elaborate and expensive . . . dolls made of dragées, little tulle-covered baskets – and lots of lovely other things as well.'

While I'm thinking that there's something about these occasions, wherever they're celebrated, that demands identical fare to the year before – and the year before that, going back to the food prepared and ceremonially eaten by *ya-ya* and *pro-ya-ya* alike – I think also of the necessity of this sameness, to bring calm and reassurance to lives shaken by political change and frequent economic disaster. Liapades had been known as one of the 'Red' villages of the area, at the time of the Civil War that succeeded the Second World War. Communists and their foes fought and died here, within living memory – indeed, within the lifespan of people who still aren't enormously old. Then, the military junta had placed its iron fist over these lives. Only the poet George Seferis had the courage to speak out against the regime – he was the first of many intellectuals exiled by the colonels' seizing of power in Greece. Seferis, Ambassador in London, issued a statement that included the warning that 'a regime has been imposed on us which is totally inimical to the ideals for which our world – and our people so resplendently – fought during the last world war . . .' For this – and for his assertion that 'in the case of dictatorial regimes the beginning may seem easy, but tragedy awaits, inevitably, in the end. The drama of this ending haunts us consciously and unconsciously – as in the immemorial choruses of Aeschylus' – Seferis had his diplomatic passport revoked.

What did the relatives and friends of the people of Liapades, those who climb ahead of us now up the steep main street, make of the regime, now in turn overthrown, with its tyranny and constrictions?

We are *xenoi*, foreigners who never can really know. But we are invited to partake in a ceremony and feast that have outlived the recent political change and upheaval. Yorgos will have lit his fires in the Nikterida charcoal grill and he'll bring up to his house *cocoretsi* – the speciality some find hard to stomach (because it is indeed made of stomach, a sheep's offal stuffed in a long stocking of fat, not unlike the Scottish haggis). There will be chicken; the ubiquitous and ever-desirable *xoriatiki* salad; and feta that is firm, moist and just right for eating. Then will come the bright, sweet-pea-coloured sugared almonds, traditional fare for a christening.

The courtyard with its lemon and orange trees in their white knee-socks – the trunks of the trees slender, and a bright array of marigolds and geraniums like flowers painted in a frieze around their base – is already crowded with relatives and guests. Aunts, grandmothers, cousins and second cousins throng the yard and climb the wooden stairs to the main rooms, as Yorgos comes beaming towards us, hand outstretched. He does his best to introduce us and explain the patchwork, here at its most intensely interwoven (though there are clans, obviously, in Liapades, who have no kin with his family at all) and we listen as he indicates sisters, nieces and a posse of very young children who will, he says with a secret grin of satisfaction, be amongst those to run out in the street and hear the child's name when it is proclaimed.

We go up the outside stairs, to find that the ceremony will shortly begin. A sudden hospitable rush: Yorgos, who makes the Nikterida restaurant, despite its site on one of the steepest hairpin bends in the locality, the most agreeable place in Liapades to sit and enjoy a meal, sees us in his home and without seats or drinks, and bustles to provide both. He remembers ouzo for my mother and myself, and beer for Tim, my partner of a few years now and as passionately interested in Rovinia and the surrounding countryside and legends as we are. How fortunate we are, I think as the inevitable shared glass of water is proffered, a drop from this turning the aniseed drink as white and cloudy as just-mixed distemper; how delicious Yorgos' olives, black and larger than ours, and with the true taste of Greece: bitter, life-giving, older even than the wine Dionysus quaffs in the bas-relief in the little museum in the town.

But just as we acclimatise to the noise up here – to the old women who shriek greetings to each other from room to room; to the young boys who run, in a desperate effort to amuse themselves, between the legs of the guests and under the table where the food is laid out – a silence falls as loud and excited as the din. The *papas* walks into the room. He's tall, bearded (as the Orthodox priest must be) and has a kindly face: my mother whispers that she had known him when she first came to live at Rovinia, when he was still a boy. He precedes what appears at first to be a large bucket, filled with water; but, as it comes closer, this can be seen to be a kind of primitive urn, deep and containing the holy element right up to the brim. No wonder, I think, it has to be sunny weather for a small child to be subjected to total immersion in this: it might be as well, too, if the candidate for baptism could already swim.

We've come to know the baby on our visits to Nikterida. Under the trellis with the vine that grows as sparse as balding hair, if you sit too far along the small terrace by the side of the road, she lies in her pram oblivious to the churn of lorries or the clip-clop of donkeys and mules as they head up the shortcut into the main street of Liapades. We've had her held up to us for inspection and seen her smile – and each time we've neglected to remember that she has no name. '*Beba*,' says her grandmother, when we search for it; she is a handsome dark-haired woman who works in the kitchen with Yorgos, producing the *calamaraki*, squid in a light batter with lemon – which we come up the path to eat, rain or shine. '*Beba*.' And we're reminded of the fact that the all-important christening has not yet taken place.

By the time the baby has had the shock of being plunged into the water – and has begun to scream, accordingly – the chatter and yell of the party have started up again. In church, the *papas* is accustomed to calling for quiet (he is always unsuccessful), so loud are the chatting, commenting voices of the congregation. Here, that moment of silence at his appearance is all God is likely to get.

Still, we're close enough to the action to be able to hear the *papas* as he speaks his (alas, incomprehensible to us) litany over the infuriated and violently shivering child. The scene, in the main front room of the house – this room one storey above ground, to give space to animals and stored hay and foodstuffs below – is one that could have taken place at any time in the past five hundred years or so. The priest, in the gloomy shade of the low room; the baby, its flesh tones vivid after the inundation in water; the proud faces of Yorgos and his wife and their daughter Marina, the baby's mother, caught in the strong beam of sunlight that comes straight into the middle of the scene – these could comprise a painting or sketch by a provincial artist, executed in the eighteenth or nineteenth century.

Now comes another kind of sound; and this time a real silence appears like a gaping hole around it. 'ATHINA,' is shouted loudly from the wooden walkway that runs along the first floor of the house, out into the street. 'ATHINA!'

So, the baby is named. The outside world has been told that Yorgos' granddaughter is Athina. And the *koumbari*, godparents, who have chosen it are joined by all the rest of the guests, everyone throwing coins down to the posse of young boys, now beyond the gates of the house and standing, palms high above their heads to catch the money, in the street.

The sugared almonds, some elaborately contrived as horses, carriages, dolls in crinolines, come round. As we crack the hard white sugar covering and crunch into the nut beneath, Yorgos comes running up. Wine flows – he tries to explain more to us – but the chattering and laughing and kissing and back-thumping are fully under way again. It's late, and the sun much lower in the sky, when we make our way down the road to Yefira and then across the terraces of olives and fig and orange trees to Rovinia.

BAREFOOT
AT SHANZU

ERROL TRZEBINSKI

ERROL TRZEBINSKI is the author of *The Kenya Pioneers*, *The Lives of Beryl Markham* and *The Life and Death of Lord Erroll*, which was short-listed for the 2000 MacAllan Golden Dagger Award for non-fiction. Her first biography, *Silence Will Speak – The Life of Denys Finch Hatton and His Relationship with Karen Blixen*, was a major source for the love story in Universal's Oscar-winning film, *Out of Africa*. She acted as consultant on the documentary *World Without Walls* about Beryl Markham, and on two BBC television documentaries, about Ernest Hemingway and Karen Blixen (the writer Isak Dinesen).

AS I WALKED across the library and felt the parquet of the floor crumble beneath the soles of my feet, it struck me that no-one is really in charge in Africa so much as the insects, white ants in particular. Nothing else is as unrelenting or as permanent. Presidents and their entourages come and go. Constitutions are rewritten. Promises made to their African subjects are but grandiloquent gestures – seldom, if ever, kept. Corruption is on the rampage, like the *crypto termes,* largely unseen but nevertheless there. Loans are doled out in huge amounts, only to be written off since the World Bank knows there is no possible hope of being repaid. Honest men in Africa are regarded as fools, if not pariahs. Only the white ants remain constant, munching steadily away through wooden furniture, drawers, legs and beams – the lot.

When we first saw this neglected villa it sat in the middle of a parking lot of levelled coral rag, facing the Indian Ocean. Two seesaws, two slides and two swings suggested twins had once lived here. A disused well added a touch of romance. Its water was brackish. The villa was really too small for my husband, Sbish, and our three children, aged eleven, seven and five. It had two single bedrooms, a split-level living room which one entered by a flight of seven steps, and on the far side, down four more stairs, an even smaller kitchen next to a bathroom with a loo and a store at the back. Every stucco wall was painted in *eau-de-nil* emulsion; the floors were black terrazzo. Our first chore was to scrub clean what we could and paint the house white inside and out. Any hint of romance faded into oblivion with an invasion of guests over our first August Bank Holiday; twenty-seven visitors from upcountry drifted in between ten in the morning and ten at night to see how we were adjusting to sweltering temperatures, and whether we were coping. We were not. We ran out of ice, drinks and food. Next day, we bought a bigger refrigerator on hire purchase and vowed to enlarge the kitchen.

Over the next thirty years, 'Shanzu' grew like Topsy. The store was converted into a bedroom with a shower for our elder son, Bruce. Later still we expanded this again, turning its passage into a dressing room with a double bedroom for ourselves. Effectively these alterations created an inner patio, which we could use as an open-air dining room. In the phase that followed we made a square six-foot-deep pool, reminiscent of a large Roman bath, in which to cool off in the hottest season. We added on a small study plus a proper dining room overlooking the pool. We moved ourselves upstairs by a spiral staircase to a bedroom, with air-conditioning. Eventually we distinguished ourselves by excavating a good-sized swimming pool in the garden so our three children could cavort or dive to their hearts' content, without being reprimanded for drenching the living space. We regarded the addition as a necessity, not an extravagance, using brackish water to fill this. But such an air of opulence did this addition bestow at Shanzu, that even when we did not know where the next school fees were coming from, outsiders imagined quite mistakenly that we were seriously well off. In due course I was to be identified as 'the woman with the house with two swimming pools' – an assumption that is still vaguely irritating. After all, I married an architect whose forte is conversions.

On the white sands of Paradise Beach everything we hoped might benefit our children took place. They discovered how the sea whispered lies in shells placed next to their ears; in the water they became agile as eels. Seven dugout canoes, each owned by a Swahili, bobbed at anchor here. When not out beyond the reef catching fish, the fishermen made friends with our children. Secrets of marine life were unlocked while goggling in rock pools at low tide or combing the reef for strange creatures. At high tide we dug for tellin clams to make chowder; with very few tourists, we could caper alone guarded by our friendly Dalmatian. Local inhabitants were nervous of him to begin with, believing he must be a member of the leopard family, but in time they were reassured by his mild manners, merely stepping out of range to avoid contact when he sniffed at a bare leg. In those carefree, sun-filled days the waves rolled in and out again, stranding flotsam and jet-sam; spring tides brought the most interesting pieces, inspired sculpture. We were spoiled for choice by fishermen bringing blue parrotfish, rock cod and langoustine to our kitchen steps. We paid so little for a huge *kikapu* of prawns.

The house was tailor-made for moveable feasts. With enough flat roof above the small colonnade surrounding the little pool, we dined on it at full moon from low circular tables. These and as many cushions as the occasion required were carried upstairs. In time, jasmine and pink and orange bougainvillaea spilled over the tiles, in a vibrant tangle. This in itself was a miracle. Each shrub, flower and tree that bloomed had been planted in a pocket of grey, weathered vesicular coral, dug out then filled with decent soil.

Sitting cross-legged on Persian carpets at night we learned to identify Venus, Castor, Pollux and (thanks to Finch Hatton) Sirius the Dog Star. The Arab room – the original living room – we transformed. Armed with a bolt of fabric from the Indian bazaar, scissors and drawing pins, a stepladder and a bottle of wine, we 'tented' the ceiling. We hung Persian carpets on the walls. The floor was strewn with carpets, too, bargained for in Mombasa's old port with the captains of trading dhows, who sailed in with the monsoon each May, bringing also exotic brass-studded chests. The room became known as 'the fornicatorium', an epithet bestowed by an elderly but witty female and a regular guest of ours. Unsurprisingly the term lived on.

We could always rely on good weather for picnics on our beach or parties in the garden where we laid out tables under a flowering acacia, which grew in the course of time into a huge green umbrella with scarlet blooms. We usually breakfasted in the pool room indoors, open to the sky bordered on three sides by arches, the fourth being the dining-room window. Underneath this was a fountain of real clam shells, over which water tumbled during daylight hours, circulating the air throughout the house.

In the study where I wrote my biography of Denys Finch Hatton on a portable typewriter, I also sat and checked

Universal's screenplay for the film that followed, *Out of Africa*; I went through the same process for the screenplay of *West with the Night*. It was here while still researching for *The Lives of Beryl Markham* that I took a call from my agent in London informing me that this proposed biography was to be optioned for film even before I began writing it. Nowadays, forget the telephone. No-one can rely on this form of communication in Kenya.

Twenty-four years of diary-keeping took place before I decided I could not deal with this topsy-turvy existence any more. The pages had always contained a ragbag of impressions; entries ranged from snippets of family conversations to, since the arrival of two grandchildren, their enchanting mispronunciations learning to talk. Excitements and disasters were inevitably interspersed with the new twists and turns in the life of my current subject. Such information *used* to come by post but nowadays the post office presents another mystery. Where do all the undelivered letters go?

My disenchantment with Kenya as a place to live festered for several years before we lost our beloved Tonio. I had voiced my unease to the point of boring my friends, holding forth about how wrong it was to continue to dwell in a place where simply by being there, one could not help but support a corrupt regime, appearing to sanction theft and cheating, and thereby contributing tacitly toward rampant dishonesty. I seemed to be gazing down the wrong end of a telescope where the joy of former times had concentrated, shrunk into miniature, become stylised, taking its place in symbolism.

With no wish to blame a country that has given me so much, what now strikes me forcibly is how life in the bush at the simplest level – with only a tent for shelter, three stones for a fire upon which to balance and boil water on safari – is really the only way of life that truly works for European interlopers such as myself. I remembered when we moved from upcountry to the coast, how the old hands advised us not to bring anything of value: paintings, books and antiques would be ruined by humidity and, if not by the climate, by termites. We paid no heed. We should have listened. We should have known about the insects.

Ironically the telephone was working that night in mid-October 2001, when a call in the early hours plunged the household into a private hell, changing our grandchildren's lives as drastically as those of the families orphaned by the terrorist attack at the World Trade Center in New York six weeks earlier.

Our white bedroom had always represented tranquillity, not least when pop music on the gramophone in the Arab room blared out. If my need to escape the throb-throb-throb was powerful, its calm atmosphere and air-conditioning were bliss. Its ceramic tiles were cool to tread upon without shoes, especially when tropical heat reached its zenith. Venetian wooden screens divided bath-room from bedroom, sliding back easily to create two rooms from one. The wall of mirror behind the bath captured a green jungle – the tops of feathery coconut palms, from which hung a colony of nests made by yellow red-capped buffalo weavers. Our antique brass four-poster bed, bought at auction for the equivalent of five English pounds, faced white fabric from ceiling to floor, obscuring the magnificent view of the Indian Ocean, before a huge plate-glass window. These curtains were seldom opened, to prevent the fierce African sun from penetrating this haven. The glare bouncing off the water three hundred yards away was instead diffused, wakening us gently. I shall miss the magnificence of the reef stretching along Kenya's largely unspoiled coastline, a ruffle of foam like a white feather boa between sea and sky; so silent, from that distance, so seemingly benign. This too is deceptive. Those waves pound savage rocks, submerged by every incoming tide. The reef is a safety barrier, keeping sharks away from Mombasa's beaches, ensuring swimmers are safe from deadly menace beyond. Even as adults, our boys would stand on the flat parts of our roof at Shanzu, checking the mood and quality of the waves; one hoped for ideal sailing conditions, the other for good surfing. Sometimes they would telephone and ask us to perform this duty, before venturing on a fool's errand.

Because the telephone upstairs sat on Sbish's bedside table rather than mine, he answered its summons. A disembodied, familiar and extremely courageous voice broke the news. The ethereal shades of white in the bedroom only added unreality.

Looking back on the hours, days, weeks that followed, I can still hear my husband's accusing response, 'Yes, you have actually . . .' (woken me up). Silence. Then an unbearable pause. 'Oh my God! How is that possible? Tonio? Shot dead – how? Where? By whom? Where are the children?'

The maternal role in the animal kingdom is eternal, unwavering: to raise her offspring, whatever age they reach and whenever circumstances demand, to protect, to buffer from pain and to comfort. How was I going to offer solace to his brother Bruce, forty-five years old, recovering in hospital from minor but vital emergency surgery and still on a drip? The ordeal had to wait until daybreak. Meanwhile, all our attempts to telephone our other child, Gabriela, in London failed, usurped as she dialled us desperately from there, getting through on Sbish's mobile an hour later. 'Tell me it's not true!' she cried, seeking reassurance only to be devastated.

That same phrase was more oft-repeated than I care to count in the hell that followed. What had happened? Nobody was sure. How then was it also that we, his parents, were not informed for five hours?

In the garden, security lights glowed, illuminating the turquoise of the big pool. Yet, like my diary on my bedside table, it too seemed unfamiliar. Even the bunches of green coconuts, like clenched green fists in the palms beyond our bathroom window, seemed menacing. Everything was unreal. I prayed I would shortly wake up when morning tea was delivered as usual, preceded by a gentle tap on the door; prayed that all would be well again, that Tonio would bound up the steps on his long legs into the Arab room, red-eyed from hours of surfing, wanting to chat about the latest antics of his two young children.

At dawn I drove alone to the hospital, vying for road space with the *matatus*, minibuses, ferrying too many workers at a time, at breakneck speed, to jobs on the island. How was I to deliver this shock? Over and over, I rehearsed what I might say without any solution. I broke the news to Bruce's wife in the hospital corridor, testing the water, establishing first whether Bruce had slept reasonably. As I walked through the door, he greeted me quizzically, 'You're up early.' His wife braced herself, taking Bruce's hand, soothing in the way partners who care for one another will rely on touch. Clasping his other wrist, I said as steadily as I was able, 'Darling, there is no easy way to break this news to you . . . Last night, T . . .' I got no further. He screamed out in increasing decibels, the words overtaking me: 'No! No! No! Not Tonio! Not Tonio! NOT TONIO!' In those split seconds the assumption that Tonio had been killed while riding his motorcycle was understandable. I stood there feeling like a traitor, appalled yet unable to take in what I was now lamely repeating, 'They think it was a carjacking. The police and . . .'

By midday, at Shanzu once more, messages of disbelief, listed by my husband, were already arriving from around the globe, relayed to us by phone, from faxes, by emails. Sitting in my wicker chair at the breakfast table near the little pool, I was now informed by an acquaintance with a strong Italian accent that random violence had been out of the question. Tonio had taken a single bullet to his heart. One shot followed by a scream was all we had to go on, in terms of evidence; an act of cold-blooded murder.

To lose a child is the worst thing that can happen to a mother. I will learn not to continue to weep but my tears could fill an ocean. Someone said that when somebody close dies young, 'all the beautiful time is yours for always, and it is time that takes away, changes and spoils so often – not death'.

The flames of his funeral pyre beneath the Ngong Hills in Kenya's magnificent Rift Valley lit up the dying light that afternoon.

Ash to ashes, dust to dust . . . perhaps I simply have a penchant for leaving, I reflected as I walked away at sundown.

For the first time since I went there in 1953, I flew out of Africa on a one-way ticket with no feeling of regret about leaving behind all the things I had imagined I once needed. Now I am back in England, living but a handful of miles from my birthplace; spring has arrived with all its promise. On a visit with my grandchildren and my daughter to Hampton Court to see the maze at last, a mass of daffodils in the tilting yard delighted us. The gentleness of the four seasons; the wind, rain and frost; the green fields; the dank and variable climate: these elements soothe my ragged soul where nothing else seems to work.

When I reached Somerset, where I was staying temporarily with a friend, a postcard from Malindi awaited me, groaning with palm trees against a blue sky above an uninhabited beach. Superimposed on the full-colour photograph was *From wonderful East Africa*. Dated March 16 – five months to the day when Tonio died – my husband had written, 'Dare I say it . . . wish you were here.'

I shall miss the smell of rain, the sound of a downpour on corrugated iron, the song of the frogs in the pond, heralding a cloudburst, the gentle greetings of our servants, their delight at accomplishing a new dish – a risen soufflé or crêpes thin enough through which to read a lover's letter – but for now, I have turned my back on the exotic, though I too may wish I was back in the bush on safari in years to come. Undoubtedly I will miss the freedom of walking barefoot at Shanzu, but for now, I know that such a thing is impossible, just as I know that the only permanent presence in Africa is insect . . .

COMING HOME IN
MASSACHUSETTS

SIMON WINCHESTER

SIMON WINCHESTER is a British writer whose book on the eruption of Krakatoa is due to be published in 2003. He is the author of the best-selling *The Surgeon of Crowthorne* (entitled *The Professor and the Madman* in the United States) and *The Map that Changed the World*, as well as *The River at the Centre of the World* and numerous other books. He divides his time between an island off the west coast of Scotland and his small farm in the Berkshire Hills of Massachusetts, where he feels now inclined to stay. Perhaps.

LAST WEEK *a man with a flat-bed trailer came to take away my tractor, so he could fit it with a backhoe.*

This sentence, which I found myself writing the other day in an email home to my aged parents in England, is not one I could have ever imagined myself writing, or even thinking of writing, as little as a year ago. Back then I lived something of a dashing existence, either wandering across the remoter parts of the planet or, when settled, inhabiting a world of gritty and costly apartments in capital cities, of business-class travel and fancy cafés and edgy urban chatter. I wasn't at all sure what a flat-bed trailer was, I certainly had no idea of the functions of a backhoe – glory be! – and to my certain knowledge tractors were merely burbling little beasts that chugged around in farmers' fields in that curious beyond one saw from train windows and which was known as 'the country'. The notion that I'd ever own or want to own one, or live and take my ease among those to whom they were a customary form of transport, was well beyond what I prided myself in considering my fairly acute powers of imagination.

Well – that was then and this is now. Now I own a tractor. I own two tractors, in fact. And last week a man with a flat-bed trailer came to take one of them away, to fix it up with a backhoe – something which weighs half a ton, needs greasing every week and costs a very great deal more than I expected. And all of this (which includes learning how to wield a mysterious device that I now know to be a grease gun) has happened because, after fifty-seven fairly exciting, exacting, sophisticated and mainly metropolitan years, I have become – voluntarily and, so far as I can tell, forever and for good – a hayseed. It is a role that I find I have slipped on as easily as a deerskin work glove, and I find also that by doing so I have become as happy as something that I was wont to eat at New York's Nobu, but which has proved as rare as hens' teeth here: and that is, to wit, *a clam*.

The notion of settling anywhere was to me once utterly alien. I was sixteen when I began to travel seriously; I hitchhiked the entire circumference of populated North America one summer, and it was then that I developed a taste for the risks and rewards of solitary wandering. Over the following years, thanks to the indulgence of a number of newspaper editors, I lived in (or perhaps more appropriately, I was *based* in) Africa, India, Ireland, China and the United States. I believe I travelled to every country on the planet – except for a scattering of those Central Asian entities that are now called 'the 'stans' – and I was able for a long while to say with the pride of an inverse snob that I had never been either to Peru or to the Hamptons. (Both I have been to lately and am happy to say that for each, once is quite enough.)

I have had more homes than I can remember, more telephone numbers, more email addresses; and friends who are kind enough to keep me in their little black books grumble at the 'W' page, dominated as it is by so many rubbings-out and fillings-in. *Can't you ever settle down?* they ask in kindly-weary exasperation. *Of course*, they add, *we envy you mightily*.

And for a while I used to think they did, especially if their lives depended on the catching of morning commuter trains and the sitting in soft-sided office cubes and the looking forward to games of golf on summer weekends. My life, *sans* both commuter trains and weekends, did seem at first blush quite appealing, I am sure. Except that they saw their daughters' bliss on wedding days, and they curled up at firesides on winter nights; and I suspect if they remembered me at all then, they saw my life a little differently – that my unsettlement and unshacklement was not quite everything, that the solitary and the empty and the rootless can also be co-equal with the joyless, and that the life of the fancy-free was often much more fancy than, in many ways, it was truly free.

And as my years began to tick on I confess that slightly, and only intermittently, I began to ponder such matters too, and to wonder at the supposed benefits of endless wanderings. This feeling gradually strengthened until, in a sudden moment of hopeful whim last year, I bought a rambling old house and a few acres of weary farmland in the Berkshire Hills of western Massachusetts. And in doing so I wondered at that very moment if I too – a little late, perhaps even a little too late – might for the first time take a shot at settling down at last. It might work, I thought. It might not. And if it didn't – well, then at least it would be another adventure out of which I could make another anecdote, to tell in some distant watering hole once the travelling had started once again.

That was nine months ago. Since then, aside from two journeys to Java and a mere handful to Europe (which approximates the stasis of a cryogenic state, compared to before), I have not budged. Eight months ago – four weeks into the experiment, in other words – came an epiphany. And this epiphany involved, just as is demanded by the symmetry of classic storytelling (and in this case, by the truth), a tractor.

I mentioned that I now own two tractors. One of them came with the property. It is not as old as the house (which was constructed a little after what, to me, an Englishman, were those melancholy events of 1776), but it sports a fair half-century of yeoman service. It is a faded blue Ford (model 8N, I mention for the aficionados out there, who I gather exist in healthy numbers). It is a little rusty. It needs to be cranked into life with much care and gentle words.

But once so eased into what passes for mechanical vivacity it runs really quite merrily, chugging and pulsing steadily like a heartbeat. It has a little exhaust pipe that emits what I am sure is the kind of blue smoke that could kill, but which in fact, when borne on country air, seems to have a rare sweetness about it. I wouldn't exactly bend down and attach my mouth to the pipe, unless I was feeling exceptionally gloomy, but when the tractor has passed by and I get the faint scent of its exhaust on the breeze, it is, I must say, an aroma most pleasing. When I mentioned this rather dull observation to the farmer who helped me, he looked at me straight in the eye and he did something farmers rarely do: he cracked a smile.

Anyway, attached to the rear of my burbling little Ford 8N, held up by what is known in hayseed-speak as a 'three-point-hitch', and powered by a shaft that emerges dangerously from a connection to what is known similarly as a 'PTO' (a power-take-off), is a spinning blade, covered by a large, yellow iron shield, which is known as a 'brush-hog'. This is what people who live in the Berkshires like to use, I was told, to mow their fields. Not to make their lawns satin-smooth, mind you, but merely to get the thistles and crab grass and timothy down to a height in which passing children and small animals don't get totally lost in the thickets.

One warm early evening, as the sun was going down over the locust trees (one of which housed a big, fat porcupine, contentedly munching twigs), I decided to have a go. I sat on the machine, lit my pipe, gently coaxed and fired up the engine, backed the brush-hog off the two baulks of timber on which it had been resting for the past many months, and set off unsteadily down the meadow.

No sweeter smell have I ever known, in any place I have ever been. In the background – I am sure the scent-makers of Grasse have a name for such a thing – were the commingled aromas of tractor exhaust and my Balkan Sobranie Mixture, with its accents of sweet Latakia leaf. But in the foreground was something nicer still: the smell of new-mown grass – new-mown *hay*, in fact, for what I was cutting in a wide swathe behind me was tall grass and blue alfalfa, which smells more unimaginably lovely than anything, except what came next. And that came when, as I directed the puttering little Ford over to a patch of richer, wilder green than the rest of the field, there wafted through the air the overwhelming aroma of fresh wild mint.

In that moment I was utterly hooked, totally transformed. Tractor smoke, fine Syrian tobacco, blue alfalfa and wild mint made a cocktail of, well, probably pheromones, someone will one day write and tell me, that produced for me a true olfactory epiphany. It was as though – and if this sounds sentimentally unreal, I make no apology for it – in that one instant the earth sang out: *Stay here*, it said. *Dig holes here*. *Put down roots*. Nurture and gentle them with sun and rain and seasons, until, like that old Ford, they burble into life as well, and show that something that grows has more point to it than anything else borne from a ceaseless wandering.

Well, to come down from the magic of the moment, to reattach to a more sober reality, you have to understand a little of farming. To dig holes in which to plant roots either real or metaphorical, one needs a far, far bigger tractor than my dear little 1952 blue monster, which serious farmers refer to only as a toy. So now in consequence, and since the epiphany lasted, and since its effects last still, I possess a great big orange monster of a new tractor, with forty-six wild horses under its hood, a big orange bucket and thick black forks at its front end, and ever since its brief flat-bed-assisted absence of last week, a backhoe attached wherever it is that backhoes hoe.

And with this machine so far, in just the last ten days, I have accomplished much. I have shifted the branches of fifty newly pruned apple trees. I have moved a ton of clay onto the floors of four stalls in a barn built for two Norwegian fjord horses. I have moved vast piles of firewood for the coming winter. I have dug out a section of the garden in which the lady who kindly partners me in this delightful madness wishes to plant rhubarb. I have helped a neighbour pull out an aged tree stump, and I have worked with another to reshape an old stone wall. I have distributed the better part of ten tons of sand onto the muddy wen that was my driveway.

Soon, when the forty tons of topsoil arrives, I will rake and smooth it around the old Vermont carriage barn that I have turned into my library, and I will plant box trees there and hope the Massachusetts winter won't make me rue the expense – for that, too, is a smell that works wonders on a flagging spirit, and might just be right for when a book is going less so.

I have plans for a thousand-and-one other tasks, as my girl-friend and I try to turn this weary old farm back into a productive little organic clutch of acres. We have plans to send out apple-finished lamb to the local restaurants (many of whom now have a policy of buying only home-made produce from local farms), of sending blossom and clover honey (for the bees arrive any day, just in time to catch the apple flowers, and we have plans for painting their hives tonight) to our friends, and to make home-smoked bacon from the pigs that soon will be snorting and snuf-fling their way in the pens we are building (with the help of the tractor, naturally) over by a new meadow that we have lately cleared for the horses' use.

Yes, we have plans all right. And I have plans, at last, to stay. I never imagined that there might one day be a place in Massachusetts for a wandering Englishman like me. And I con-fess I still find it difficult to believe that the wandering will ever stop – for, mistakenly and foolishly I now realise, there was a long time in my life when such *persona* as I had was perhaps defined by the fact of travel. I was only useful to people when I wasn't around – amusing to them when I came back and told the tales, but someone to be prodded back to the airport or the dock-side, and made to go away again.

Well, that is no more (or more or less no more: I am off to London tomorrow, and Hong Kong in July, and briefly back to Java after that). No, it was that evening of aromas that convinced me, and the simple fact that I was at that moment performing a task that is ageless and eternal, and should, were we all so lucky, be done at some moment by us all. *I was making hay while the sun shines* – as good a way to run a life, I know at last, as any I can suppose.